Intellectual Property in the 21st Century

Creative Works and the Right of Making Them Available: In Depth Analyses

INTELLECTUAL PROPERTY IN THE 21ST CENTURY

Additional books in this series can be found on Nova's website under the Series tab.

Additional e-books in this series can be found on Nova's website under the e-book tab.

INTELLECTUAL PROPERTY IN THE 21ST CENTURY

CREATIVE WORKS AND THE RIGHT OF MAKING THEM AVAILABLE: IN DEPTH ANALYSES

BRANDON S. CASEY
EDITOR

nova publishers
New York

Library of Congress Cataloging-in-Publication Data

ISBN: 978-1-63485-522-8

Published by Nova Science Publishers, Inc. † New York

CONTENTS

PREFACE

The growth of new technologies in the digital age has rapidly expanded the availability of copyrighted works. Along with this expansion have come questions central to copyright jurisprudence as whether and how the creative works of authors may be accessed and disseminated.

Two international treaties to which the United States is a party—the WIPO Copyright Treaty and the WIPO Performances and Phonograms Treaty (collectively, the "WIPO Internet Treaties")—require member states to recognize the right of "making available," which gives authors, producers, and performers the exclusive right to authorize the transmission of their works and sound recordings to the public through interactive platforms that enable members of the public to choose where and when to access them.

This book provides a thorough assessment of the state of U.S. law recognizing and protecting copyright holders' exclusive right of "making available" and how both U.S. and foreign laws have interpreted and implemented the relevant provisions of the WIPO Internet Treaties.

In: Creative Works …
Editor: Brandon S. Casey
ISBN: 978-1-63485-522-8

Chapter 1

THE MAKING AVAILABLE RIGHT IN THE UNITED STATES*

Kevin Amer and Kimberley Isbell

EXECUTIVE SUMMARY

In the digital age, few questions are as central to copyright jurisprudence as whether and how the creative works of authors may be accessed and disseminated on the Internet. These issues frequently turn upon the application of national copyright laws to new or improved technologies and emerging business models. As discussed in this Report, however, national copyright laws do not operate in a vacuum. Rather, they reflect the binding provisions of treaties and other intergovernmental agreements that are essential to modern commerce.

In the early days of the digital economy, member states of the World Intellectual Property Organization ("WIPO"), including the United States, met in Geneva, Switzerland to update the international copyright framework. In 1996, they completed a pair of treaties, widely regarded as balanced and forward thinking, together referred to as the WIPO Internet Treaties. Among other achievements, the Treaties affirmed the operation of exclusive rights in the online environment, including the prerogative of authors to authorize "the making available to the public of works in such a way that members of the

* This is an edited, reformatted and augmented version of a report of the Register of Copyrights, issued by the United States Copyright Office, February 2016.

public may access these works from a place and at a time individually chosen by them."[1]

In crafting the making available right, the treaty parties anticipated the impact of continuing technological advancement, and worked to create language that would be both effective for copyright owners and adaptable to future fact patterns. For example, the making available right is technology neutral. This means that it covers all formats in which a work may be digitally communicated, including downloads, streams, and any other existing or future- developed methods of online transmission.[2] The making available right also focuses on access rather than receipt.[3] This ensures that a copyright owner can establish an infringement claim by, for example, showing that the defendant uploaded a copyrighted work to a publicly accessible file sharing network without authorization. And, the making available right extends to the delivery of works through one-to-one on-demand transmissions—*i.e.*, those that can be received by members of the public individually in separate places and at different times.[4] This ensures that a party engaging in unauthorized communication of a copyrighted work cannot evade the reach of the right by delivering the work to the public in many separate individualized transmissions.

The United States ratified and implemented the WIPO Internet Treaties in 1998, incorporating a number of newly stated obligations in amendments that comprise the Digital Millennium Copyright Act ("DMCA"). Congress made no express changes regarding the making available right, however, concluding instead that the exclusive rights enumerated in Section 106 of the Copyright Act are sufficient in any given instance to support and effect the substance of the relevant treaty provisions. This determination was consistent with the understanding among the negotiators at the time of the Treaties' adoption that the making available right could be "implemented in national legislation through application of any particular exclusive right . . . or combination of exclusive rights, as long as the acts described in [the treaty] Articles were covered by such rights."[5]

During the past two decades, U.S. government officials have uniformly maintained that the Copyright Act's exclusive rights, taken together, cover the full range of conduct encompassed by the making available right, meaning that such conduct will implicate and be governed by one or more of the Section 106 exclusive rights, including, for example, the distribution, public display, and public performance rights.[6] Subsequent Congresses have reaffirmed this conclusion through their approval, between 2003 and 2011, of a dozen free trade agreements with foreign nations obliging the United States to provide a making available right, determining in each case that adoption would not require changes to U.S. copyright law.[7]

The courts of the United States have been less consistent in their analyses and decisions. On the one hand, the Supreme Court's recent decision in *American Broadcasting Cos. v. Aereo, Inc.* confirms that the public performance right encompasses the transmission of copyrighted works to the public through individualized streams. On the other hand, in the context of offers of access to copyrighted content, some district courts have questioned the existence of the right under U.S. law, ultimately failing to recognize a cause of action where copyright owners cannot prove that downloads or receipt occurred. Others have wholly rejected the right out of hand, failing to discuss or even acknowledge the international obligations of the United States.[8] At the appellate level, courts have yet to conclusively resolve these issues in cases involving works in digital format. There are, however, two appellate decisions holding that, in the context of a library offering physical copies of a work to the public, distribution does not necessarily require an actual transfer of copies.[9]

Evidentiary requirements are among the issues that would benefit from clarification sooner rather than later, to ensure that the rules for bringing a *prima facie* infringement case are clear and consistent. In the context of file sharing cases, for example, some courts have attempted a practical fix. Effectively, they have permitted plaintiffs to proceed with their claims using circumstantial or investigator evidence that infers or suggests that downloading has occurred, even when it cannot be proven directly. Unfortunately, this solution is difficult to reconcile with a proper construction of the treaty language, in that it turns upon receipt rather than access. More practically, it creates factual quagmires and burdensome litigation costs that affect all involved, including the courts themselves. This is not to say that circumstantial evidence could not be helpful in proving appropriate factual questions, such as, for example, whether and how defendants allegedly offered access.

In accordance with the congressional assignment that triggered this study, the Copyright Office has focused its review of the legal landscape on three key issues. These are: "(1) how the existing bundle of rights under Title 17 covers the making available . . . right[] in the context of digital on-demand transmissions such as peer-to-peer networks, streaming services, and music downloads, as well as more broadly in the digital environment; (2) how foreign laws have interpreted and implemented the relevant provisions of the

WIPO Internet Treaties; and (3) the feasibility and necessity of amending U.S. law to strengthen or clarify our law in this area."[10]

The Copyright Office engaged in an extensive public process while analyzing these issues, and received the views of stakeholders representing a broad range of interests and perspectives. These submissions captured the historical and policy underpinnings of the relevant legal provisions, as well as their practical application in litigation and business transactions. The Copyright Office also took into account the experiences of other nations in applying the exclusive rights of copyright owners to emerging technologies.

Based on all of these considerations, the Copyright Office reaches the following conclusions:

- Consistent with its prior analyses and testimony, as well as the views of Congress, multiple Administrations, appellate courts, and leading academic authorities, the Copyright Office concludes that the exclusive rights of copyright owners set forth under 17 U.S.C. § 106 collectively meet and adequately provide the substance of the making available right.
- Consistent with the plain language of the Treaties, which defines the making available right in terms of whether members of the public "*may* access" a copyrighted work, U.S. law should be read to include the offer of public access, including through on- demand services, without regard to whether a copy has been disseminated or received. Doing so is also consistent with the judicial opinions of foreign jurisdictions on this point.
- Within the particular context of downloads, U.S. law provides the making available right through the exclusive right of distribution under Section 106(3). While some courts have failed to find distribution in the absence of evidence of completed transfers, and therefore declined to recognize claims based solely on making copies available to the public for download, the Copyright Office concludes that the appropriate reading of Section 106(3) in the context of making available claims is that it covers offers of access.
- Within the context of Internet streaming or the display of an image online, the United States provides the making available right through the rights of public performance and public display under Section 106(4)–(6), respectively. Moreover, in the context of on-demand transmissions, the Supreme Court's *Aereo* decision confirms that the public performance right covers transmissions to the public via

individualized streams. Further still, where an act of file sharing or streaming involves the creation of a digital copy of a work, it also may implicate the right of reproduction under Section 106(1).

- Although the United States' approach to the making available right differs from that of its treaty partners, the majority of which have implemented the right through a broadly worded right to communicate copyrighted works to the public, both approaches are reasonable and effective, and indeed, both are sanctioned by the treaty language. It would not necessarily be beneficial for the United States to amend its approach by enacting a separate making available or communication-to-the-public right at this time, for example to respond to disparate court opinions or to confirm the application of the Treaties to new and emerging online activity. On the contrary, such an endeavor would likely prove more disruptive, not less, to the rule of law in this area.

At this time, the Copyright Office's recommendation is that Congress continue to monitor the opinions of both district and appellate courts regarding the scope and application of the making available right in the United States, especially because the publication of this Report and the analyses contained herein should prove helpful to both courts and practitioners looking for guidance in this area in the future. To the extent it becomes necessary, Congress could choose to provide legislative clarity. Such clarity might come in the form of a Section 101 definition, *i.e.*, stating that the right of distribution includes the right to offer access, and/or it might come in the form of a clarifying amendment to Section 106, *i.e.*, providing that a copyright owner's exclusive rights thereunder encompass the right to make a work available to the public, including in such a way that members of the public may access the work from a place and at a time individually chosen by them.

Alternatively, Congress could adopt the language of the right of communication to the public that is used by some other countries. As noted above, however, this approach is exponentially more complex, and would likely require a reordering of the existing Section 106 rights and corresponding changes to applicable exceptions and limitations.

Finally, the Copyright Office notes that this Report's analysis of U.S. law is limited to the question of whether the Copyright Act provides authors with a cause of action for the making available of copyrighted works to the public, as required by the WIPO Internet Treaties. Questions about the application of the right will continue to arise as business models evolve, and the Report expresses no opinion as to facts, technologies, or activities that have not yet been addressed by courts.

Moreover, it is important to note that even where a court finds a particular form of online access to implicate an exclusive right, that determination means only that a copyright owner may establish a *prima facie* infringement case on that ground; it does not mean that the defendant in any given case ultimately will be found liable. As always, the fair use doctrine and other enumerated copyright exceptions in the law will provide important bulwarks against overbroad claims that could impede desirable online activities. The role of the courts will be critical to effecting this overall balance.

I. Introduction and Study History

The growth of new technologies in the digital age has rapidly expanded the availability of copyrighted works through both legal and illicit sources. In the mid-1990s, when the Internet was relatively new but growing exponentially, the international copyright community sought to ensure that copyrighted works would be adequately protected online. To further this goal, the World Intellectual Property Organization ("WIPO")[11] and its member states (including the United States) began discussions on how to best ensure that copyright law could be applied effectively to the new medium. These discussions led to the WIPO Internet Treaties—the WIPO Copyright Treaty ("WCT") and the WIPO Performances and Phonograms Treaty ("WPPT").[12] Among other obligations, the WCT requires member states to recognize authors' exclusive right to authorize "any communication to the public of their works, by wire or wireless means, including the making available to the public of their works in such a way that members of the public may access these works from a place and at a time individually chosen by them."[13] The WPPT extends the right to performers and phonogram producers.[14] These treaty provisions ensure that copyright owners have the exclusive right to provide on-demand access to their works on the Internet and elsewhere.[15]

The United States implemented the WIPO Internet Treaties in 1998 via the DMCA.[16] The DMCA did not, however, add a specific making available right and did not otherwise amend the Copyright Act's enumeration of exclusive rights in Section 106. Instead, Congress found that the WCT and WPPT did "not require any change in the substance of copyright rights or exceptions in U.S. law."[17] Since then, U.S. government officials consistently have stated that the Copyright Act's existing exclusive rights cover the making available right,[18] and Congress has affirmed that understanding by approving numerous international agreements without any changes to U.S. law.[19]

Some courts, however, have struggled to determine the application of particular exclusive rights under the Act to various online activities, including newly developed forms of on-demand access. In light of these challenges, then-Representative Melvin L. Watt, Ranking Member of the House Judiciary Committee's Subcommittee on Courts, Intellectual Property, and the Internet, asked the Copyright Office to study the current state of the making available right under U.S. law.[20] Specifically, he asked that the Office review and assess how the existing bundle of rights under Title 17 covers the right "in the context of digital on-demand transmissions . . . as well as more broadly in the digital environment."[21] In addition, Representative Watt asked the Office to address how foreign nations have implemented the making available right, and to assess the feasibility and necessity of amending U.S. law in this area.[22]

The Office issued a request for public comments on February 25, 2014,[23] and received twenty-seven written responses from a range of parties, including academics, industry groups, and public interest organizations.[24] The Office then held a roundtable discussion in Washington, D.C. on May 5, 2014, during which members of the copyright community discussed a variety of issues relating to the making available right.[25] The Office provided the public with an additional opportunity to provide written comments via a July 15, 2015 Request for Additional Comments, which resulted in twenty-eight additional comments.[26]

The comments submitted in response to the two notices fell into roughly three categories of views. Many copyright owner representatives took the view that no legislative change is currently necessary because U.S. law already provides a making available right, and that the law, properly interpreted, encompasses the provision of access to copyrighted works, even without evidence that a user received a copy.[27] A smaller number of commenters agreed with that interpretation, but argued that Congress should strongly consider amending the law to provide greater clarity.[28] Others, including some public interest and technology groups, conceded the obligation to recognize such a right, but urged a narrower understanding of its scope, arguing that the making available right does not necessarily require U.S. law to cover mere offers of access.[29] Some commenters also contended that the addition of express "making available" language to U.S. copyright law would have significant adverse consequences, including creating uncertainty as to the legality of commonplace online activities.[30] Importantly, no one challenged the view that the United States is obligated by international agreements to recognize the making available right, or that the exclusive rights in Section 106 could serve as a basis for the fulfillment of those obligations.[31]

II. THE WIPO INTERNET TREATIES AND THE MAKING AVAILABLE RIGHT

Beginning in the early 1970s, WIPO embarked upon almost two decades of study and analysis to consider the most effective way to adapt the international copyright regime to new and emerging technologies.[32] Member countries were keenly aware that the primary treaty governing international copyright, the Berne Convention for the Protection of Literary and Artistic Works, was first adopted in the late 1800s and had been most recently amended in 1971. Thus, the international copyright regime lagged well behind subsequent developments in computers, photocopying, and satellite technology. In 1991, WIPO convened two Committees of Experts to consider the negotiation of new instruments to address these issues.[33] The "digital agenda," as it became known, concerned "certain definitions, rights applicable for the storage of works and objects of neighboring rights in digital systems, transmission of works and objects of neighboring rights in digital networks, limitations on and exceptions to rights in a digital environment, technological protection measures and rights management information."[34]

Throughout the digital agenda discussions, the United States and other countries highlighted the "immediate, costless, and widespread"[35] copying facilitated by the Internet, which "allow[ed] users of electronic media to send and retrieve perfect reproductions of copyrighted material easily and nearly instantaneously, to or from locations around the world."[36] As a result, the Internet posed several legal challenges—including the ease with which infringement could be carried out across international borders—that increased the importance of harmonizing international copyright standards.[37] The work of these Committees ultimately resulted in the WCT, which provides protection for authors of literary and artistic works (including writings, computer programs, musical works, audiovisual works, fine art works, photographs, and databases); and the WPPT, which includes protections for performers and producers of phonograms.

During the negotiation of the WIPO Internet Treaties, the Committees discussed the need to address authors' rights in light of the advent of digital interactive, on-demand transmissions and agreed "that the transmission of works and objects of neighboring rights on the Internet and in similar networks should be subjected to an exclusive right of authorization of the owners of the rights."[38] The Committees did not agree, however, on *how* to grant authors the right to authorize such transmissions. Instead, the member states debated two competing bundles of exclusive rights through which to provide this protection—either the right of reproduction plus a broad right of distribution, or reproduction plus the Berne Convention's right of communication to the public.[39] The United States argued that the distribution right properly encompassed digital transmissions, but several other countries preferred to cover such transmissions through a communication-to-the-public right.[40] The European Community was a strong proponent of the latter view and proposed draft treaty language that housed an author's right to make works available by wire or wireless means within the right of communication to the public.[41] After it became clear that neither the United States' nor the European Community's preferences would generally be accepted, a compromise solution, referred to as the "umbrella solution," was developed and incorporated into the WCT and WPPT.[42]

The umbrella solution, in attempting to close the Berne Convention gaps in coverage for the distribution and communication to the public rights, provides treaty members with flexibility in how they implement the exclusive right to authorize on-demand and interactive digital transmissions into national law.[43] This flexibility was particularly important for the United States. At the 1996 Diplomatic Conference that yielded the final text of the WIPO Internet Treaties, the U.S. delegation, according to the official minutes, "stressed the understanding—which had never been questioned during the preparatory work . . .—that those rights might be implemented in national legislation through application of any particular exclusive right . . . or combination of exclusive rights, as long as the acts described in [the treaty] Articles were covered by such rights."[44] Though the applicable treaty provisions used the terms "communication to the public" and "making available," treaty members were free to implement the obligations either as a subset of the right of communication to the public, as a stand-alone "making available" right, or through some other exclusive right or combination of rights found in their national laws.[45] The goal was to provide a vehicle for "grant[ing] effective and efficient protection in the digital environment, and [for] facilitat[ing] 'interoperability' between different systems."[46] Thus, "the most basic element of the 'umbrella solution' [was] the neutral, legal-characterization-free description of interactive transmissions (neutral in the sense that it should not be characterized either as distribution or communication to the public)" covered by the newly articulated right.[47]

The WCT and the WPPT reflect the umbrella solution in slightly different ways. WCT Article 8, entitled "Right of Communication to the Public," first provides an exclusive right for authors of literary and artistic works to authorize any "communication to the public . . . by wire or wireless means," and then extends that exclusive right to transmissions via interactive services, without legally characterizing the nature of the right:

> Without prejudice to the provisions of Articles 11(1)(ii), 11*bis*(1)(i) and (ii), 11*ter*(1)(ii), 14(1)(ii) and 14*bis*(1) of the Berne Convention, authors of literary and artistic works shall enjoy the exclusive right of authorizing any communication to the public of their works, by wire or wireless means, including the making available to the public of their works in such a way that members of the public may access these works from a place and at a time individually chosen by them.[48]

The WPPT reflects the umbrella solution[49] by providing an exclusive right of making available in Articles 10 for performers[50] and 14 for producers of sound recordings.[51] The WPPT uses the phrase "communication to the public" in an entirely different context, referring not to the interactive element but to more traditional communications to the public, similar to the public performance right in the United States.[52]

During the Diplomatic Conference, the Chairman of the Committees of Experts provided guidance on what types of activities the making available right was intended to reach. The Chairman stressed that one of the main objectives of WCT Article 8 was "to make it clear that interactive on-demand acts of communication are within the scope of the provision."[53] Similarly, WPPT Articles 10 and 14 are "based on interactivity and on on-demand access" by transmission, rather than physical distributions of copies.[54] In addition, the Chairman explained that the action covered by the exclusive right is the "making available of the work by providing access to it. What counts is the initial act of making the work available, not the mere provision of server space, communication connections, or facilities for the carriage and routing of signals."[55] Finally, the Chairman noted that "[i]t is irrelevant whether copies are available for the user or whether the work is simply made perceptible to, and thus usable by, the user."[56]

Since the Treaties' adoption, most authorities—including judicial decisions in countries that have incorporated explicit "making available" language into national law—have interpreted the right to cover not only the actual transmission of a work, but also the offering to the public of access to a work on demand.[57] They note that the treaty text refers to making works available in such a manner that members of the public "may access" them.[58] Thus, as one leading treatise concludes, "simply offering the work on an undiscriminating basis, so that any member of the general public may access the work, should come within the scope of the right. . . . It is not necessary that the offer be accepted: 'making available' embraces incipient as well as effected communications."[59] The majority of participants in this study agreed with that interpretation.[60]

III. U.S. IMPLEMENTATION OF THE MAKING AVAILABLE RIGHT

As noted above, the umbrella solution grants countries flexibility in how they implement the making available right—as a stand-alone exclusive right, or through a combination of other exclusive rights. Ultimately, however, the making available right as incorporated into the WCT and the WPPT sought to reserve to copyright owners the right to control interactive, on-demand dissemination of copyrighted works over the Internet, including provision of access to streams or downloads. In evaluating U.S. implementation of the making available right, then, we must look to how U.S. law addresses these and similar forms of communicating copyrighted works to the public under its exclusive rights scheme.

A. United States Treaty Ratification

The U.S. Senate passed a resolution to ratify the WIPO Internet Treaties in November 1998.[61] During deliberations on implementing the Treaties' exclusive rights provisions, including making available, officials from both the Copyright Office and the U.S. Patent and Trademark Office testified that the Treaties would not require amendment to the exclusive rights set forth in Section 106 of the Copyright Act. The Register of Copyrights stated that "[a]fter an extensive analysis the Copyright Office concluded that existing protections [in Title 17 were] adequate to fulfill . . . the substantive treaty obligations" implicating copyright owners' exclusive rights, and therefore there was "no need to alter the nature and scope of the copyrights and exception[]s, or change the substantive balance of rights embodied in the Copyright Act."[62] The Assistant Secretary of Commerce and Commissioner of Patents and Trademarks testified that "nothing in these Treaties . . . affects the issue of liability for particular acts of copyright infringement."[63]

In October 1998, President Clinton signed the DMCA, Title I of which is entitled the WIPO Copyright and Performances and Phonograms Treaties Implementation Act of 1998.[64] The Conference Report accompanying the legislation states that Title I "implements two new intellectual property treaties, the WIPO Copyright Treaty and the WIPO Performances and Phonograms Treaty, signed in Geneva, Switzerland in December 1996."[65] The DMCA did not modify any of the exclusive rights provided under Section 106 of Title 17. Consistent with the view of the Register and the Administration, the House Judiciary Committee Report on the legislation concluded that "[t]he treaties do not require any change in the substance of copyright rights or exceptions in U.S. law."[66]

Since then, the U.S. government has maintained consistently that the Copyright Act satisfies the WIPO Internet Treaties' making available obligations. For example, in 2002, the Register of Copyrights stated that "[w]hile Section 106 of the U.S. Copyright Act does not specifically include anything called a 'making available' right, the activities involved in making a work available are covered under the exclusive rights of reproduction, distribution, public display and/or public performance," and that the specific right "invoked in any given context will depend on the nature of the 'making available' activity."[67] Additionally, in formal statements to the World Trade Organization, the United States affirmed that it "provides full rights of making available as required by the WCT and WPPT"[68] and that "[t]he WCT and WPPT obligation to provide a right of making available . . . is fully satisfied through" provisions of Section 106.[69] And in 2013, the Department of Commerce's Internet Policy Task Force noted that the United States implements the making available right in part through the Act's exclusive right of distribution, and concluded that that right was intended to encompass "the mere offering of copies to the public."[70]

The United States also has reaffirmed its obligation to recognize the making available right in numerous bilateral and multilateral free trade agreements ("FTAs") entered into with other nations. Eleven FTAs (involving sixteen foreign countries) incorporate language based closely on WCT Article 8.[71] For example, the United States-Korea Free Trade Agreement, which entered into force in 2012, provides:

> Without prejudice to Articles 11(1)(ii), 11*bis*(1)(i) and (ii), 11*ter*(1)(ii), 14(1)(ii), and 14*bis* of the Berne Convention, each Party shall provide to authors the exclusive right to authorize or prohibit the communication to the public of their works, by wire or wireless means, including the making available to the public of their works in such a way that members of the public may access these works from a place and at a time individually chosen by them.[72]

Another FTA provides a general obligation to give effect to provisions of the WCT and WPPT, including the articles establishing the making available right.[73]

Pursuant to statute, the Executive Branch submitted these agreements to Congress for approval.[74] Each of the FTAs expressly referencing the making available right was accompanied by a formal Statement of Administrative Action setting out the Executive Branch's views regarding how implementation of the agreement would change or affect existing law.[75] In each case, the Administration concluded that no statutory or administrative change would be required to implement the chapter on intellectual property rights, which included the provisions on making available.[76] Congress specifically approved each of these Statements in the legislation implementing the respective FTAs.[77]

B. Exclusive Rights Relevant to "Making Available"

The United States implements the making available right principally through the Copyright Act's exclusive rights of distribution, public performance, and public display. In addition, to the extent that the act of making a work available to the public involves the creation of a copy, it may also implicate the right of reproduction.[78]

1. Right of Distribution

It is generally settled that the exclusive right of distribution gives a copyright owner the right to control the transmission of her work to the public in the form of digital downloads. Courts considering the issue have uniformly agreed that providing public access to downloadable copies of a copyrighted work without authorization—for example, by uploading a file to a publicly accessible peer-to-peer network—may give rise to liability under Section 106(3) in certain circumstances. Nonetheless, there is significant disagreement among courts and commentators over the evidentiary showing necessary to establish an infringement of the right in this context. We consider that issue in Part III.B.1.b below. First, however, we address a threshold issue raised by a few participants in this study.

> [T]he owner of copyright under this title has the exclusive rights to do and to authorize any of the following:
>
> . . . .
>
> (3) to distribute copies or phonorecords of the copyrighted work to the public by sale or other transfer of ownership, or by rental, lease, or lending
>
> . . . .
>
> 17 U.S.C. § 106(3)

a. Digital Files as Material Objects

A small number of commenters argued that the right of distribution does not cover digital transmissions at all, such as digital downloads or uploads. In support of that view, they noted that Section 106(3) speaks to the distribution of "copies or phonorecords," which are defined in Section 101 as "*material objects* . . . in which a work is fixed by any method now known or later developed, and from which the [work/sounds] can be perceived, reproduced, or otherwise communicated, either directly or with the aid of a machine or device."[79] In their view, the "transmission of bits" over the Internet does not involve the distribution of a material object.[80] Additionally, these commenters pointed to language in Section 106(3) limiting the scope of the right to distributions made "by sale or other transfer of ownership, or by rental, lease, or lending," which they interpret to require a change in ownership or possession of a material object from transferor to transferee. A digital transmission fails to satisfy that requirement, they argued, because it does not divest the sender of her copy of the relevant file; it merely creates a duplicate at the recipient's location.[81]

Such a narrow view of the distribution right, of course, would wholly upend protections for copyright owners online and therefore defeat the very purpose of the WIPO Internet Treaties—that is, to confirm exclusive rights for copyright owners in the digital age.[82] And, we are aware of no court in the United States that has adopted this extreme position. Each court to have considered this issue has concluded that digital transmissions are within the scope of Section 106(3).[83] As one court noted, such arguments "are unsupported by law and run contrary to the policies underlying the application of copyright law to internet communications."[84]

The District of Massachusetts's opinion in *London-Sire Records, Inc. v. Doe 1* provides a particularly thorough analysis.[85] There, the court noted as a preliminary matter that electronic files are "material objects" within the meaning of the Copyright Act, explaining that "any object in which a sound recording can be fixed"—including "the appropriate segment of [a] hard disk"—qualifies as such.[86] The court then determined, based on the distribution right's overall purpose of "allow[ing] the author to control the rate and terms at which copies or phonorecords of the work become available to the public," that electronic file transfers are "distributions" under Section 106(3).[87] It noted that "while the statute requires that distribution be of 'material objects,' there is no reason to limit 'distribution' to processes in which a material object exists throughout the entire transaction—as opposed to a transaction in which a material object is created elsewhere at its finish."[88] Finally, the court held that an electronic transmission can constitute a "transfer of ownership" under Section 106(3), reasoning that the statute "is concerned with the ability of a transferor to create ownership in someone else—not the transferor's ability simultaneously to retain his own ownership."[89]

In addition, as several commenters noted, other Copyright Act provisions indicate that Congress understood digital file transfers to implicate the distribution right.[90] Section 115, which establishes a compulsory license for making and distributing phonorecords of nondramatic musical works, repeatedly refers to distribution "by means of a digital phonorecord delivery,"[91] and gives a licensee the right "to distribute or authorize the distribution of a phonorecord . . . by means of a digital transmission which constitutes a digital phonorecord delivery."[92] A "digital phonorecord delivery" is defined to mean "each individual delivery of a phonorecord by digital transmission of a sound recording which results in a specifically identifiable reproduction by or for any transmission recipient of a phonorecord of that sound recording . . . ."[93] The statute thus provides a limitation on the distribution right of copyright owners of musical works, and defines that right to include the delivery of phonorecords by digital transmission.

In light of this unbroken line of authority, the Office readily concludes that Section 106(3) extends to the digital transfer of copies or phonorecords in electronic formats and is not limited to the conveyance of tangible objects.[94]

b. Evidence Required to Establish Distribution

A second, more widespread area of disagreement is the question of whether a party can infringe the distribution right by offering a copyrighted work to the public for download, or whether evidence of an actual download is an essential element of such a violation.[95] To date, neither the U.S. Supreme Court nor any of the circuit courts has had occasion to directly rule on the issue,[96] and the district courts that have considered the question have come to differing conclusions. Several of the district courts to consider the issue have found, at least preliminarily, that offering copyrighted material online for download, without actual evidence of third party downloads, may be sufficient to support a claim for unauthorized distribution.[97] In contrast, other district courts have held that evidence of an actual download is required to support a finding of infringement of the right to distribute.[98] Among the courts adopting this latter view, some have concluded that plaintiffs nevertheless are not required to offer direct proof of a download to establish distribution, but may do so through circumstantial or investigator evidence from which it reasonably can be inferred that a download took place.[99]

For the reasons discussed below, the Copyright Office adheres to the view that Section 106(3) is properly construed to cover the making available of copies of works to the public in the form of downloads, regardless of whether the plaintiff proves that an actual download occurred.

While the issue is not free from ambiguity, we conclude that this construction produces the more internally consistent reading of Title 17 and best reflects congressional intent. The statutory language, context, and legislative history all support this conclusion.

i. Statutory Language and Context

As noted, Section 106(3) gives the owner of a copyright the exclusive right "to distribute copies or phonorecords of the copyrighted work to the public by sale or other transfer of ownership, or by rental, lease, or lending."[100] The term "distribute" is not defined in the statute, and its meaning generated little case law prior to the emergence of electronic transmission technologies. During that period, "few plaintiffs alleged violation of the distribution right apart from violation of the reproduction right" under Section 106(1), since, in most cases, copies of works *distributed* without a rightsholder's authorization were also *made* without authorization.[101] Thus, a plaintiff could establish a *prima facie* infringement case simply through proof of unauthorized copying, making it unnecessary for courts to construe the scope of the distribution right.[102]

Cases that did turn solely on the distribution right typically "involved unusual scenarios, such as placing a copyrighted work in a library that was open to the public."[103] In *Hotaling v. Church of Jesus Christ of Latter-Day Saints*, the Fourth Circuit held that a church distributed copies of a work for purposes of Section 106(3) when it made them available to the public at its libraries.[104] The court did not address the ordinary meaning of "distribute," but it held that the copies were distributed notwithstanding the lack of record evidence that the libraries had in fact loaned them to members of the public. The court explained:

> When a public library adds a work to its collection, lists the work in its index or catalog system, and makes the work available to the borrowing or browsing public, it has completed all the steps necessary for distribution to the public. At that point, members of the public can visit the library and use the work. Were this not to be considered distribution within the meaning of § 106(3), a copyright holder would be prejudiced by a library that does not keep records of public use, and the library would unjustly profit by its own omission.[105]

The key element for the court, then, was not that there was direct proof that someone actually checked out library copies, but that the library had offered the copies to the public and completed all steps necessary to fulfill that offer.[106]

More recently, in *Diversey v. Schmidly*, the Tenth Circuit held that the distribution right is infringed by the unauthorized listing of a work in a library catalog for public lending.[107] Agreeing with *Hotaling*, the court concluded that "[t]he essence of distribution in the library lending context is the work's availability 'to the borrowing or browsing public.'"[108] Like the Fourth Circuit, the *Diversey* court did not provide a detailed analysis of the statutory text. Nevertheless, both courts determined, at least implicitly, that the term "distribute" can encompass the making available of copies in such a manner that the only action necessary for a transfer to occur is that of an offeree in acquiring a copy.

With the development of digital transmission technologies, the question of what it means to "distribute" copies has attained far greater salience, and the resulting litigation has produced substantial disagreement among courts and commentators. In peer-to-peer file sharing cases, some courts have disagreed with *Hotaling*, one concluding that "the ordinary dictionary meaning of the word 'distribute' necessarily entails a transfer of ownership or possession from one person to another"[109] and another stating that "[m]erely because the defendant has 'completed all the steps necessary for distribution' does not necessarily mean that a distribution has actually occurred."[110] In response, a number of commentators have observed that not all dictionary definitions of "distribute" refer to the receipt of material by another person,[111] arguing that, in at least some contexts, the term is "sufficiently broad to include providing copies for people who wish to acquire them."[112]

In any event, the definitional issue is only part of the statutory construction equation. When construing statutory language, courts do not examine the relevant terms in isolation. Rather, "[i]t is a 'fundamental canon of statutory construction that the words of a statute must be read in their context and with a view to their place in the overall statutory scheme.' A court must therefore interpret the statute 'as a symmetrical and coherent regulatory scheme,' and 'fit, if possible, all parts into an harmonious whole.'"[113] Here, two other Copyright Act provisions addressing the scope of the distribution right suggest that Section 106(3) is properly construed to cover offers to distribute copyrighted works via download.

First, a criminal copyright provision in Section 506 of Title 17 demonstrates Congress's intention to treat the making available of works on publicly accessible computer networks as a violation of the distribution right. Section 506(a)(1)(C) provides that a person may criminally infringe copyright "by the distribution of a work being prepared for commercial distribution, by making it available on a computer network accessible to members of the public, if such person knew or should have known that the work was intended for commercial distribution."[114] This provision, which was added to the Copyright Act by the Family Entertainment and Copyright Act of 2005,[115] indicates both Congress's intent to proscribe making works available for download before their authorized commercial release, and its understanding that the exclusive right implicated by such conduct is that of distribution.[116]

The district court in *In re Napster, Inc. Copyright Litigation* discounted the significance of this legislation on the ground that it did not amend Section 106(3) and thus does not speak explicitly to the scope of civil liability under the distribution right.[117] Other courts have found that the statute actually indicates that Congress did *not* intend to cover offers in the civil context. In their view, Section 506(a)(1)(C) shows that "when Congress intends distribution to encompass making available or offering to transfer, it has demonstrated that it is quite capable of explicitly providing that definition within the statute."[118] To be sure, Congress could have combined the new criminal provision with language directly addressing "making available" activity in the civil context. The Office is not persuaded, however, that the absence of such a provision carries the significance ascribed to it by some courts. To read the 2005 amendment as wholly irrelevant to civil claims, or to treat it as evidence that offers are excluded in that context, requires interpreting the statute to mean that the same conduct that is a criminal infringement under Section 506(a)(1)(C) cannot be the subject of a civil infringement claim. Such a construction seems highly implausible. As noted in one analysis, there is no other instance under the Copyright Act "in which an act that gives rise to criminal liability for copyright infringement could not provide the basis for civil liability."[119] Moreover, the statutory language makes clear that the conduct described in Section 506(a)(1)(C) is an infringement of the copyright owner's distribution right: a person who acts willfully is criminally liable for "infring[ing] a copyright . . . if the infringement was committed . . . by the distribution of a work . . . by making it available on a computer network accessible to members of the public . . . ."[120] In the Copyright Office's view, it is more consistent with "a symmetrical and coherent regulatory scheme"[121] to construe Section 506(a)(1)(C) as an extension of criminal sanctions to a specific subset of "making available" conduct, the broader universe of which was already covered by Section 106(3).

The second Copyright Act provision relevant to the construction of the distribution right is Section 602, which concerns the unauthorized importation of copies or phonorecords. Section 602(a)(1) provides that "[i]mportation into the United States, without the authority of the owner of copyright under this title, of copies or phonorecords of a work that have been acquired outside the United States is an infringement of the exclusive right to distribute copies or phonorecords under section 106 . . . ."[122] The statute does not require evidence that copies were actually disseminated to members of the public to establish a violation. The legislative history confirms that "any unauthorized importer of copies or phonorecords acquired abroad, could be sued for damages and enjoined from making use of them, even before any public distribution in this country has taken place."[123] Therefore, as one participant in this study has noted, "this provision indicates that Congress was interested in protecting the copyright owner's exclusive right to distribute without concern for technical requirements. Someone who imports copies of a work violates the distribution right unless that person fits within one of the specific exceptions."[124] Nor is there any indication that Congress intended to provide a lower standard of proof for violations of the distribution right arising out of unauthorized importations than for distribution violations generally. Indeed, Professor Nimmer concludes that such a construction would be "entirely fanciful," finding it highly unlikely that Congress intended not to require proof of actual dissemination "for activity at an international border, . . . [but] harbored the opposite intention with respect to entirely domestic activity."[125] The Office agrees that the better approach is to construe Section 602(a)(1) and Section

106(3) consistently, with the former providing clarification that infringement of the distribution right does not require evidence of receipt by a third party.

In light of this analysis, the Office respectfully disagrees with the conclusion reached by some courts that the phrase "by sale or other transfer of ownership, or by rental, lease, or lending" in Section 106(3) indicates that the distribution right is implicated only where a copy of a work changes hands.[126] That reading might be persuasive were the relevant analysis confined to Section 106(3) itself, but it is difficult to reconcile with Sections 506 and 602, which demonstrate that infringement of the distribution right does not require such a transfer in all circumstances. At a minimum, these provisions would seem to create an ambiguity in the statute, making consideration of its legislative history appropriate. As discussed in the next section, that history strongly indicates that Congress intended Section 106(3) to encompass offers of public distribution. Furthermore, under the statutory construction canon discussed in Part III.C.2, the statute should be interpreted consistently with international norms where fairly possible. In the Office's view, it is reasonable to read the "sale or other transfer of ownership" language not as a requirement for actual dissemination, but simply as a means of distinguishing the types of communication methods covered by the distribution right from those covered by other exclusive rights. By referring to distribution "by sale or other transfer of ownership, or by rental, lease, or lending," the statute makes clear that the distribution right applies only to activities that enable a member of the public to obtain possession of a copy of a work, as opposed to those that merely allow a work to be perceived, which generally fall under the public performance or public display rights. Based on all of these considerations, the Office concludes that this is the preferable interpretation.

Nor is the Office persuaded that a provision in Chapter 9 of Title 17 is indicative of congressional intent to limit the distribution right to completed transfers. Noting that Section 901 expressly defines "distribute" to include "offer[ing] to sell, lease, bail, or otherwise transfer,"[127] a few commenters argued—and one court has concluded[128]—that this language demonstrates that when Congress intends to include offers within the meaning of "distribution," it is capable of making that intention explicit in the statutory text.[129] Section 901, however, is a provision of the Semiconductor Chip Protection Act of 1984, which, although codified in Title 17, "neither amends the preceding chapters nor constitutes any part of the Copyright Act."[130] It does not speak to the exclusive rights of copyright owners but instead creates a *sui generis* form of protection limited to "mask works" fixed in semiconductor chip products.[131] The Office is not convinced that definitional language from this separate statute warrants significant weight in the construction of the Copyright Act's distribution right, particularly in relation to the statutory provisions discussed above expressly addressing that right.[132]

In sum, there is substantial support in the text of the Act that the exclusive right of distribution encompasses the making available to the public of copies of works for download. The term "distribute" as commonly defined extends to making items available for persons to acquire, as the two federal appellate courts in *Hotaling* and *Diversey* recognized in construing Section 106(3) in the analog context. To the extent that the ordinary meaning of the term does not fully resolve the issue in the digital realm, reading Section 106(3) in the context of related statutory provisions suggests that Congress did not intend to condition liability on proof of actual dissemination.

It should be noted that the statutory text also reflects an important limitation on the scope of "offering" liability under the distribution right. Under both Sections 506(a)(1)(C) and 602(a)(1), it is clear that the defendant actually must have possession of the relevant work for liability to attach. This limitation likewise is embodied in the *Hotaling* formulation, which looks to whether the defendant has "completed all the steps necessary for distribution to the public,"[133] and thus permits a finding of infringement only where a party has a copy of a work and makes one or more copies available for members of the public to obtain.[134] Accordingly, while a person who uploads a copyrighted work to a share folder for downloading by the public has made an offer sufficient to implicate Section 106(3), one who simply makes a statement purporting to "offer" copies that she does not in fact possess has not done so.

ii. Legislative History

Some have expressed the view that the Copyright Act is ambiguous with respect to whether Section 106(3) includes a right of making available.[135] In the event that courts in future cases reach the same conclusion, they may look to legislative history for further insight into Congress's intent to provide such a right.[136] In particular, the history surrounding the relationship between the distribution right and certain exclusive rights under the Copyright Act of 1909 reflects Congress's understanding that Section 106(3) would encompass offers to distribute copies to the public. Most courts that have construed the right have not had the full benefit of this history, instead relying on prior editions of the *Nimmer on Copyright* treatise to conclude that the statute is limited to completed transfers. In light of recent historical scholarship, however, the treatise has been updated to conclude that Congress intended the distribution right to extend to offers of access.

(a) Relationship to Historic Rights to Publish and Vend

An examination of the development of the 1976 Act reveals compelling evidence that the distribution right was intended to broaden the scope of the exclusive rights to "publish" and to "vend" provided under the Copyright Act of 1909, which had long been understood to encompass offers to distribute copies to the public.

The 1909 Act did not include an exclusive right of distribution. Instead, Section 1(a) of that law provided that a copyright owner had the exclusive right to "print, reprint, publish, copy, and vend the copyrighted work."[137] In its 1961 *Report of the Register of Copyrights on the Revision of the U.S. Copyright Law*, the Copyright Office concluded that "[t]hese various terms are redundant. Printing and reprinting are modes of copying, and vending is a mode of publishing. . . . In substance, as several courts have observed, the right embraced in the repetitive terms of section 1(a) is the twofold right to make and to publish copies."[138] After a series of public meetings, the Office released a preliminary draft of a revised copyright law in 1962.[139] Section 5 of the draft reframed the exclusive rights to make and publish copies as the "right to copy or record" and the "right to distribute copies and sound recordings," respectively.[140] The change in terminology was explained in a February 1963 Copyright Office hearing by Abe Goldman, General Counsel of the Office: "Subsection (b) [establishing the distribution right], I believe, would cover everything that's covered in section 1(a) of the present law by reference to the terms 'publish' and 'vend'—broadened, I would say, to avoid any questions as to whether 'publish' or 'vend' is used in such a narrow sense that there might be forms of distribution not covered."[141] Case law construing the 1909 Act (as well as prior versions of the copyright law) had consistently interpreted the publication right "to encompass the offering of copyrighted works to the public."[142] In fact, according to one analysis, "[n]o court recognized a requirement to prove actual distribution of copies."[143]

The decision to substitute "distribute" for "publish" in the new legislation appears to have been motivated in part by a desire to avoid confusion that had arisen in the case law over other aspects of the publication right. Under the 1909 Act, the publication of a work could carry severe consequences for copyright owners because "the act of publication forfeited common law copyright protection for the work and improper notice [upon publication] surrendered statutory protection."[144] As a result, "[j]urists developed doctrines to avoid such harsh effects," but these often resulted in "dubious distinctions" in the concept of publication that generated confusion among litigants and criticism from commentators.[145] At the February 1963 Copyright Office hearing, Edward Sargoy, representing the American Bar Association, suggested that the use of the term "distribute" in place of "publish" could help to remedy this concern:

> I am heartily in accord with the omission of the use of the words "published" or "publication." I think that the use of the words "publication" or "published," in hundreds of common law and statutory cases, dissertations, and otherwise, has made the terms archaic today in the light of our recent technological progress. Reference to such materials where the word derived its meaning from conditions existing in the 18th, 19th, and early part of the 20th century, will only lead to confusion. I think it is an excellent idea to use the word "distribute" and, just as the draft here has done, have "distribute" expressly include the right "to sell," (which is strictly one of the rights of publication), "or otherwise transfer ownership of, rent, lease, or lend one or more copies or sound recordings of the work."[146]

Ultimately, this proposed change was reflected in legislation introduced in Congress in 1965, which included under Section 106(a)(3) the exclusive right of the copyright owner "to distribute copies or phonorecords of the copyrighted work to the public by sale or other transfer of ownership, or by rental, lease, or lending . . . ."[147] No subsequent changes to this language were made, and Section 106(3) of the current act is identically worded. Underscoring the intended relationship to publication, the 1965 Supplementary Report of the Register of Copyrights notes that the language of the proposed clause containing the distribution right "is virtually identical with that in the definition of 'publication' in section 101, but for the sake of clarity we have restated the concept here."[148]

Perhaps even more revealing, the 1976 reports of the House and Senate Judiciary Committees on the legislation that ultimately became the current Copyright Act repeatedly use the term "publication" in place of "distribution" when describing the exclusive rights provided. The reports state: "The five fundamental rights that the bill gives to copyright owners—the exclusive rights of reproduction, adaptation, *publication*, performance, and display—are stated generally in section 106."[149] Under the heading "*Rights of reproduction, adaptation, and publication*," the reports provide that "[t]he first three clauses of section 106" include exclusive rights that "can generally be characterized as rights of copying, recording, adaptation, and publishing."[150] The Senate report then explains: "Clause (3) of section 106 establishes the exclusive right of publication: The right 'to distribute copies or phonorecords of the copyrighted work to the public by sale or other transfer of ownership, or by rental, lease, or lending.'"[151] Read together with the earlier drafting history, these statements strongly suggest that "Congress understood 'distribute' to encompass 'publish' explicated through its long-established meaning and chose the term 'distribute' to limit any confusion that had emerged over judicial efforts to avoid the severe consequences of publication without proper notice."[152]

Some courts have rejected the proposition that the distribution right fully incorporates publication. Their analysis, however, does not take into account the full legislative record, much of which did not receive widespread attention from copyright stakeholders until the publication of an article by Professor Peter S. Menell in 2011.[153] Instead, these courts have focused primarily on the definition of "publication" in Section 101 of the current Act, which provides:

> "Publication" is the distribution of copies or phonorecords of a work to the public by sale or other transfer of ownership, or by rental, lease, or lending. The offering to distribute copies or phonorecords to a group of persons for purposes of further distribution, public performance, or public display, constitutes publication. A public performance or display of a work does not of itself constitute publication.[154]

In the view of these courts, the presence of the phrase "the offering to distribute" within the definition suggests that Congress intended "distribution" and "publication" to have different meanings. In *London-Sire Records*, for example, the court read that language to indicate that "the statute explicitly creates an additional category of publications that are not themselves distributions."[155] Under that construction, an offer to distribute copies to a group of persons for purposes of further distribution, public performance, or public display would constitute a publication but not a distribution within the meaning of Section 106(3).

Yet while the statutory text may permit such a reading, it does not compel it: the fact that Congress chose to clarify that certain offers to distribute were to be treated as publications does not necessarily mean that it intended to exclude offers from the scope of the distribution right. Moreover, placing such weight on that portion of the definition seems at odds with congressional intent. The sentence containing the "offering to distribute" language was added to the draft legislation by a 1971 Senate bill[156] that, according to the House report accompanying the final legislation in 1976, provided only "minor amendments" to the previous version of the proposed Act.[157] Indeed, as Professor Nimmer notes, "there is no accompanying commentary" for the 1971 bill.[158] Had Congress intended to reject the well-established view that the distribution right "would cover everything" encompassed by the prior rights to publish and vend[159]—and, in so doing, to narrow the rights long afforded copyright owners under existing law—it seems highly unlikely that it would have done so through a "minor" definitional amendment and without comment.[160] The Office accordingly is not persuaded that this language contradicts the extensive and consistent evidence of congressional intent to preserve those protections under the distribution right.[161]

(b) Role of *Nimmer on Copyright* Treatise

Prior to the publication of Professor Menell's article, the academic source most frequently relied on by courts construing the distribution right was the *Nimmer on Copyright* treatise. Numerous courts cited a statement in previous editions of the treatise that "infringement of [the distribution right] requires an actual dissemination of either copies or phonorecords" in support of their conclusion that the statute does not cover offers of access.[162] For example, the treatise was the sole authority cited by the Eighth Circuit in *National Car Rental System, Inc. v. Computer Associates International, Inc.*, in support of its statement that Section 106(3) requires an actual distribution of copies.[163] Several courts have in turn relied on *National Car Rental* for the proposition that Section 106(3) does not provide a making available right.[164]

After reviewing Professor Menell's legislative history scholarship, however, Professor Nimmer removed the statement from the treatise and invited Professor Menell to co-author a revised section on the origins and scope of the distribution right.[165] Based in part on the newly examined legislative history, the current edition concludes that "[n]o consummated act of actual distribution need be demonstrated in order to implicate the copyright owner's distribution right," and that "the act of making available sound recordings for downloading by the public through file-sharing networks suffices to show actionable copyright infringement."[166] Moreover, the current edition clarifies that its earlier "offhand statement" regarding "actual dissemination" was merely intended to contrast the concept of distribution with that of performance.[167]

The first court of appeals case to interpret Section 106(3) following the publication of the revision was the Tenth Circuit's *Diversey* decision noted above. The court cited both Professor Menell's research and the updated treatise in support of its conclusion that, at least in the library lending context, making a work available to the public is sufficient to implicate the distribution right.[168]

* * *

In light of all of the foregoing evidence, the Copyright Office concludes that a person who has "completed all the steps necessary for distribution to the public,"[169] such that members of the public may access downloadable copies of a work on demand, has engaged in a "distribution" within the meaning of Section 106(3). The text and legislative history of the Act indicate that Congress intended to afford copyright owners the exclusive right to control not only the actual dissemination of copies of their works, but also the making available of copies to the public. Our conclusion in this regard is further supported by the need, discussed below, to construe the statute consistently with our international obligations where fairly possible.[170]

2. *Right of Public Performance*

> [T]he owner of copyright under this title has the exclusive rights to do and to authorize any of the following:
>
> . . . .
>
> (4) in the case of literary, musical, dramatic, and choreographic works, pantomimes, and motion pictures and other audiovisual works, to perform the copyrighted work publicly;
>
> . . . .
>
> (6) in the case of sound recordings, to perform the copyrighted work publicly by means of a digital audio transmission.
>
> 17 U.S.C. § 106(4), (6)

In addition to digital downloads, the WIPO Internet Treaties sought to address other acts of making copyrighted works available online, including the streaming of copyrighted content.[171] As noted above, acts of Internet streaming primarily implicate the right of public performance, since such transmissions often do not result in the creation of a permanent file on the user's computer (and thus may not be completely covered by the reproduction or distribution rights).

Under Section 101 of the Copyright Act, to "perform" a work means "to recite, render, play, dance, or act it, either directly or by means of any device or process or, in the case of a motion picture or other audiovisual work, to show its images in any sequence or to make the sounds accompanying it audible."[172] The definition of what constitutes a "public" performance encompasses two types of activities: performances or displays that occur in a public setting or before a public group,[173] and performances or displays that occur via a "device or process" that transmits the performance to the public or to a public place. The latter category is defined by Section 101's "Transmit Clause":

> To perform or display a work 'publicly' means—
>
> . . . .
>
> (2) to transmit or otherwise communicate a performance or display of the work . . . to the public, by means of any device or process, whether the members of the public capable of receiving the performance or display receive it in the same place or in separate places and at the same time or at different times.[174]

As discussed, most authorities interpret the making available right under the Treaties to cover the offering of access to a work to the public on-demand.[175] Thus, for purposes of evaluating U.S. implementation with respect to streaming, the key considerations are whether the Transmit Clause encompasses (1) offers to stream, rather than just completed transmissions, and (2) on-demand communications—*i.e.*, those that individual members of the public can receive at a time and place of their choosing. The first issue has not been squarely resolved by courts, but the Office concludes that the statute is properly construed to reach such offers. As to the second issue, the Supreme Court has confirmed that the Transmit Clause does in fact reach performances communicated in individualized streams.

a. Offers to Stream

Through the Transmit Clause, Congress intended to focus on the *act* of engaging in public performance or public display, without regard to whether or not the public actually *received* the performance or display. To "transmit" a performance or display is defined to mean "to communicate it by any device or process whereby images or sounds are received beyond the place from which they are sent."[176] The House report accompanying the 1976 Act makes clear that Congress intended that definition to turn on the accessibility of a performance or display to the public, not on its actual receipt by any individual:

> Each and every method by which the images or sounds comprising a performance or display are picked up and conveyed is a 'transmission,' and if the transmission reaches the public in my [sic] form, the case comes within the scope of clauses (4) or (5) of section 106.

> Under the bill, as under the present law, a performance made available by transmission to the public at large is 'public' even though the recipients are not gathered in a single place, and even if there is no proof that any of the potential recipients was operating his receiving apparatus at the time of the transmission.[177]

The report also notes that Congress intended to give the statute sufficient flexibility to accommodate changes in technology: "The definition of 'transmit' . . . is broad enough to include all conceivable forms and combinations of wired or wireless communications media, including but by no means limited to radio and television broadcasting as we know them."[178]

Outside the streaming context, courts have looked to this legislative history to conclude that infringement of the public performance right does not require a showing that any users actually received the transmitted performances. For example, in a case involving retransmission of broadcast signals, the District of Maine noted that "for purposes of demonstrating transmission 'to the public,' [a plaintiff] need not prove that a substantial number of people actually viewed the challenged transmission."[179] Instead, the plaintiff needed to prove that "despite restrictions imposed by [the defendant] on viewership, the challenged transmission was *capable* of being viewed by a substantial number of people."[180] Likewise, in a case involving a video system designed to transmit films from a central bank of video cassette players to potential viewers' hotel rooms, the Northern District of California determined that "whether the number of hotel guests viewing an On Command transmission is one or one hundred . . . the transmission is still a public performance since it goes to members of the public."[181]

Of course, on-demand streaming differs from traditional broadcasting and cable systems in that the latter typically "transmit[] constantly," and the "signals, in a sense, lurk[] behind the screen, ready to emerge when the subscriber turn[s] the knob."[182] In a streaming service, by contrast, the content is available to users, but a transmission begins only after a user selects the desired work through an online interface. Few courts have addressed whether the offering of works for streaming is enough to implicate the public performance right absent such a transmission. Some courts have avoided resolution of the issue by allowing plaintiffs to establish claims based on evidence other than direct evidence of streaming to third parties. For example, in *Capitol Records, Inc. v. MP3tunes, LLC*, the court noted that "the jury heard evidence from which it could infer that Sideload.com's features, including the playback feature, encouraged new users to sign up at MP3tunes.com," and thus "the jury could conclude reasonably that potential users had likely taken advantage of this feature."[183] Similarly, in *China Central Television v. Create New Technology (HK) Ltd.*, the court held that plaintiffs were likely to succeed on a public performance claim based on evidence that the plaintiffs and their investigators observed and recorded portions of copyrighted television episodes streamed through the defendant's peer-to-peer streaming service.[184] Meanwhile, the Seventh Circuit has discussed the issue without deciding it, observing that a construction that covers offers would be "better at giving meaning to 'public' in public performance but worse at giving meaning to 'performance.'"[185]

While acknowledging the lack of direct judicial authority, the Office concludes that reading the statutory provisions in light of the purposes articulated by Congress indicates that the public performance right encompasses offers to stream.[186] To begin with, excluding such offers would require reading the text in a manner that is inconsistent with Congress's clear intention to make a performance's accessibility, not its actual receipt, the determining factor under the Transmit Clause. As one commenter observed, if the phrase "transmit . . . to the public" is to be read literally, "it would follow there is no transmission to 'the public' if the service does not in fact communicate the performance of the work to a substantial number of people."[187] Indeed, "[t]he Act . . . suggests that 'the public' consists of a large group of people outside of a family and friends."[188] But, as shown, "what matters, in determining whether the audience for a transmission is 'the public,' is *capacity* by 'members of the public' to receive the transmission, not actual receipt."[189]

Furthermore, the narrow construction seems inconsistent with congressional intent given the functional equivalency between traditional communications systems and on-demand streaming. Although the legislative history of the Transmit Clause describes the covered activities in terms of actual transmissions (unsurprisingly given then-existing technologies), it strongly suggests that the critical inquiry is whether the performance or display has been made available in such a manner that members of the public need only activate a receiving apparatus in order to access it: "[A] performance made available by transmission to the public at large is 'public' even though the recipients are not gathered in a single place, and even if there is no proof that any of the potential recipients was operating his receiving apparatus at the time of the transmission."[190] The lack of an actual transmission in the streaming context would not seem to make a substantive difference since, as the Supreme Court recently recognized, the distinction in delivery mechanisms "means nothing to the [streaming service] subscriber. It means nothing to the broadcaster" or other copyright owner.[191] Under both communication methods, all that is required for an offeree to receive the performance or display is for her to activate the relevant reception device. In the case of streaming, that action—"today's 'turn of the knob'"—is as simple as "a click on a website."[192] We believe it unlikely that Congress would have intended to exclude such services, particularly in light of its stated desire not to limit the statute's coverage to technologies existing in 1976.[193]

b. Individualized Streams

Case law involving the application of the public performance right to on-demand streaming has focused largely on two issues to date. First, several courts have considered whether streams delivered separately to individual recipients can qualify as "public" performances. Until recently, conflicting lower court decisions on that issue were in tension with the Treaties' on-demand access requirement, but the Supreme Court's recent decision in *American Broadcasting Cos. v. Aereo, Inc.*[194] confirmed that U.S. law covers such transmissions. Second, courts have disagreed over whether, or to what extent, a streaming service must exercise "volitional conduct" to infringe the public performance right.

i. Streams as "Public" Performances

Before the Supreme Court resolved the issue, courts were divided over whether the public performance right could encompass the delivery of a performance in individualized streams. In a pair of cases, the Second Circuit interpreted the Transmit Clause to limit the public performance right to transmissions for which multiple individuals were capable of viewing a single stream, effectively exempting from the public display and performance rights all forms of unicast streaming,[195] as well as any technologies that create separate copies of a work for multiple users. In *Cartoon Network LP, LLLP v. CSC Holdings, Inc.* ("*Cablevision*"), the court noted that the Transmit Clause uses the words "capable of receiving the performance" instead of "capable of receiving the transmission," and reasoned that "a transmission of a performance is itself a performance" for purposes of determining whether the performance was to the "public."[196] Extrapolating from this, the court concluded that a work is publicly performed within the meaning of the Transmit Clause and Section 106(4) only when multiple individuals are capable of receiving the same transmission. The court then applied this construction to Cablevision's system, which allowed a single subscriber to direct a server maintained by Cablevision to record a copy of a television program, and then to later transmit a video stream of the file to the subscriber. The court held that this later transmission did not constitute a public performance under Section 106(4), because only the subscriber who directed the making of the copy could receive the later transmission of that copy. Significantly, the Second Circuit rejected the district court's holding that, because multiple customers would receive the same underlying work, Section 106(4) was implicated even if each transmission originated from a distinct copy.[197]

The Second Circuit expanded its *Cablevision* holding to find that the Aereo Internet broadcast television streaming service did not engage in a public performance in *WNET v. Aereo, Inc.*[198] When an individual user logged into the service, Aereo would dedicate an individual dime-sized antenna to that user, who could then select from a list of local programming currently being aired. Aereo would capture the broadcast signal using the dedicated antenna, and with the assistance of a transcoder, translate the broadcast signals into data and save a copy to an Aereo hard drive in a directory reserved for that user. Once six or seven seconds of programming had been saved, the system would begin streaming the program to the user from that copy. The user could then watch the program on an Internet-connected device, delayed just slightly behind the original network broadcast. Consistent with its *Cablevision* holding, the Second Circuit interpreted the word "performance" in the Transmit Clause ("capable of receiving the performance") to mean the individual transmission, rather than the underlying performance of the copyrighted work. The consequence of this was that if only a single person were able to receive any individual transmission, then the performance would not be public. The Second Circuit further held that "private transmissions—that is those not capable of being received by the public—should not be aggregated."[199] Thus, if only one person would be capable of receiving each individual transmission of the work, the court reasoned, that transmission would not constitute a public performance within the meaning of Section 106(4), even if several people received identical performances of the work through several transmissions.

After the Second Circuit's *Cablevision* and *Aereo* decisions, a divide among the courts on this issue began to emerge. Courts in the Second and First Circuits applied *Cablevision* to limit the public display and performance right to cases where the stream or file being transmitted was a "master" file, excluding from liability any technology that created separate copies of a work for its users.[200] Courts elsewhere, however, rejected the master file test, finding liability where a defendant transmitted a work to multiple users, even if the work was embodied in multiple copies.[201]

The Supreme Court took up the question of the proper contours of the public performance right on the Internet when it granted certiorari in *Aereo*. In reaching its conclusion that the Aereo technology infringed the plaintiffs' right of public performance, the Supreme Court addressed two questions: was Aereo the *entity* that performed the works, and did Aereo perform the works *publicly*? On the first question, the Court held that Aereo performed within the meaning of Section 106(4). Rejecting Aereo's argument that it merely provided the equipment for users to perform plaintiffs' works themselves, the majority focused on the legislative intent behind the 1976 Act, noting "Aereo's overwhelming likeness to the cable companies targeted by the 1976 amendments."[202]

On the second question, the Court held that Aereo performed "publicly," notwithstanding that it transmitted to individual subscribers from personal copies. Looking again to the Act's purposes, the Court concluded that Aereo's use of dedicated copies did "not render Aereo's commercial objective any different from that of cable companies" or "significantly alter the viewing experience of Aereo's subscribers."[203] In addition, it read the Transmit Clause to mean that an "entity may transmit a performance through one or several transmissions, where the performance is of the same work,"[204] and thus, in contrast to the Second Circuit's interpretation, the "performance" at issue is not the individual transmission, but the underlying performance of the copyrighted work itself. The Court explained, by way of illustration, that "[o]ne can sing a song to his family, whether he sings the same song one-on-one or in front of all together . . . . By the same principle, an entity may transmit a performance through one or several transmissions, where the performance is of the same work."[205]

This interpretation, the Court held, is compelled by the language in the Transmit Clause providing that a performance may be public "whether the members of the public capable of receiving the performance . . . receive it . . . at the same time or at different times."[206] "Were the words 'to transmit . . . a performance' limited to a single act of communication," the Court reasoned, "members of the public could not receive the performance communicated 'at different times.'"[207] The Court thus concluded that "when an entity communicates the same contemporaneously perceptible images and sounds to multiple people, it transmits a performance to them regardless of the number of discrete communications it makes."[208]

The Court's decision accordingly addresses concerns expressed by some commenters regarding U.S. treaty implementation.[209] The Court's ruling makes clear that the public performance right extends to streams accessible "from a place and at a time individually chosen by" members of the public.[210]

ii. Volitional Conduct Requirement

The Second Circuit's decision in *Cablevision* and a 2007 decision by the Ninth Circuit, *Perfect 10, Inc. v. Amazon.com, Inc.*,[211] have been interpreted by some courts as imposing a "volitional conduct" requirement in public performance and public display cases involving the Internet. At its most basic, the volitional conduct doctrine requires a showing of active participation by the defendant in the infringing activities in order to support a claim for direct infringement.[212] One commenter expressed concern that such a requirement taken to an extreme—for example, requiring that the defendant select every copyrighted work transmitted to users—could effectively bar direct infringement claims against on-demand services, thereby substantially undermining copyright owners' making available rights.[213]

Perfect 10 has been cited for the proposition that there can be no claim for direct copyright infringement where "software or hardware schemes automatically produce copies of the allegedly infringing images and the defendants do not actively participate in such activity."[214] Other courts have reached a similar conclusion based on a portion of the *Cablevision* decision in which the court held that copies of television programming recorded using a remote storage DVR system were "made" by individual customers, not by the company offering the service.[215] Courts have relied on that holding to expand the volitional conduct doctrine to bar liability for defendants that provide a service that performs for the user actions the user could lawfully perform for themselves.[216] Such a formulation has been rejected by other courts, including district courts in the Ninth Circuit.[217]

In *Aereo*, the majority was silent on whether volitional conduct is essential for finding that a defendant publicly performed copyrighted works. Having concluded "that Aereo is not simply an equipment provider,"[218] the Court emphasized that Aereo actively participates in the transmission and analogized Aereo to the types of traditional cable companies that Congress intended to bring within the reach of copyright law via the 1976 Act.[219] In doing so, the majority did not directly address the dissent's discussion of a "volitional-conduct requirement" as necessary to separating direct infringement liability from secondary liability.[220] Yet, the majority noted that "[i]n other cases involving different kinds of service or technology providers, a user's involvement in the operation of the provider's equipment and selection of the content transmitted may well bear on whether the provider performs within the meaning of the Act."[221]

Some courts have continued to apply the volitional conduct doctrine post-*Aereo*. For example, the Central District of California rejected the argument that *Aereo* had eliminated the doctrine, instead applying it to hold that the DISH Anywhere service did not infringe Fox Broadcasting's right of public performance.[222] In analyzing the service, the court identified three factors relied upon by the Supreme Court to find the Aereo system similar to traditional cable providers, and thus find Aereo was the entity engaging in the public performance: (1) the fact that "Aereo sold a service that allowed subscribers to watch television programs almost as they were being broadcast"; (2) the fact that "Aereo used its own equipment, housed in a centralized warehouse, outside of its users' homes"; and (3) the fact that "Aereo's system received programs that had been released to the public and carried them by private channels to the additional viewers."[223] In rejecting the claim that DISH directly infringed Fox's public performance right, the court found dispositive the fact that DISH, unlike Aereo, had a license for the initial retransmission of the programming to users via satellite, and thus the DISH Anywhere system could "only be used by a subscriber to gain access to *her own home STB/DVR* and the authorized recorded content on that box."[224] Thus, the court reasoned, the operative transmission is the one that occurs when the recorded programming is streamed to a connected device, after the programming has been recorded. Such transmission, the court found, occurs as the result of the subscriber's actions, not DISH's.[225]

In another recent case, however, the court rejected the argument that a DVR-like service allowing users to record broadcast television programming and watch it at a later time lacked sufficient volition to "perform."[226] The court held that the case was controlled by Aereo, noting that "the Supreme Court did not find it necessary to address the 'volitional conduct' requirement . . . to hold that both Aereo and its subscribers perform within the meaning of the Transmit Clause."[227]

As these cases suggest, the continued applicability of the volitional conduct doctrine in the wake of *Aereo* is a matter of dispute, and commenters were divided on the question.[228] At a minimum, however, *Aereo* establishes that the performance right does not require "volition" at the level of individually selecting the works to be transmitted.[229] As one scholar explained, the decision makes clear that, in the case of on-demand and "cable-like" services, "[t]he end user may be choosing what copyrighted work to view or hear, and when and where to receive it, but the entity that offers the user those choices is 'performing' the works, even when it merely responds automatically to the end-user's choice."[230] A contrary interpretation might have raised concerns in that it would have limited the ability of copyright owners to bring direct infringement claims against services engaged in unauthorized streaming of copyrighted works.

3. Right of Public Display

> [T]he owner of copyright under this title has the exclusive rights to do and to authorize any of the following:
>
> . . . .
>
> (5) in the case of literary, musical, dramatic, and choreographic works, pantomimes, and pictorial, graphic, or sculptural works, including the individual images of a motion picture or other audiovisual work, to display the copyrighted work publicly . . . .
>
> 17 U.S.C. § 106(5)

As defined in the Copyright Act, to "display" a work means "to show a copy of it, either directly or by means of a film, slide, television image, or any other device or process or, in the case of a motion picture or other audiovisual work, to show individual images non-sequentially."[231] It is well established that this right protects against the unauthorized uploading of a copyrighted image for display to the public online. While the Internet service provider safe harbors contained in the DMCA limit the situations in which website owners can be held secondarily liable for content uploaded by users,[232] courts consistently have found violations of the public display right where the defendant (itself or through an agent) uploads a copy of a copyrighted work to a publicly accessible website.[233] Moreover, because the Transmit Clause applies to the transmission of displays as well as performances,[234] *Aereo*'s construction of the Clause establishes that the display right extends to the delivery of a copyrighted image to the public in individualized communications. And, based on the above analysis of the Clause, the Copyright Office concludes that the right is properly construed to encompass the *offering* to transmit such an image. Thus, consistent with the making available obligation, Section 106(5) provides an exclusive right to offer the public access to images on demand.

Some cases involving the display right have been interpreted to bar infringement claims where the work is perceptible on the defendant's website or service, but the actual copy of the work rests on a third party server—applying the so-called "server" test. The leading case from which the server test derives is the Ninth Circuit's decision in *Perfect 10, Inc. v. Amazon.com, Inc.*[235] In response to search queries, Google's Image Search provided low-resolution "thumbnails" of images that it had indexed from third-party websites. When a user clicked on a thumbnail image, the user's browser would connect to the website where the image was located, download a full- size version, and display that version in a window on the user's screen, "framed" by information from Google's webpage. This technique—in which an image, audio file, or video seems to be part of the webpage being viewed, even though it is actually located on a different server—is known as "inline linking."[236] "Framing," meanwhile, "refers to the process by which information from one computer appears to frame and annotate the in-line linked content from another computer."[237] The court was asked to consider whether both the communication of the low-resolution thumbnail images to users and the framing of the inline-linked images from a third party's website constituted violations of the plaintiff's public display right.

Applying the server test, the court held that Google's use of thumbnails was a *prima facie* infringement of the plaintiff's display right because Google stored those images on its servers and communicated copies to users.[238] It held, however, that Google's use of inline linking and framing was not a direct infringement because Google did not store the full-size images on its own servers, but instead provided HTML instructions that directed the user's browser to access another website. Noting that Section 101 defines "display" as "to show a copy of [a work]," the court concluded that Google did "not have a copy of the images for purposes of the Copyright Act" and "thus [could not] communicate a copy."[239] "Providing these HTML instructions," the court concluded, "is not equivalent to showing a copy."[240] The Ninth Circuit's reasoning in *Perfect 10* has been relied on to bar direct infringement claims for instances of inline linking and framing.[241]

A group of several visual arts trade associations submitted comments arguing that the server test is inconsistent with the making available obligation. In their view, the test "eviscerates visual artists' [making available] right" by allowing a website operator to avoid the need for licenses for the use of copyrighted images hosted on third-party servers, notwithstanding that the images may appear to users to be part of the operator's own site.[242]

These issues came to the fore in a recent case in which Getty Images contended that its display rights were infringed by an image embedding tool offered by Microsoft. Microsoft marketed its Bing Image Widget to website publishers as a means to enhance their sites by incorporating images retrieved using the Bing search engine.[243] The Image Widget consisted of a "snippet" of computer code displayed on a Bing website. The site also provided a box in which web publishers could enter search terms. Publishers were invited to copy the snippet and paste it into the source code of their own web pages. This would cause the publisher's page to display a panel in which images responsive to the search query would appear. The publisher could choose to have the images appear either in a "collage" format, which would fill the panel with a collection of thumbnail-sized images, or a "slideshow" format, which would show larger images one-by-one at intervals of a few seconds. The images were delivered using methods similar to those in *Perfect 10*: the thumbnails displayed in the collage format were generated from copies stored on Microsoft's servers, while the larger images in the slideshow format were communicated directly from third-party websites via inline linking.

Among other disputed issues, the parties disagreed over the applicability of the server test to the latter images. Getty contended that *Perfect 10* had been superseded by *Aereo*, which it argued had "rejected the very sort of technical distinctions that underpinned the 'server test.'"[244] It further argued that Microsoft's use of inline links was materially different from that at issue in *Perfect 10* in that "the Bing Image Widget [was] neither functioning nor promoted as a search engine," but instead was "a means of providing content for the purpose of encouraging users to remain on a given website and, ultimately, to enter [Microsoft's] own universe of websites."[245] Microsoft responded that *Aereo*'s holding was limited to the technologies before the Court and had no bearing on the server test.[246] Relying on *Perfect 10*, it contended that it did not display copies within the meaning of the Act because "the Widget merely provide[d] a location address or pointer, not a copy of the image itself."[247]

Ultimately, the parties settled the case prior to the court's reaching a decision on these issues. As a result, it remains uncertain whether a court might deem certain forms of inline linking or framing distinguishable from the technology in *Perfect 10* for purposes of the server test. As will be discussed further below, application of the making available right to activities such as these raises complex issues that require consideration of a number of important factors.[248] While some of these issues have been addressed preliminarily, U.S. courts have not made definitive rulings as to how the server test might apply to activities potentially raising greater concerns for visual artists' ability to exploit their works online than have been addressed so far.[249]

Conclusive resolution of these issues will require further guidance from the courts.[250]

4. Right of Reproduction

> [T]he owner of copyright under this title has the exclusive rights to do and to authorize any of the following:
>
> (1) to reproduce the copyrighted work in copies or phonorecords . . . .
>
> 17 U.S.C. § 106(1)

The final stick in the bundle of exclusive rights constituting the making available right in the United States is the right of reproduction under Section 106(1). Often in Internet streaming and file sharing cases, the same activity can give rise to liability for violations of more than one exclusive right. For example, if the process of making a work available to the public involves the creation of an unauthorized copy—such as by uploading a file to a peer-to-peer network—then the uploader's conduct may implicate the reproduction right in addition to the distribution, performance, or display rights.[251] And if another party then downloads a copy, that separate reproduction may provide a basis for a direct infringement claim against the downloader, as well as a claim against the service provider under a theory of secondary liability.[252] Finally, the reproduction right also may be implicated in online streaming cases as a result of the creation of a temporary copy of a work, or portion of it, in a computer's random access memory ("RAM") during the delivery of content to the ultimate user.[253]

Some study participants suggested that the availability of these types of claims may make it unnecessary to construe the distribution, performance, or display rights in relation to the making available right.[254] The Copyright Office is not persuaded, however, that the reproduction right can satisfy the obligation independently of those rights. With respect to direct infringement claims against persons who make copies available to the public online, it is likely true that in many cases a reproduction claim will be available because the file being offered will itself have been created without the copyright owner's authorization.[255] That need not always be case, however. While earlier forms of file sharing required the uploading of a file to a centralized location, and thus the making of a copy, file sharing services today typically enable users to share material directly from their own hard drives, including files that were lawfully acquired (*e.g.*, files stored in an iTunes folder). In such circumstances, a reproduction claim against the offering party may not be available.[256]

Nor does the Office believe that relying on secondary liability would be adequate to fill any purported gaps in U.S. implementation in this area. Through secondary liability theories,[257] a copyright owner may be able to establish an indirect infringement claim against the operator of an online service for facilitating or otherwise contributing to an unauthorized reproduction by an end-user.[258] Secondary liability, however, requires a showing of direct infringement by a third party. Therefore, to bring a claim against a service for contributing to a downloader's unauthorized reproduction, a plaintiff still would have to prove that a download in fact occurred. Thus, secondary liability would not allow the copyright owner to bring a claim against the service based solely on the ground that it has offered access to the work to the public.

This is not to discount the importance of secondary liability to copyright owners in the digital context. As one music industry representative noted during the roundtable, "you have to go after the facilitators. . . . And it is these doctrines of secondary liability which are extremely important and do allow us to go after those who are really creating the problem of copyright infringement on the internet."[259] Because, however, it does not permit an independent cause of action for the unauthorized offering of access to a work to the public, secondary liability alone is not sufficient to guarantee U.S. implementation of that aspect of the making available obligation.[260]

C. Factors Relevant to All Exclusive Rights

In addition to the foregoing analysis of the individual exclusive rights, two considerations relevant to the interpretation of Section 106 as a whole lend substantial support for construing it to provide the substance of a making available right, including the right to offer access to copyrighted works to the public.

1. Legislative History of Treaty Implementation

First, the legislative history surrounding the United States' implementation of the WIPO Internet Treaties reflects Congress's reasoned determination that U.S. law already satisfied all treaty obligations implicating the exclusive rights of copyright owners. As noted, during Congress's deliberations on implementation of the Treaties in 1997 and 1998, both the

Register of Copyrights and the Commissioner of Patents and Trademarks testified that implementation would not require changes to the exclusive rights under Title 17. The Register noted that "existing protections [were] adequate to fulfill . . . the substantive treaty obligations" pertaining to exclusive rights, and that there accordingly was "no need to alter the nature and scope of the copyrights and exception[]s, or change the substantive balance of rights embodied in the Copyright Act."[261] The Commissioner, who led the U.S. delegation to WIPO, stated that "nothing in these Treaties . . . affects the issue of liability for particular acts of copyright infringement."[262] The House Judiciary Committee report accompanying the implementing legislation endorsed this view.[263]

Furthermore, the Senate's resolution on ratification of the Treaties required that "[t]he United States shall not deposit the instruments of ratification for these Treaties until such time as the President signs into law a bill that implements the Treaties,"[264] and it is clear that Congress believed that the DMCA constituted such legislation. Title I of the DMCA is entitled the WIPO Copyright and Performances and Phonograms Treaties Implementation Act of 1998,[265] and the Conference Committee Report confirms that it "implements two new intellectual property treaties, the WIPO Copyright Treaty and the WIPO Performances and Phonograms Treaty, signed in Geneva, Switzerland in December 1996."[266] All of this evidence demonstrates that Congress was fully cognizant of the obligations imposed by the Treaties when it drafted the DMCA and that it made a considered judgment that that legislation was sufficient to implement them.

The Supreme Court has recognized that "once an agency's statutory construction has been 'fully brought to the attention of the public and the Congress,' and the latter has not sought to alter that interpretation although it has amended the statute in other respects, then presumably the legislative intent has been correctly discerned."[267] In the case of the DMCA, two expert agencies formally advised Congress of their view that treaty implementation would require certain additions to Title 17 (relating to copyright protection systems and copyright management information), but would not require changes to the exclusive rights under Section 106. Congress enacted implementing legislation reflecting that interpretation. Accordingly, "the total combination of what Congress did and did not do" in amending Title 17 through the DMCA is "probative of its understanding of the compliance of the unamended portions with treaty norms."[268]

2. *The Charming Betsy Canon*

The conclusion that U.S. law includes a right of making available is further supported by the *Charming Betsy* canon—a longstanding principle of statutory interpretation directing that "an act of Congress ought never to be construed to violate the law of nations if any other possible construction remains."[269] Thus, a court should interpret a federal statute consistently "with international law or with an international agreement of the United States" where such a construction is "fairly possible."[270]

As noted above, the United States is obligated to provide a making available right not only under the WIPO Internet Treaties, but also under no fewer than twelve free trade agreements, all of which have been approved by Congress, the most recent in 2011.[271] There is no indication that Congress has had any intention to depart from these obligations. To the contrary, as just discussed, it is clear that Congress intended to fully implement the Internet Treaties through the DMCA and concluded that no substantive changes to existing exclusive rights were necessary to do so. Moreover, Congress gave specific approval to multiple Executive Branch determinations that no statutory change would be required to implement FTA chapters containing a making available obligation.[272] The question thus is whether interpreting the Copyright Act to provide a making available right in substance is fairly possible. For all the reasons noted above, the Office concludes that such a construction is not only possible but is the reading most consistent with the text of the statute as a whole and the clearly expressed purposes of both the 1976 Act and the DMCA. Therefore, *Charming Betsy* counsels that courts should adopt that interpretation.

The district court in *Capitol Records, Inc. v. Thomas* reached a different conclusion as to the canon's applicability in this context.[273] While the court acknowledged that "the *Charming Betsy* doctrine directs the Court to adopt the reasonable construction that is consistent with the United States' international obligations" and that "past Presidents, Congresses, and the Register of Copyrights have indicated their belief that the Copyright Act implements WIPO's make-available right," it concluded that interpreting the right of distribution to cover peer-to-peer filesharing activity in the absence of evidence of downloading "is simply not reasonable."[274] This holding was in turn cited with approval in the Eastern District of Virginia's recent decision in *BMG Rights Management (US) v. Cox Communications, Inc.*, which also declined to apply the canon to Section 106.[275] The court in *Thomas*, however, based its statutory interpretation in part on the Eighth Circuit's *National Car* decision (which it deemed binding authority) and on the prior version of the

Nimmer treatise, both of which, as noted above, are now of limited analytical value on this issue.[276] Viewing the statute in its full context, the Office concludes that construing the Copyright Act to include a making available right is, at the very minimum, a reasonable interpretation. The *Charming Betsy* canon accordingly provides an additional basis for recognizing such a right.[277]

***

For all of the foregoing reasons, the Copyright Office adheres to the longstanding U.S. government view that the exclusive rights under Section 106 collectively provide the substance of the making available right in the WIPO Internet Treaties. In reaching this conclusion, we recognize that there are a number of online contexts in which U.S. courts have yet to fully address whether, or to what extent, particular exclusive rights may be implicated. As noted, the Office does not attempt to resolve such questions here. Some of these issues, however, have generated significant litigation in other WIPO member states in the context of those countries' national laws. We briefly review those cases in the discussion of Emerging Issues in the next Part.

IV. Making Available Implementation by Other Treaty Partners

As part of this study, the Office was asked to assess whether alternative implementation approaches may be beneficial in the United States.[278] The Office identified the statutory language other countries have used to incorporate the making available right into national law and sorted them into three groups: (i) countries that adopted the WIPO Internet Treaties language near verbatim to implement the making available right, (ii) countries that adopted alternative language to implement the right, and (iii) countries that, like the United States, have not adopted explicit making available language, but instead have implemented the right through an existing right or rights.

The Office then considered how the courts in each of these categories have interpreted the making available right as it relates to the two issues that have arisen in the United States that form the *sine qua non* of the making available right: the treatment of one-to-one transmissions, which secures to copyright owners the right to control delivery of their works to members of the public individually in separate places and times, and the treatment of "offers" of copyrighted works, which secures to copyright owners the right to control access to their content. At the end of the section, we briefly discuss a third area of law that has received significant attention in foreign jurisdictions (although the jurisprudence regarding this issue is less developed in the United States), namely the treatment of offering access to content hosted elsewhere on the Internet (typically through some form of hyperlinking).[279]

The three categories into which we grouped the legislative approaches adopted by other treaty signatories are:

(1) *Internet Treaties Language*
Under this approach, implementing legislation adopted a making available right using language that tracks that of WCT Article 8, either identically or with non-substantive differences. It may be couched as part of a broader communication-to-the-public right or it may be a separately enumerated right.[280]

(2) *Alternative Language*
Under this approach, a new, explicit making available right was adopted, but the statutory text does not directly track the language from the WIPO Internet Treaties. The new right may be included as part of a broad communication-to-the-public right or it may be a standalone right.[281]

(3) *Statutory Silence*
This approach covers the act of making available through a pre-existing right or rights, without adopting a specific reference to the making available right.

A. Internet Treaties Model

The most common approach to implementation of the making available right has been for a foreign jurisdiction to adopt the language of the WIPO Internet Treaties in its copyright statute. This model has been adopted by roughly 49 of the 94 contracting parties that have ratified the WCT.[282] Although a number of countries have taken this approach, the overwhelming majority of related court decisions the Office has been able to identify have come from Europe,[283] along with a few from Singapore. Despite nearly identical implementation language, the courts in Singapore and the EU have come to different conclusions on several questions regarding the scope of the making available right. Some of this inconsistency may be traced to the treaty language itself. As multiple decisions of the Court of Justice of the European Union ("CJEU") have noted, while the InfoSoc Directive text incorporates the WCT language, neither the Directive nor the WCT defines the right of "communication to the public."[284]

> Member States shall provide authors with the exclusive right to authorise or prohibit any communication to the public of their works, by wire or wireless means, including the making available to the public of their works in such a way that members of the public may access them from a place and at a time individually chosen by them.
>
> —EU InfoSoc Directive Art. 3(1)

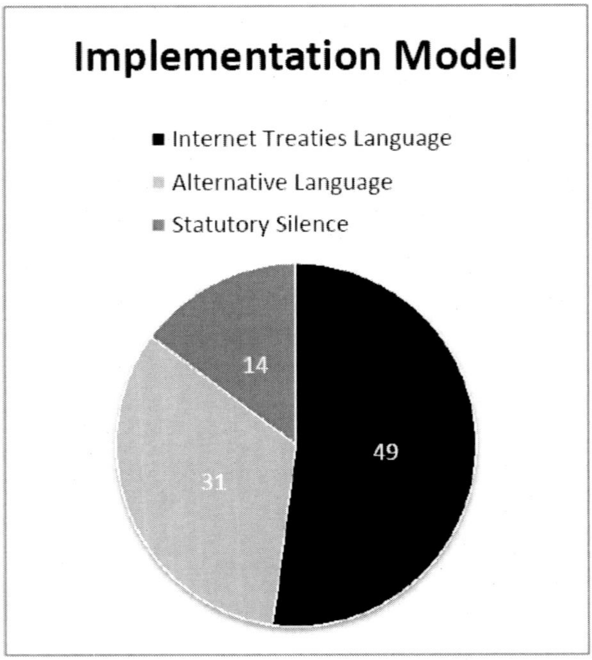

1. One-to-One Transmissions

The WIPO Internet Treaties sought to anticipate the continued evolution of the technology used to deliver copyrighted works digitally, defining the making available right broadly as encompassing delivery through interactive, on-demand wireless transmissions.[285] Nonetheless, changes to the technologies used to stream copyrighted works have posed challenges for courts interpreting the making available right in those countries that incorporate the right within a broader right of communication to the public. With the advent of technology that creates individual streams to transmit copyrighted works to each user, courts have struggled with how to handle such activity. Are such transmissions directed at the public, thus implicating the right of communication to the public? Or does the use of such technology render each transmission a non-public communication that is not subject to any of the exclusive rights of the copyright owner?[286] Courts in countries that have adopted the Internet Treaties Language approach have reached different conclusions on this issue. While courts in the European Union have focused their analysis on the availability to the public of such one-to-one transmissions, courts in Singapore have focused their analysis on whether a *particular* transmission constituted a communication to the public.

In cases presenting the question of one-to-one transmissions, the CJEU[287] has concluded that "the cumulative effect of making the works available to potential recipients should be taken into account," finding that the transmission of a terrestrial television broadcast over the Internet to individual subscribers' private viewing devices implicated the copyright owner's right of communication to the public in the 2013 case of *ITV v. TVCatchup*.[288] In reaching this conclusion, the CJEU reasoned that "it is irrelevant whether the potential recipients access the communicated works through a one-to-one connection" because doing so "does not prevent a large number of persons having access to the same work at the same time."[289] Similarly, the CJEU determined in *SGAE v. Rafael Hoteles* that broadcast signals received by a hotel and provided to customers through individual transmissions to in-room television sets constituted a communication to the public.[290]

In contrast, an appellate court in Singapore declined to find infringement by a service that provided individualized transmissions of televised programming that was requested by a user and only accessible by that user.[291] The case, *Record TV v. Media Corp TV*, involved an Internet- based DVR service, Record TV. A user could select a "free-to-air" Media Corp show broadcast in Singapore to record, after which the DVR would capture the show on a television tuner, record it on Record TV's on-site computers, and then stream the recording to the user's computer over the Internet.[292] The lower court held that the recording infringed Media Corp's right of communication to the public, but did not infringe its reproduction right because the recordings merely enabled users to "time-shift."[293] The Court of Appeal reversed on the right of communication to the public, holding that "any communications made by Record TV to Registered Users . . . were made privately and individually."[294] The court stated that the relevant question "was not whether

Record TV's iDVR service was available to 'the public,'" but instead "should have been whether a particular . . . show had been transmitted to the public."[295] Framed in this manner, the court determined that the operative "communication" did not occur until a show was downloaded to the user's playlist and thus available for viewing by that user.[296] Since the user controlled the content of the playlist, the court concluded that the user was the "communicator" for purposes of the Copyright Act,[297] not RecordTV.[298] Consequently, the court found that RecordTV did not infringe MediaCorp's right of communication to the public.[299] In reaching this conclusion, the court broadly followed the pre-*Aereo* U.S. decision in *Cablevision*, which it extensively cited early in the opinion.[300] It is difficult to ascertain the full implication of this case on the interpretation of the interactive element of the making available right in Singapore, beyond the facts of this particular case.

As one commenter in our study noted, such disagreements regarding the status of one-to- one transmissions, by focusing on the act of receipt of the communication by an individual rather than the offer of the communication to the public, appear to be out of step with the intent behind the WCT making available right. Professor Jane Ginsburg expressed the view that "[t]he act that triggers the making available right is the offer to communicate the work to the public on an on- demand basis; while actual individualized communications to members of the public are of course covered as well, the innovation of the WIPO Treaties was to enable authors to license, or to seek redress from, persons or entities who hold works out to the public as available for access by streaming or download."[301] Yet, despite acknowledging that the Singapore Copyright Act had incorporated the WCT Article 8 language almost verbatim, the Singapore appellate court devoted most of its analysis to parsing the phrase "communication to the public," not the interactive element of that definition. In comparison, the courts in the EU decisions discussed above focused their interpretation on the phrase "making available," thus finding one-to-one transmissions offered to the public to be subject to the exclusive right.

2. Offers

As noted above, in the United States, the most contested question with respect to the scope of the making available right has been whether offering to distribute a copyrighted work online, without evidence of a completed download, may constitute an infringement.[302] In contrast, our review did not reveal any cases in the Internet Treaties Model countries that have focused on whether a mere offer to communicate violates the making available right. This may be because their adoption of explicit "making available" language renders the answer to the question obvious.[303] Indeed, language from various CJEU opinions indicates that the court considers it a settled matter of law that Article 3(1) of the InfoSoc Directive covers offers. For example, in *Rafael Hoteles*, the CJEU stated that "it is sufficient that the work is made available to the public in such a way that the persons forming that public may access it."[304] Regardless of whether hotel customers ever turned on their televisions, they had "access to the works," and that, the court said, was enough to implicate the making available right in Article 3(1).[305] Similarly, in a subsequent case the court asserted that it "is apparent from Article 3(1) of Directive 2001/29, [that] for there to be an 'act of communication', it is sufficient, in particular, that a work is made available to a public in such a way that the persons forming that public may access it, irrespective of whether they avail themselves of that opportunity."[306] Academics and others reviewing EU law agree that mere offers are covered by Article 3(1).[307] As one group of commenters noted, "the [InfoSoc] Directive applies to all types of transmissions, so the *means of transmission* is irrelevant. The focus is *on access to the works*. . . . In short, merely uploading a work for potential receipt is an act of communication falling within the copyright owner's exclusive right."[308]

B. Alternative Language Model

Many countries have opted for a different statutory implementation approach, using language to codify a making available right that differs from the WIPO Internet Treaties language, although each of these countries has adopted an explicit making available right as part of a communication-to-the-public right or as a standalone right. As noted previously, in some of these countries, the statutory language appears to closely track the language from WCT Art. 8 but includes phrases such as "telecommunication" or "information network" that incorporate into the right separate statutory and regulatory schemes, while in other countries the language deviates more significantly from the WIPO Internet Treaties language. Among the countries that chose this model, relevant case law has developed around the scope of the making available right in Australia, Canada, China, and Japan.

1. One-to-One Transmissions

Three of the four Alternate Language Model countries we examined have addressed the making available right in the context of one-to-one transmissions. While several of the opinions predate those countries' amendments to implement the WIPO Internet Treaties, it appears that each of them would consider one-to-one transmissions to implicate the right of communication to the public, and thus the making available right.

> *[C]ommunicate* means make available online or electronically transmit (whether over a path, or a combination of paths, provided by a material substance or otherwise) a work or other subject- matter, including a performance or live performance within the meaning of this Act.
>
> —Copyright Act, Law No. 63 of 1968, as amended by Act No. 80 of 2015, Article 10 (Australia)

Australia provides copyright owners a right to communicate to the public, and defines "communicate" as to "make available online or electronically transmit (whether over a path, or a combination of paths, provided by a material substance or otherwise) a work or other subject-matter."[309] Before this statutory language was added via the Copyright Amendment (Digital Agenda) Act 2000, the Australian High Court already had concluded that private, one-to-one transmissions could be to the "public."[310] This conclusion appears unchanged after adoption of the Digital Agenda amendments in 2000 to incorporate an explicit making available right. Similarly, Canadian copyright law provides a right "in the case of any literary, dramatic, musical or artistic work to communicate the work to the public by telecommunication,"[311] which was amended by the Copyright Modernization Act of 2012 to incorporate an explicit right of making a work available online.[312] Applying this pre-2012 communication-to-the-public right, the Canadian Supreme Court similarly held that one-to-one communications are to the public when, for example, music files are streamed to users accessing the works in different locations and at different times.[313] It is premature to know how this new statutory definition may be applied in future Canadian cases.

Finally, Japan amended its Copyright Act in 1997 to, among other things, add a "public transmission" right[314] that "encompasses a large range of acts contributing to transmissions to members of the public via various media."[315] This right, read in conjunction with various definitions in the law, entitles copyright owners to "control the Internet transmission of works, including uploading them into a server."[316] Japanese case law seems to indicate that this right is also implicated when services make personalized, or one-to-one, transmissions to private users.[317] The 2011 *Maneki TV* case dealt with the question of whether Maneki TV's "Location Free" device, which converted terrestrial broadcast television programs into digital formats and transmitted the digitally converted broadcasts to users on request via the Internet, infringed the broadcasters' transmission rights.[318] Reversing the Intellectual Property High Court,[319] the Supreme Court of Japan found that even though the device technically transmitted only to a single apparatus designated in advance, the transmissions were to the public because they were to unspecified persons.[320] Additionally, the court held that the party who "creates a condition in which [a] device can automatically transmit information upon request" is the one who performs the transmission.[321] It further noted that "[w]here such device is connected with a telecommunications line provided for use by the public and information is continuously input into said device, it is appropriate to consider the person who inputs information into said device to be the party who performs transmission."[322] The court found that Maneki TV enabled each transmission. Thus, even though each transmission was made at the request of a user, the court found that Maneki TV, not the user, was the infringer.[323]

2. Offers

We were unable to locate much case law on the issue of offers in the Alternate Language Model countries. The few cases we did find, however, hold that unauthorized offers both implicate and violate the making available right under the circumstances at hand.

One Australian case suggests that mere offers implicate the making available right there. In *Roadshow Films Pty Ltd. v iiNet Ltd.*,[324] the Federal Court held that peer-to-peer file sharers made films available online, and thereby communicated them to the public, each time the users connected their computers to the Internet with movie in their BitTorrent folders.[325] The court concluded explicitly that "[t]he act of communication by making available online does not require that there be any actual communication in the ordinary sense of that word. A person who uses a computer to make a film available online 'communicates' it for the purpose of s 86(c) whether or not it is transmitted to or accessed by any other person."[326] Thus, the right of making available to the public does not appear to require proof of an actual transmission.

Chinese law includes a "right of communication through information network."[327] Like courts in Australia, Chinese courts have found that mere offers can violate this right. Chinese courts have construed the term "making available" broadly. For example, a judicial interpretation issued in 2012 by the Supreme People's Court on the right of communication through information network found that when a network user or a "network service provider"[328] makes another person's copyrighted work available online without authorization, including by uploading it to a publicly-available server or using file sharing software, the actor has violated the right of communication, without requiring further evidence that the content was actually downloaded.[329]

C. Statutory Silence Model

The third model that the remaining countries fit into involves cases where there is no explicit statutory language that mentions either a communication-to-the-public right that includes a making available right or a stand-alone making available right. Under this model, the statute is silent on the making available right but the country maintains that existing law or laws provide rights that together comprise the making available right. The United States takes this approach, as do roughly thirteen other countries we identified.330 In some cases, it is unclear which countries are silent because of reliance on a patchwork of existing laws, and which are silent because the treaty is self-executing or the member state has yet to amend its copyright statute.

Outside of U.S. case law, we are aware of little litigation in these countries that has helped to flesh out the scope of a making available right.[331] The exception appears to be Belgium. The copyright statute is silent on the making available right for copyright, but national courts have interpreted its laws as providing a making available right.[332] For example, Professor Guido Westkamp notes in a 2007 study that, in a pre-Internet Treaties case, Belgian courts applied the making available right to the authorized storing of newspaper articles in a database and the delivering of them to users upon request.[333] "Therefore," he argues, "one can consider that the communication right already covered non-simultaneous reception of electronic communication or acts of making copyrighted content available to the members of the public at a place and at a time individually chosen by them."[334]

D. Emerging Issues Relating to the Making Available Right

Beyond the issues of one-to-one transmissions and offers, which form the primary focus of this Report, foreign jurisdictions have begun to grapple with another intersection of technology and the making available right—the legal consequences of a defendant providing access to copyrighted content that is hosted on a server controlled by someone else. Providing access to content hosted elsewhere on the Internet can be accomplished in a number of ways, although the most frequent methods are various forms of hyperlinking, including framing and inline linking.[335] A handful of foreign courts have begun to address these issues, but they have by far received the most attention in the European Union, where the CJEU has issued a number of closely-followed decisions addressing whether, and under what circumstances, hyperlinking to content can violate a plaintiff's making available right.

The CJEU has already issued a number of decisions regarding the extent of potential liability for such conduct, finding that this activity does not generally give rise to liability under a making available theory outside of a narrow set of circumstances. In these opinions, the CJEU does not differentiate among the types of hyperlinking activities that could, in any instance, permit audiences on one website to access content from another site. Rather, its approach has been to compare the audience for the original communication to the public (as authorized by the copyright owner) with the audience of the allegedly infringing communication. Specifically, the court asks whether the audience for the allegedly infringing communication of the copyrighted content is comprised of the same public targeted by the original communication, or whether the defendant's actions instead made the content available to a "new public" that did not have access to the original communication.[336] For example, did the copyright owner post the content online without restriction, making the original audience for the work coextensive with the public to which the defendant has made the work available? Or did the defendant make available content to which the copyright owner had limited access, for example to those paying subscriptions or other fees (such as content hosted behind a website paywall)?

In crafting and applying this new test, the CJEU has denied liability for claims against a defendant providing deep links to access copyrighted content hosted on the plaintiff's server,[337] although the court has indicated that there may be liability for such deep links if the plaintiff employed technological restrictions to restrict access to a limited set of individuals, such as its subscribers.[338] The CJEU has not yet directly reached the question of whether liability should be imposed for providing access to unauthorized copies hosted on third-party servers, although this issue is raised by several cases currently pending before the court.[339]

The CJEU's test, frequently referenced as the "new public test," has generated some debate within the European Union.[340] The European Commission is currently considering whether modifications to the definitions of the rights of "communication to the public" and "making available" are needed to address the ambiguities introduced by the *Svensson* line of cases as part of its broader work on the Digital Single Market.[341] This consultation, combined with the pending referrals to the CJEU,[342] may result in a further refinement of the new public test, or may supersede the new public test and replace it with a new rule regarding what constitutes a communication to the public online.

Other courts in Internet Treaty Model jurisdictions have found that liability may exist when a defendant assists its users to bypass the plaintiff's protection measures or provides access to infringing third-party content.[343] In contrast, while there does not appear to have been significant litigation regarding such activities in most Alternative Language Model countries, in the few reported cases we were able to identify the courts rejected infringement claims based upon hyperlinking to content found on the Internet, regardless of whether the hyperlinked content was itself unauthorized.[344]

* * *

The foregoing review of cases from jurisdictions representing the three different implementation models reveals a few trends.

First, the degree of consistency among countries regarding the interpretation of the making available right differs with respect to the different factual scenarios we reviewed. The case law is generally consistent across jurisdictions with respect to the application of the making available right to offers. The only cases we located rejecting liability for offers were the district court cases in the United States discussed above.[345] Likewise, one-to-one transmissions have been found to be covered by the making available right in most of the jurisdictions we studied, with the principal exception being Singapore.[346] There has been some greater divergence in jurisprudence with regards to the emerging issue of making available content already hosted elsewhere on the Internet (such as through some form of hyperlinking), although a majority of courts have declined to find liability. The outcomes in such cases appear to be highly fact-specific, and the full contours of how the courts will apply the making available right in such situations are still evolving. It does appear, however, that even courts in countries that have adopted the verbatim language of the Treaties have been careful to construe the right to avoid imposition of liability in cases that may involve everyday online activity, such as providing deep links to otherwise freely available content.[347]

Second, there is no approach that provides crystal clear legal guidance in all making available cases, either in terms of the activity that will be covered by the right or the ability to ensure that its application will easily address new and emerging technologies. Although most of the countries that have ratified the WIPO Internet Treaties adopted language from the WCT nearly verbatim into national law, courts across the spectrum of implementation approaches—whether verbatim WIPO Internet Treaties language, alternative language providing a making available right, or existing language that is silent on a making available right—have struggled with the application of the statutory language to specific factual situations in the digital age. Thus, even adopting the making available language from the WIPO Internet Treaties has not guaranteed clarity, but has instead resulted in sometimes conflicting results when applied by courts in different countries.[348] Many of these challenges have their roots in new factual circumstances and technological capabilities not fully understood, or even known, when the WIPO Internet Treaties were concluded in 1996.

V. Conclusions and Recommendations

As part of this study, the Copyright Office was asked to assess "the feasibility and necessity of amending U.S. law to strengthen or clarify our law" with respect to the making available right.[349] No commenters disputed that the United States has an obligation to recognize the right. At the same time, nearly all expressed the view that it is currently unnecessary to amend U.S. law for purposes of implementing that obligation, though, as noted, there was some disagreement over the exact scope of the treaty requirement. Under the interpretation adopted overwhelmingly by scholarly authorities and foreign courts, as well as by a substantial majority of commenters, the making available right covers the offering of on-demand access to a work to the public, regardless of whether there is evidence of actual receipt.[350] The Office agrees that this reading best comports with the plain language of the Treaties, which define "making available" in terms of whether members of the public "may access" a work.[351]

Assessing U.S. law in light of this understanding, the Office concludes that no statutory change is needed at this time from a treaty perspective. For the reasons explained below, and in light of the foregoing analysis, the Office continues to be of the view that the exclusive rights under Section 106 collectively give copyright owners the exclusive right to offer access to their works online, including through individualized on-demand transmissions. To the extent that the statute is ambiguous with respect to particular aspects of that right, both the legislative history of U.S. treaty implementation and the *Charming Betsy* canon instruct that it should be interpreted in accordance with the United States' international obligations in this area. In the event that courts adopt a narrower construction in the future, such that certain international legal questions might arise, Congress may wish to consider various legislative clarifications. Any such change, however, would need to be carefully drawn so as not to produce unintended consequences or upset settled expectations, and may require consideration of corresponding changes to maintain the copyright law's existing balance.

A. Sufficiency of Current Statute

The Office maintains its longstanding view that the act of making a copyrighted work available in such a way that members of the public may access it at a time and place of their choosing will implicate one or more of the exclusive rights under Section 106 of the U.S. Copyright Act. In general, where a party offers members of the public access to a work in the form of a download, the offer implicates the right of distribution. Where access is offered in the form of a stream or the showing of an image, the relevant right is that of public performance or public display. In each case, the applicable statutory provision satisfies the essential elements of the treaty obligation, including specifically the requirements that the exclusive right cover (1) offers to communicate a work, not just completed transmissions, and (2) individualized communications that can be received in separate places and at different times.

Again, it is important to note that the analysis here is limited to the showings necessary to support a *prima facie* claim for infringement, which is a separate issue from that of the defendant's ultimate liability. Should a plaintiff succeed in establishing a claim on one of these bases, the defendant will be entitled to assert the same defenses that are available to copyright defendants generally, including reliance on any relevant exception or limitation under the Copyright Act.[352]

1. Offers to Communicate

The Office interprets both the right of distribution under Section 106(3) and the rights of public performance and public display under Section 106(4)–

(6) to cover offers of access. In the case of the distribution right, as discussed in Part III.B.1, the statutory language, context, and legislative history all indicate that Congress intended to reserve to copyright owners the right to determine whether and how their works are made available to the public in copies, including digital files. References to the distribution right in other sections of the Copyright Act demonstrate that Congress did not intend for infringement claims to require a completed transfer of copies in all instances. Moreover, Congress's adoption of criminal sanctions for the distribution of pre-release copies of a work "by making it available on a computer network accessible to members of the public,"[353] indicates that Congress understood such conduct to be an infringement of the distribution right. This understanding is confirmed by the legislative history, which shows that Congress intended the right to be synonymous with the historic right of publication, which had long been understood to include offers to distribute copies to the public. Therefore, a copyright owner can establish a *prima facie* infringement of Section 106(3) by showing that the defendant had possession of a copy of a work and offered to electronically transmit copies to the public in the form of downloadable files. No evidence that any individual member of the public in fact downloaded a copy need be offered.

Nevertheless, the case law on this question is far from uniform, and a number of courts have concluded that Section 106(3) applies only to completed transfers. To date, however, the cases that have directly held to that effect are limited to district courts.[354] Moreover, nearly all of those decisions either cited directly, or relied on prior cases citing, the *Nimmer on Copyright* language that Professor Nimmer has since retracted in light of Professor Menell's recent legislative history scholarship. Since the publication of those findings and the updated *Nimmer* treatise, the Tenth Circuit has cited both to conclude, albeit in the analog context, that "distribution" does not require an actual transfer of copies.[355] Based partly on these developments, most commenters who agreed that Section 106(3) is properly construed to cover offers argued that it is not currently necessary to amend the statute to resolve the lack of judicial consensus.[356] They instead suggested that Congress and the Office monitor the case law and, in the event that courts in future cases interpret the statute to exclude making available claims, to consider legislative changes at that time.[357] The Office agrees that the existing precedent taking that narrow view of Section 106(3) is not so widespread or settled as to require congressional action to confirm U.S. treaty implementation at this time.[358]

We also are cognizant of the concern expressed by some study participants that interpreting the distribution right to cover offers "could create liability for commonplace and harmless activities such as the use of common file storage in a business setting, or personal use of Internet-based 'cloud storage' systems that may inadvertently be accessible by the public."[359] In our view, however, these concerns, while worth noting, are overstated. Application of the making available right is unlikely to give rise to a substantial number of claims targeting activities such these, because the fair use doctrine, the safe harbors under Section 512, and other copyright exceptions and limitations will continue to provide robust accommodations for users.[360]

In the context of file sharing, moreover, failure to recognize a making available right can impose real costs on copyright owners, courts, and third parties. It is true that some courts that have been unwilling to permit claims based on offers of access have nonetheless allowed file sharing cases to move forward on the basis of circumstantial or investigator evidence of completed downloads.[361] As Professor Nimmer testified in the congressional review hearing on this issue, however, a requirement that plaintiffs prove actual downloading would in many cases generate costly discovery and evidentiary disputes.[362] To the extent that such investigations might involve the issuance of subpoenas to Internet Service Providers "in order to furnish the identity of the subscribers behind the Internet Protocol addresses that have engaged in downloading," there also could be considerable implications for user privacy.[363] The Office agrees that, as a policy matter, rejecting the making available right would have the effect of "unduly rais[ing] the costs of enforcing the copyright owner's distribution right, with the unfortunate concomitant of reducing the deterrent effects of copyright enforcement."[364]

With respect to the public performance and public display rights, the Copyright Office likewise concludes that the proper construction is to permit claims based on offers to transmit. In contrast to the distribution right, the availability of offer-based claims under these rights has not been a central focus of litigation; indeed, the Office is not aware of any case in which a court has squarely decided the issue. The Office nevertheless believes that its interpretation follows from reading the statutory language in light of its expressed purpose. Both the text and legislative history of the Transmit Clause indicate that Congress intended to define the statute's coverage on the basis of whether members of the public are "capable of receiving" the transmission of a performance or display, not whether any person actually has done so.[365] The Office is not convinced that the distinction in delivery methods between traditional services and on-demand streaming—*i.e.*, that the latter requires user action to initiate the transmission—makes a substantive difference. In any event, given the apparent infrequency with which this question has arisen in litigation, there would not seem to exist an immediate need for statutory clarification.

2. Individualized Communications

The treaty language giving copyright holders the exclusive right to make their works available for access "from a place and at a time individually chosen by" members of the public requires member states to cover the delivery of works via individualized communications. The United States' implementation of this obligation seems clear. With respect to the distribution right, there appears to be no dispute (with the exception of those who argue that the right does not apply at all in the digital context[366]) that Section 106(3) covers the transmission of copies to recipients who are separated in space and time. In the public performance context, conflicting lower court decisions had created some uncertainty over whether on-demand transmissions qualify under Section 106(4), but *Aereo* has resolved that question in the affirmative.

As discussed, prior to *Aereo*, courts had divided on whether the term "performance" in the Transmit Clause refers to the underlying performance of a work or to a particular transmission of a performance. The latter reading, adopted by the Second Circuit in *Cablevision*, might have raised concerns from a treaty perspective because a particular on-demand transmission is receivable only by one person, and therefore would not constitute a transmission "to the public." In *Aereo*, however, the Court rejected that construction. It held instead that "when an entity communicates the same contemporaneously perceptible images and sounds to multiple people, it transmits a performance to them regardless of the number of discrete communications it makes."[367] The Court's ruling thus confirms that U.S. law, consistent with the treaty requirement, protects the delivery of works to the public via individualized, asynchronous streams, and therefore no legislative change is necessary in this area.[368]

This is not to say that the application of the public performance right to particular streaming technologies will always be clear. In fact, *Aereo* indicates that the inquiry is highly fact-specific. For example, while the Court held that Aereo "performed" even though the content to be transmitted was selected by individual subscribers, it observed that "[i]n other cases involving different kinds of service or technology providers, a user's involvement in the operation of the provider's equipment and selection of the content transmitted may well bear on whether the provider performs within the meaning of the Act."[369] This suggests that a storage service whose relationship to a transmission is sufficiently passive might be argued to be merely a supplier of equipment or facilities rather than a performer of works. As noted, one court recently reached that conclusion in the case of a DISH service allowing subscribers to remotely access television programming that they already were licensed to receive on a home set-top box.[370]

Similarly, the *Aereo* Court noted that the "public" nature of a performance may turn on the recipients' "relationship to the underlying work," explaining that "an entity that transmits a performance to individuals in their capacities as owners or possessors does not perform to 'the public,' whereas an entity like Aereo that transmits to large numbers of paying subscribers who lack any prior relationship to the works does so perform."[371] The Court also emphasized that it had "not considered whether the public performance right is infringed when the user of a service pays primarily for something other than the transmission of copyrighted works, such as the remote storage of content."[372] Thus, the application of the performance right to certain activities may involve difficult questions concerning users' legal relationship to the relevant content and the nature of the services for which they are paying.[373]

The fact, however, that there may be close cases does not alter the overall scope of U.S. law in this area.[374] In light of *Aereo*, it is now clear that the public performance and display rights cover transmissions accessible "from a place and at a time individually chosen by" members of the public. The limitations on the scope of the rights articulated by the Court—which, together with the statutory exceptions and limitations under the Act, provide important checks against overbroad applications—are consistent with the flexibility afforded by the Treaties. In the Office's view, therefore, additional legislation is not currently necessary from a treaty perspective.

B. Legislative Options

The Office has briefly examined various options that Congress could consider should courts in future cases construe Section 106 inconsistently with the making available obligation. These range from narrow definitional clarifications to a more fundamental restructuring under which certain existing exclusive rights would be combined into a general communication-to-the-public right similar to those in place in other countries.

To the extent Congress wishes to address only the aspect of this issue on which courts are presently divided, it could do so by adding a definition of "distribute" to Section 101 that includes offers. For example, Congress could adopt a definition similar to that in the Semiconductor Chip Protection Act, which provides: "to 'distribute' means to sell, or to lease, bail, or otherwise transfer, or to offer to sell, lease, bail, or otherwise transfer."[375] Should Congress also wish to clarify that the public performance and display rights cover offers to communicate a work, it could consider amending the Transmit Clause[376] to provide that offering to transmit or otherwise communicate a performance or display to the public satisfies the definition of performing or displaying a work "publicly." These two changes would confirm the Office's understanding of current law by clarifying that the three exclusive rights most directly relevant to the making available obligation—distribution, public performance, and public display—all include the right to offer online access to a work to the public. Congress also could consider a more basic explanatory amendment—for example, the addition of a statement in Section 106 providing that a copyright owner's exclusive rights thereunder encompass the right to make a work available to the public, including in such a way that members of the public may access the work from a place and at a time individually chosen by them.[377]

Alternatively, Congress could depart from the United States' historical practice of implementation through multiple exclusive rights and instead adopt a general right of communication to the public that includes offers of on-demand access. This could take a variety of forms, but under the WCT, the term "'Communication' implies transmission to a public not present in the place where the communication originates."[378] If Congress were to follow that model, the existing rights of distribution, public performance, and public display likely would be subsumed under the communication-to-the-public right insofar as they cover transmissions to remote locations. The separately enumerated distribution, performance, and display rights would remain in the statute, but presumably would be limited only to physical or in-person communications going forward.

This approach would represent a sweeping reconfiguration of U.S. copyright law. The addition of a communication-to-the-public right to Section 106 would necessitate corresponding changes throughout Title 17. Virtually every existing provision referring to the distribution, performance, or display rights would have to be updated to address which right or combination thereof would be implicated under the new structure.[379] As several commenters observed, such changes would introduce substantial uncertainty into the marketplace by disrupting established licensing models and other business practices based around the current exclusive-rights framework.[380] "Existing limitations and exceptions, as well, may need to be updated and new ones created" in order to avoid upsetting the current balance within the copyright law.[381] It is not clear that the costs of these disruptions would be justified by any additional clarity that such a right might produce.

This conclusion is bolstered by the fact that communication-to-the-public rights have not always been applied consistently among foreign jurisdictions that have implemented them. In particular, courts have reached differing conclusions over whether and under what circumstances individualized transmissions may constitute communications "to the public." In the EU, "it is irrelevant whether the potential recipients access the communicated works through a one-to-one connection," because doing so "does not prevent a large number of persons having access to the same work at the same time."[382] Conversely, Singapore's Court of Appeal has held that a communication requested by a user and accessible only by that user is *not* "to the public."[383] These divergent results indicate that countries providing a communication-to-the-public right are experiencing many of the same challenges over the application of exclusive rights to emerging technologies that have faced U.S. courts. The Office accordingly is not persuaded that the addition of such a right to our law would generate substantially greater predictability than exists currently.

* * *

In adopting the WIPO Internet Treaties, member states recognized the "profound impact of the development and convergence of information and communication technologies on the creation and use of literary and artistic works."[384] Of all these effects, none is more significant than the unprecedented ease with which copyrighted works can be made available to vast numbers of would-be recipients throughout the world. By granting copyright owners the exclusive right of making available, the Treaties seek to ensure that authors may continue to exercise meaningful control regarding whether and how their works are accessed and disseminated to the public, including through on-demand access.

For all the reasons discussed, the Copyright Office concludes that U.S. law provides the full scope of protection required by the making available obligation. The Office hopes that the analysis presented here will be useful to courts and stakeholders considering the possible application of the Copyright Act's exclusive rights to particular communications technologies and activities. Should Congress determine, based on future judicial developments or otherwise, that statutory clarification would be advisable, the Office stands ready to assist with its consideration of any proposed changes.

APPENDIX A. STUDY REQUEST FROM REPRESENTATIVE MELVIN L. WATT

MELVIN L. WATT
12TH DISTRICT
NORTH CAROLINA

COMMITTEES
JUDICIARY
RANKING MEMBER, SUBCOMMITTEE ON
COURTS, INTELLECTUAL PROPERTY
AND THE INTERNET

FINANCIAL SERVICES
SUBCOMMITTEE ON FINANCIAL
INSTITUTIONS AND CONSUMER CREDIT
SUBCOMMITTEE ON CAPITAL MARKETS AND
GOVERNMENT SPONSORED ENTERPRISES

Congress of the United States
House of Representatives
Washington, DC 20515–3312
December 19, 2013

The Honorable Maria A. Pallante
Register of Copyrights
U.S. Copyright Office
101 Independence Avenue, S.E.
Washington, D.C. 20540

Dear Ms. Pallante:

Earlier this session of the 113th Congress, I introduced H.R. 3219, the Free Market Royalty Act (FMRA), to address the unequal treatment of performers and musicians under U.S. copyright law. The FMRA was well-received in the press and supported across philosophical lines. The legislation would correct a long-standing inequity by granting musicians and performers the same power to negotiate rights to their sound recordings for broadcast terrestrial radio as musical composers have under current law. The legislation also instructed the U.S. Copyright Office to assess the state of U.S. law recognizing and protecting "making available" and "communicating to the public" rights for copyright holders. In light of the positive reaction to my bill and ongoing interest in the issues it raises, I would like the Office to begin its study now so that any recommendations may be considered as part of the ongoing congressional review of copyright law convened by the Subcommittee on Courts, Intellectual Property and the Internet.

The right of communication to the public and "making available" are explicitly included in two international treaties to which the United States is a party- the WIPO Copyright Treaty (WCT Article 8) and the WIPO Performance and Phonograms Treaty (WPPT Article 10, WPPT 15) (together the "WIPO Internet Treaties"). The WIPO Internet treaties recognize the importance of these rights for copyright holders in the digital environment and obligate contracting states to recognize these rights in national law. The United States implemented the treaties by enacting the Digital Millennium Copyright Act (DMCA) in 1998. The DMCA did not, however, amend U.S. copyright law to include specific references to "making available" or "communication to the public" because Congress concluded at the time that these rights already were covered by Title 17's panoply of exclusive rights and thus no implementing legislation was necessary. Since then, courts and commentators have struggled to adapt the various exclusive rights set forth in Title 17 to the digital environment, and specifically to address the variety of ways in which content is disseminated and transmitted today. As a result, some conflicting court decisions have created inconsistency about the strength and scope of protection for those rights in the United States.

In light of the rapidly changing technology and inconsistency in the various court discussions of these rights, I think it is important that the Copyright Office study the current state of the law in the United States. Specifically, it would be useful for the Office to review and assess: (1) how the existing bundle of exclusive rights under Title 17 covers the making available and communication to the public rights in the context of digital on-demand transmissions such as peer-to-peer networks, streaming services, and music downloads, as well as more broadly in the digital environment; (2) how foreign laws have interpreted and implemented the relevant provisions of the WIPO Internet Treaties; and (3) the feasibility and necessity of amending U.S. law to strengthen or clarify our law in this area. The report should include any recommendations to meet the objectives of fully recognizing and protecting such rights under section 106 of title 17, U.S.C. As an initial step in the examination, I trust that the Office will meet with and solicit comments from stakeholders and work closely with the staff of the Judiciary Committee throughout the review process.

Thank you for your expert assistance in this matter.

Sincerely,

Melvin L. Watt
Ranking Member

House Judiciary Subcommittee on the Courts, Intellectual Property and the Internet

cc: Hon. Bob Goodlatte, Chairman, House Judiciary Committee
Hon. John Conyers, Jr., Ranking Member, House Judiciary Committee

APPENDIX B. FEDERAL REGISTER NOTICES

Library of Congress
United States Copyright Office
[Docket No. 2014–2]
Study on the Right of Making Available; Comments and Public Roundtable

Agency: U.S. Copyright Office, Library of Congress.

Action: Request for comments and notice of public roundtable.

Summary: The United States Copyright Office is undertaking a study at the request of Congress to assess the state of U.S. law recognizing and protecting "making available" and "communication to the public" rights for copyright holders. The Office is requesting public comments on how the existing bundle of rights under Title 17 covers the making available and communication to the public rights, how foreign laws have addressed such rights, and the feasibility and necessity of amending U.S. law to strengthen or clarify our law in this area. The Copyright Office also will hold a public roundtable to discuss these topics and to provide a forum for interested parties to address the issues raised by the comments received.

Dates: Comments are due on or before April 4, 2014. The public roundtable will be held on May 5, 2014, from 9:00 a.m. to 5:00 p.m. EDT.

Addresses: All comments should be submitted electronically. To submit comments, please visit *http:// www.copyright.gov/docs/ making_available/*. The Web site interface requires submitters to complete a form specifying name and organization, as applicable, and to upload comments as an attachment via a browser button. To meet accessibility standards, commenting parties must upload comments in a single file not to exceed six megabytes ("MB") in one of the following formats: The Portable Document File ("PDF") format that contains searchable, accessible text (not an image); Microsoft Word; WordPerfect; Rich Text Format ("RTF"); or ASCII text file format (not a scanned document). The form and face of the comments must include both the name of the submitter and organization. The Office will post all comments publicly on the Office's Web site exactly as they are received, along with names and organizations.

The public roundtable will take place in the Copyright Office Hearing Room, LM–408 of the Madison Building of the Library of Congress, 101 Independence Avenue SE., Washington, DC 20559. The Copyright Office strongly prefers that requests for participation be submitted electronically. A participation request form will be posted on the Copyright Office Web site at *http://www.copyright.gov/docs/ making_available/* on or about April 7, 2014. If electronic submission of comments or requests for participation is not feasible, please contact the Office at 202–707–1027 for special instructions.

For Further Information Contact: Maria Strong, Senior Counsel for Policy and International Affairs, by telephone at 202–707–1027 or by email at *mstrong@loc.gov*, or Kevin Amer, Counsel for Policy and International Affairs, by telephone at 202–707–1027 or by email at *kamer@loc.gov*.

Supplementary Information:

I. Background

The WIPO Internet Treaties—the WIPO Copyright Treaty ("WCT")[385] and the WIPO Performances and Phonograms Treaty ("WPPT")[386]— require member states to recognize the rights of "making available" and "communication to the public" in their national laws. The treaties obligate member states to give authors of works, producers of sound recordings, and performers whose performances are fixed in sound recordings the exclusive right to authorize the transmission of their works and sound recordings, including through interactive platforms, such as the Internet, where the public can choose where and when to access them. In the specific context of interactive, on-demand situations, WCT Article 8 and WPPT Articles 10 and 14 provide treaty members with flexibility in the manner in which they implement this right.[387]

The United States implemented the WIPO Internet Treaties through the Digital Millennium Copyright Act ("DMCA") in 1998.[388] Based on advice received from the Copyright Office, among many other experts, Congress did not amend U.S. law to include explicit references to "making available" and "communication to the public," concluding that Title 17 already provided those rights.[389] As former Register of Copyrights Marybeth Peters observed:

> While Section 106 of the U.S. Copyright Act does not specifically include anything called a "making available" right, the activities involved in making a work available are covered under the exclusive rights of reproduction, distribution, public display and/or public performance. . . . Which of these rights are invoked in any given context will depend on the nature of the "making available" activity.[390]

Indeed, both Congress and the Executive Branch have continued to support this view since the enactment of the DMCA.[391]

The lack of explicit references to these rights in U.S. law, however, has led some courts and commentators to express uncertainty over how the existing rights in Title 17 may apply to various methods of making of copyrighted works available to the public, including in the digital environment. Especially in the Internet era, in any given case several of these rights (reproduction, distribution, public performance, and public display) may be at issue, depending on the facts involved.

Courts, academics, and practitioners particularly have focused on the scope of the distribution right under Section 106 and have debated whether it fully encompasses the making available of a copyrighted work without proof of an actual distribution.[392] For example, two early Eighth and Fourth Circuit cases discussing making available yielded conflicting results. The Eighth Circuit in *National Car Rental System, Inc.* v. *Computer Associates International, Inc.* rejected the notion that making a work available without more violated the distribution right.[393] The principal authority to the contrary is the Fourth Circuit's decision in *Hotaling* v. *Church of Jesus Christ of Latter-Day Saints,* in which the defendants made several unauthorized microfiche copies of genealogical research materials, one of which ended up in a library collection.[394] The library did not keep records of public use, and therefore there was no evidence of the copy being loaned to the public.[395] The court found that making a work available to the public constituted distribution because "[w]hen a public library adds a work to its collection, lists the work in its index or catalog system, and makes the work available to the borrowing or browsing public, it has completed all the steps necessary for distribution to the public."[396]

A recent Tenth Circuit decision, *Diversey* v. *Schmidly,*[397] followed *Hotaling*'s conclusion that making a work available to the public constitutes distribution under Section 106(3). *Diversey* involved a similar situation to *Hotaling* and addressed a library lending an unauthorized copy of a work to the public. The Tenth Circuit noted, however, that there has not been consensus on *Hotaling's* applicability to Internet file-sharing cases, and the court avoided extending its holding to those digital situations.[398]

Other courts have addressed the scope of the distribution right in the online context and have reached similarly conflicting results. The Ninth Circuit in *A&M Records* v. *Napster, Inc.* concluded that distribution encompasses "making available," observing that "Napster users who upload file names to the search index for others to copy violate plaintiffs' distribution rights."[399] Other courts have disagreed and required actual distribution. Thus, the court in *London- Sire Records, Inc.* v. *Doe 1,* which considered infringement of the distribution right through peer-to-peer file sharing, cast doubt on *Hotaling,* asserting that "[m]erely because the defendant has 'completed all the steps necessary for distribution' does not necessarily mean that a distribution has actually occurred."[400] Notably, however, while the *London-Sire* court required actual distribution, it did not require direct evidence of dissemination over peer-to-peer networks, holding instead that a reasonable fact-finder may infer that distribution actually took place where the defendant has completed all necessary steps for a public distribution.[401] Other courts have also relied on the language of Section 106(3) to require actual distribution in order to find a violation of that right.[402]

In sum, while Congress and the Copyright Office have agreed that U.S. law covers the making available right of the WCT, courts have encountered difficulties in evaluating the scope of this interactive right, and the level of evidence needed to establish liability, in the specific cases before them.[403]

In a letter dated December 19, 2013, Representative Melvin L. Watt requested that the Copyright Office "assess the state of U.S. law recognizing and protecting 'making available' and 'communicating to the public' rights for copyright holders. . . . In light of the rapidly changing technology and inconsistency in the various court discussions of these rights . . . it is important that the Copyright Office study the current state of the law in the United States." Specifically, Representative Watt asked the Office to review and assess: "(1) How the existing bundle of exclusive rights under Title 17 covers the making available and communication to the public rights in the context of digital on-demand transmissions such as peer-to-peer networks, streaming services, and music downloads, as well as more broadly in the digital environment; (2) how foreign laws have interpreted and implemented the relevant provisions of the WIPO Internet Treaties; and (3) the feasibility and necessity of amending U.S. law to strengthen or clarify our law in this area."

On January 14, 2014, the House Judiciary Committee's Subcommittee on Intellectual Property, Competition, and the Internet held a hearing during which two witnesses were asked to address the issue of the making available right.[404] These witnesses expressed a variety of views on whether current U.S. copyright law provides sufficient clarity on this issue and whether adding an explicit making available right to Title 17 would be beneficial.[405] They agreed, however, that current law is properly construed to provide such protection.[406]

II. Request for Comment

In light of uncertainty among some courts regarding the nature and scope of the making available and communication to the public rights, and to facilitate the study requested by Representative Watt, the Copyright Office seeks public comments on the three main issues listed above. The Office poses additional questions on these three topics below, and requests that commenters identify the questions they are answering in their responses.

1. Existing Exclusive Rights under Title 17

a. How does the existing bundle of exclusive rights currently in Title 17 cover the making available and communication to the public rights in the context of digital on-demand transmissions such as peer-to-peer networks, streaming services, and downloads of copyrighted content, as well as more broadly in the digital environment?
b. Do judicial opinions interpreting Section 106 and the making available right in the framework of tangible works provide sufficient guidance for the digital realm?

2. Foreign Implementation and Interpretation of the WIPO Internet Treaties

a. How have foreign laws implemented the making available right (as found in WCT Article 8 and WPPT Articles 10 and 14)? Has such implementation provided more or less legal clarity in those countries in the context of digital distribution of copyrighted works?
b. How have courts in foreign countries evaluated their national implementation of the making available right in these two WIPO treaties? Are there any specific case results or related legislative components that might present attractive options for possible congressional consideration?

3. Possible Changes to U.S. Law

a. If Congress continues to determine that the Section 106 exclusive rights provide a making available right in the digital environment, is there a need for Congress to take any additional steps to clarify the law to avoid potential conflicting outcomes in future litigation? Why or why not?
b. If Congress concludes that Section 106 requires further clarification of the scope of the making available right in the digital environment, how should the law be amended to incorporate this right more explicitly?
c. Would adding an explicit "making available" right significantly broaden the scope of copyright protection beyond what it is today? Why or why not? Would existing rights in Section 106 also have to be recalibrated?
d. Would any amendment to the "making available" right in Title 17 raise any First Amendment concerns? If so, how can any potential issues in this area be avoided?
e. If an explicit right is added, what, if any, corresponding exceptions or limitations should be considered for addition to the copyright law?

If there are any pertinent issues not discussed above, the Office encourages interested parties to raise those matters in their comments.

III. Public Roundtable

On May 5, 2014, the Copyright Office will hold a public roundtable to hear stakeholder views and to initiate discussion of the three topics identified above. The agenda and the process for submitting requests to participate in the public roundtable will be available on the Copyright Office Web site on or about April 7, 2014.

IV. Requests to Participate

Requests to participate in the public roundtable should be submitted online at *http://www.copyright.gov/docs/ making_available/.* Nonparticipants who wish to attend and observe the discussion should note that seating is limited and, for nonparticipants, will be available on a first come, first served basis.

Dated: February 20, 2014.

Maria A. Pallante,

Register of Copyrights.

[FR Doc. 2014–04104 Filed 2–24–14; 8:45 am]

Billing Code 1410–30–P

Library of Congress

U.S. Copyright Office

[Docket No. 2014–2]

Notice of Room Change: Public Roundtable on the Right of Making Available

Agency: U.S. Copyright Office, Library of Congress.

Action: Notice of room change for public roundtable.

Summary: The U.S. Copyright Office has changed the location of the May 5, 2014 public roundtable announced in the Office's February 25, 2014 Notice of Inquiry for its study on the rights of "making available" and "communication to the public." The roundtable will be held in 2226 Rayburn House Office Building, Washington, DC 20515, from 9:00 a.m. to 5:00 p.m. EDT.

For Further Information Contact: Maria Strong, Senior Counsel for Policy and International Affairs, by telephone at 202–707–1027 or by email at *mstrong@loc.gov*, or Kevin Amer, Counsel for Policy and International Affairs, by telephone at 202–707–1027 or by email at *kamer@loc.gov*.

Supplementary Information: On February 25, 2014, the Copyright Office published a Notice of Inquiry requesting public comments and announcing a May 5, 2014 public roundtable on the state of U.S. law recognizing and protecting "making available" and "communication to the public" rights for copyright holders. Interested members of the public were directed to submit written comments and to request participation in the public roundtable using forms posted on the Office's Web site.

The Office is announcing that the location of the public roundtable has been changed to 2226 Rayburn House Office Building, Washington, DC 20515. As previously scheduled, the roundtable will be held on May 5, 2014, from 9:00 a.m. to 5:00 p.m. EDT.

Individuals selected for participation in one or more roundtable sessions will be notified directly by the Office. The Office will post the agenda for the roundtable on or about April 28, 2014 at *http://www.copyright.gov/docs/making_available/*. Nonparticipants who wish to attend and observe the discussion should note that seating is limited and, for nonparticipants, will be available on a first come, first served basis.

Dated: April 23, 2014.

Maria A. Pallante,

Register of Copyrights.

[FR Doc. 2014–09656 Filed 4–28–14; 8:45 am]

Billing Code 1410–30–P

Library of Congress

U.S. Copyright Office

[Docket No. 2014–2]

Study on the Right of Making Available; Request for Additional Comments

Agency: U.S. Copyright Office, Library of Congress.

Action: Request for additional comments.

Summary: The U.S. Copyright Office seeks further comments on the state of U.S. law recognizing and protecting "making available" and "communication to the public" rights for copyright holders. This request provides an opportunity for interested parties to address issues raised in prior written comments and during the public roundtable held on May 5, 2014, as well as express their views on recent legal developments.

Dates: Comments must be received no later than 5:00 p.m. EDT on August 14, 2014.

Addresses: All comments should be submitted electronically. To submit comments, please visit http:// www.copyright.gov/docs/ making_available/. The Web site interface requires submitters to complete a form specifying name and organization, as applicable, and to upload comments as an attachment via a browser button. To meet accessibility standards, commenting parties must upload comments in a single file not to exceed six megabytes ("MB") in one of the following formats: A Portable Document File ("PDF") format that contains searchable, accessible text (not an image); Microsoft Word; WordPerfect; Rich Text Format ("RTF"); or ASCII text file format (not a scanned document). The form and face of the comments must include both the name of the submitter and organization. The Office will post all comments publicly on the Office's Web site exactly as they are received, along with names and organizations. If electronic submission of comments is not feasible, please contact the Office at 202–707–1027 for special instructions.

For Further Information Contact: Maria Strong, Senior Counsel for Policy and International Affairs, by telephone at 202–707–1027 or by email at mstrong@loc.gov, or Kevin Amer, Counsel for Policy and International Affairs, by telephone at 202–707–1027 or by email at kamer@loc.gov.

Supplementary Information:

I. Background

The Copyright Office is undertaking a study at the request of Congress to assess the state of U.S. law recognizing and protecting "making available" and "communication to the public" rights for copyright holders, particularly in the digital age. As part of its review, the Office issued a Notice of Inquiry (the "Notice") on February 25, 2014,[407] seeking comments from the public on the following general issues: (1) How the existing bundle of exclusive rights under Title 17 covers the making available and communication to the public rights in the context of digital on- demand transmissions such as peer-to- peer networks, streaming services, and music downloads, as well as more broadly in the digital environment; (2) how foreign laws have interpreted and implemented the relevant provisions of the WIPO Internet Treaties;[408] and (3) the feasibility and necessity of amending U.S. law to strengthen or clarify our law in this area. The Office also posed additional questions on each of these topics.

The Office received twenty-seven written comments from various interested parties in response to the Notice. On May 5, 2014, the Office held a public roundtable in Washington, DC to hear stakeholder views on these issues. Commenters and participants in the roundtable expressed a variety of views on a broad range of topics. The Notice, public comments, the agenda for the public roundtable, and the transcript of the roundtable proceedings are posted on the Copyright Office Web site.[409] A video recording of the roundtable will be posted on the Web site when it becomes available.

Commenters and roundtable participants generally agreed that current U.S. law, properly interpreted, provides rights that are equivalent to the making available and communication to the public rights required by the WIPO Internet Treaties. There was disagreement, however, over whether and how particular provisions of Title 17 may apply to various activities in the digital context. For example, several stakeholders argued that the unauthorized uploading of a copyrighted work to a shared network folder that is accessible to the public constitutes a violation of the exclusive right of distribution under

17 U.S.C. 106(3). Others disagreed, arguing that direct or circumstantial evidence that another user has downloaded a copy of that file is necessary to establish an infringement of the distribution right by the uploader. The roundtable discussion and initial written comments also highlighted issues such as whether a digital file is a "material object[]" for purposes of the statutory definitions of "copies" and "phonorecords"; [410] the relevance of legislative history to the construction of the distribution right; the role of secondary liability theories in assessing the United States' implementation of the relevant treaty provisions; and the use of evidence provided by a copyright owner's investigator in digital filesharing cases.

Following the Office's roundtable discussions, on June 25, 2014, the Supreme Court decided *American Broadcasting Cos., Inc.* v. *Aereo, Inc.*[411] The case involved a service, Aereo, that used thousands of dime-sized antennas to allow subscribers to capture and watch television programs over the Internet as the programs were being broadcast over the air. When a subscriber selected a program to watch on Aereo's Web site, the system would create a subscriber-specific copy of the program that would then be streamed to the subscriber's computer or Internet- connected device. The Court held that this activity infringed the exclusive right of the owners of the copyrights in the programs to perform those works publicly.[412]

A critical aspect of the Court's decision was its interpretation of Title 17's "Transmit Clause." That clause provides that the public performance right afforded to copyright owners under Section 106 includes the exclusive right "to transmit or otherwise communicate a performance . . . of the work . . . to the public, by means of any device or process, whether the members of the public capable of receiving the performance . . . receive it in the same place or in separate places and at the same time or at different times."[413]

Finding Aereo's activities "substantially similar to those of the [cable television] companies" that Congress intended to reach when it updated the public performance right in 1976, the Court held that "Aereo, and not just its subscribers, 'perform[ed]' (or 'transmit[ted]')" within the meaning of the statute.[414] The Court further concluded that Aereo performed copyrighted works "publicly," notwithstanding that each transmission was made to a single subscriber from a personal copy, holding that "when an entity communicates the same contemporaneously perceptible images and sounds to multiple people, it transmits a performance to them regardless of the number of discrete communications it makes." [415]

Justice Scalia, joined by Justices Thomas and Alito, dissented, concluding that Aereo did not "perform" within the meaning of Section 106(4). The dissenting Justices reasoned that, because Aereo's subscribers, not the company itself, selected the programs to be streamed, the resulting performances were not "the product of Aereo's volitional conduct," and therefore Aereo could not be held directly liable for infringement.[416]

II. Request for Comment

The Office invites further written comments on the issues raised in the Notice, including from parties who did not previously address those subjects, or those who wish to amplify or clarify their earlier comments or respond to issues raised during the public roundtable. In addition, the Office is interested in commenters' views regarding the Supreme Court's opinion in *Aereo* and how that opinion may affect the scope of the rights of making available and communication to the public in the United States. Specifically, commenters may wish to address the following questions:

1. To what extent does the Supreme Court's construction of the right of public performance in *Aereo* affect the scope of the United States' implementation of the rights of making available and communication to the public?
2. How should courts consider the requirement of volitional conduct when assessing direct liability in the context of interactive transmissions of content over the Internet, especially in the wake of *Aereo*?
3. To what extent do, or should, secondary theories of copyright liability affect the scope of the United States' implementation of the rights of making available and communication to the public?
4. How does, or should, the language on "material objects" in the Section 101 definitions of "copy" and "phonorecord" interact with the exclusive right of distribution, and/or making available and communication to the public, in the online environment?
5. What evidentiary showing should be required to prove a copyright infringement claim against an individual user or third-party service engaged in unauthorized filesharing? Should evidence that the defendant has placed a copyrighted work in a publicly accessible shared folder be sufficient to prove liability, or should courts require evidence that another party has downloaded a copy of the work? Can the latter showing be made through circumstantial evidence, or

evidence that an investigator acting on the plaintiff's behalf has downloaded a copy of the work?

6. Please provide any additional comments or suggestions regarding recommendations or proposals the Copyright Office might wish to consider as it concludes its study.

A party choosing to respond to this request need not address all of these topics, but the Office requests that responding parties clearly identify and separately address those subjects for which a response is submitted. Commenters also may address any other issues pertinent to the Office's review.

Dated: July 10, 2014.

Karyn A. Temple Claggett,

Associate Register of Copyrights.

[FR Doc. 2014–16537 Filed 7–14–14; 8:45 am]

Billing Code 1410–30–P

Library of Congress

U.S. Copyright Office

[Docket No. 2014–02]

Extension of Comment Period; Study on the Right of Making Available; Request for Additional Comments

Agency: U.S. Copyright Office, Library of Congress.

Action: Extension of comment period.

Summary: The U.S. Copyright Office is extending the deadline for public comments that address topics listed in the Office's July 15, 2014 Request for Additional Comments.

Dates: Comments are now due no later than 5:00 p.m. EDT on September 15, 2014.

Addresses: All comments should be submitted electronically. To submit comments, please visit http:// www.copyright.gov/docs/making_ available/. The Web site interface requires submitters to complete a form specifying name and organization, as applicable, and to upload comments as an attachment via a browser button. To meet accessibility standards, commenting parties must upload comments in a single file not to exceed six megabytes ("MB") in one of the following formats: a Portable Document File ("PDF") format that contains searchable, accessible text (not an image); Microsoft Word; WordPerfect; Rich Text Format ("RTF"); or ASCII text file format (not a scanned document). The form and face of the comments must include both the name of the submitter and organization. The Office will post all comments publicly on the Office's Web site exactly as they are received, along with names and organizations. If electronic submission of comments is not feasible, please contact the Office at 202–707–1027 for special instructions.

For Further Information Contact: Maria Strong, Senior Counsel for Policy and International Affairs, by telephone at 202–707–1027 or by email at mstrong@loc.gov, or Kevin Amer, Counsel for Policy and International Affairs, by telephone at 202–707–1027 or by email at kamer@loc.gov.

Supplementary Information: On July 15, 2014, the Copyright Office issued a Request for Additional Comments on the state of U.S. law recognizing and protecting "making available" and "communication to the public" rights for copyright holders.[417] The Request listed several questions for interested members of the public to address in the context of U.S. implementation of the WIPO Copyright Treaty (WCT) and the WIPO Performances and Phonograms Treaty (WPPT) rights of "making available" and "communication to the public," and also invited views on specific issues raised during the public roundtable held in Washington, DC on May 5, 2014. To provide sufficient time for commenters to respond, the Office is extending the time for filing additional comments from August 14, 2014 to September 15, 2014.

Dated: July 28, 2014.

Karyn A. Temple Claggett,

Associate Register of Copyrights.

[FR Doc. 2014–18097 Filed 7–31–14; 8:45 am]

Billing Code 1410–30–P

APPENDIX C. COMMENTING PARTIES

Parties Who Submitted Comments in Response to the February 25, 2014 Notice of Inquiry

1. American Society of Composers, Authors and Publishers; Broadcast Music, Inc.; Songwriters Guild of America; SESAC, Inc.; and National Music Publishers' Association
2. American Society of Media Photographers
3. Association of American Publishers, Inc.
4. Association of Learned and Professional Society Publishers
5. Bridges, Andrew P.

6. Computer and Communications Industry Association
7. Copyright Alliance
8. Corporation for National Research Initiatives
9. Digital Public Library of America
10. Entertainment Software Association
11. Ginsburg, Jane C.
12. International Association of Scientific, Technical and Medical Publishers
13. Internet Commerce Coalition
14. Library Copyright Alliance
15. Lunney, Glynn S., Jr.
16. Menell, Peter S.
17. Motion Picture Association of America, Inc. and Recording Industry Association of America, Inc.
18. Oppenheimer, David
19. Pangasa, Maneesh
20. Public Knowledge and Electronic Frontier Foundation
21. Sanders, Rick G., Jr.
22. Society of American Archivists
23. Software and Information Industry Association
24. Sydnor, Thomas D., II
25. University of North Carolina at Chapel Hill University Libraries, Scholarly Communications Office
26. U.S. Chamber of Commerce, Global Intellectual Property Center

Parties Who Submmitted Reply Comments in Response to the July 15, 2014 Request for Additional Comments

1. American Association of Independent Music
2. American Photographic Artists
3. Barkman, Alex
4. Bridges, Andrew P.
5. Broadcast Music, Inc.; American Society of Composers, Authors and Publishers; National Music Publishers' Association; SESAC, Inc.; and Songwriters Guild of America, Inc.
6. BSA | The Software Alliance

7. Cablevision Systems Corp.
8. Campbell, John
9. Computer and Communications Industry Association
10. Copyright Alliance
11. Devorah, Carrie
12. DISH Network Corporation
13. Ginsburg, Jane C.
14. Internet Association
15. Internet Commerce Coalition
16. Motion Picture Association of America, Inc. and Recording Industry Association of America, Inc.
17. Music Managers' Forum and Featured Artists' Coalition
18. PACA, Digital Media Licensing Association, Inc.; National Press Photographers Association; American Society of Media Photographers; and Graphic Artists Guild
19. Pala
20. Pangasa, Maneesh
21. Public Knowledge and Electronic Frontier Foundation
22. Sanders, Rick G., Jr.
23. Society of Composers and Lyricists
24. Software and Information Industry Association
25. Sydnor, Thomas D., II
26. U.S. Chamber of Commerce, Global Intellectual Property Center
27. Wade, Brandon

APPENDIX D. AGENDA FOR PUBLIC ROUNDTABLE HELD ON MAY 5, 2014

Introduction 9:00 am **Opening Remarks by the U.S. Copyright Office**

Session 1 9: 10 am – 10:45 am **Existing Exclusive Rights under Title 17 (Part One)**

This session will explore how the exclusive rights in Title 17 cover the making available and communication to the public rights in the context of digital on-demand transmissions such as peer-to-peer networks, streaming services, and music downloads, as well as more broadly in the digital environment. This session will also address evidentiary issues in infringement actions.

John C. Beiter SESAC, Inc.
Andrew P. Bridges Attorney
George M. Borkowski Senior Vice President, Litigation and Legal Affairs, Recording Industry Association of America
Eugene DeAnna Library of Congress
Professor Jane Ginsburg Columbia University School of Law
Terry Hart Director of Legal Policy, Copyright Alliance
Professor Glynn Lunney Tulane University School of Law
Professor Peter Menell University of California – Berkeley School of Law
Sam Mosenkis Vice President, Legal Affairs, American Society of Composers, Authors and Publishers
Matthew Schruers Vice President of Law and Policy, Computer and Communications Industry Association
Nancy Wolff PACA: Digital Media Licensing Association

10:45 am – 11:00 am **Break**

Session 2 11:00 am – 12:30 pm **Existing Exclusive Rights under Title 17 (Part Two)**

Like Session 1, this session will explore how the exclusive rights in Title 17 cover the making available and communication to the public rights in the context of digital on-demand transmissions such as peer-to-peer networks, streaming services, and music downloads, as well as more broadly in the digital environment. This session will also address evidentiary issues in infringement actions.

Jonathan Band Counsel, Library Copyright Alliance
Joseph J. DiMona Vice President, Legal Affairs, Broadcast Music, Inc.
Jim Halpert Internet Commerce Coalition
Lawrence Husick Delaware County IP Roundtable
Lee Knife Executive Director, Digital Media Association
Keith Kupferschmid General Counsel and Senior Vice President, Intellectual Property, Software and Information Industry Association

	Patrice A. Lyons General Counsel, Corporation for National Research Initiatives Laura Moy Staff Attorney, Public Knowledge Jay Rosenthal General Counsel, National Music Publishers' Association Ben Sheffner Vice President, Legal Affairs, Motion Picture Association of America, Inc. Steven Tepp Global Intellectual Property Center, U.S. Chamber of Commerce
12:30 pm – 1:45 pm	**Lunch Break**
SESSION 3 1:45 pm – 3:15 pm	**Benefits of Clarification/Possible Changes to U.S. Law** This session will explore the feasibility and necessity of amending U.S. law to strengthen or clarify U.S. law in this area. Allan Adler General Counsel, Association of American Publishers Sandra Aistars Chief Executive Officer, Copyright Alliance Jonathan Band Counsel, Library Copyright Alliance Gregory A. Barnes General Counsel, Digital Media Association John C. Beiter SESAC, Inc. Andrew P. BridgesAttorney Mitch Glazier Senior Executive Vice President, Recording Industry Association of America Keith Kupferschmid General Counsel and Senior Vice President, Intellectual Property, Software and Information Industry Association Patrice A. Lyons General Counsel, Corporation for National Research Initiatives Professor Peter Menell University of California – Berkeley School of Law Laura Moy Staff Attorney, Public Knowledge Nancy Wolff PACA: Digital Media Licensing Association
SESSION 4 3:15 pm – 4:15 pm	**Foreign Implementation and Interpretation of the WIPO Internet Treaties** This session will explore how foreign laws have interpreted and implemented the relevant provisions of the WIPO Internet Treaties. Sofia Castillo Legal Fellow, Copyright Alliance Joseph J. DiMona Vice President, Legal Affairs, Broadcast Music, Inc. Christian Genetski Senior Vice President and General Counsel, Entertainment Software Association Professor Jane Ginsburg Columbia University School

	of Law Professor Glynn Lunney Tulane University School of Law Jay Rosenthal General Counsel, National Music Publishers' Association Matthew Schruers Vice President of Law and Policy, Computer and Communications Industry Association Steven Tepp Global Intellectual Property Center, U.S. Chamber of Commerce
Session 5 4:15 pm – 5:00 pm	**Audience Participation** This session will allow the audience to add final comments and views on the issues discussed during the day. Audience members will be able to sign-up throughout the day. Statements will be limited to 2 minutes in order to accommodate a maximum number of participants. Session participants will also be able to sign-up after the public audience members, time permitting.

APPENDIX E. SURVEY OF FOREIGN LAWS REGARDING STATUTORY APPROACHES TO THE RIGHT OF MAKING AVAILABLE

Survey of Foreign Laws Regarding Statutory Approaches to the Right of Making Available

This chart identifies the statutory structure of countries' implementation of Article 8 of the WCT. In order to conduct this survey, the Office developed a structure that grouped the manner of implementation of the right of making available into three categories.[418]

(1) *Internet Treaties Language*
Under this approach, implementing legislation adopted a making available right using language that tracks that of WCT Article 8, either identically or with non-substantive differences. It may be couched as part of a broader communication-to-the-public right or it may be a separately enumerated right.[419]

(2) *Alternative Language*

Under this approach, a new, explicit making available right was adopted, but the statutory text does not directly track the language from the WIPO Internet Treaties.

The new right may be included as part of a broad communication-to-the-public right or it may be a standalone right.[420]

(3) *Statutory Silence*

This approach covers the act of making available through a pre-existing right or rights, without adopting a specific reference to language reflecting the making available right.

This approach includes those countries whose statutes may be silent but there is case law that covers the making available right.

Also included in this category are laws that may be self-executing (hence there is no reason to change statutory language) as part of countries' WCT accession/ratification.

Finally, this category also may include national laws that that have not yet been amended to reflect WCT language.

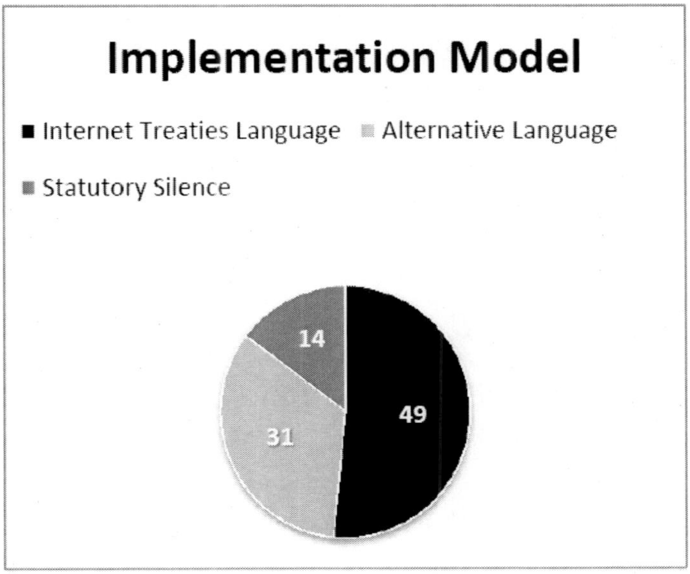

The Office used its expertise, based on available information, to evaluate the situation in each country and make a subjective determination resulting in the relevant category placement.

Survey Chart
(WCT = 94 members as of April 12, 2016)

Internet Treaties Model		Alternative Language Model		Statutory Silence Model	Reference(s)
Part of the CTTP Right	**Standalone Right Apart from CTTP**	**Part of the CTTP Right**	**Standalone Right Apart from CTTP**		**in National Law**
	Albania				Copyright and Other Rights Related to It, Law No. 9380 of 2005, Article 13.
				Algeria	Copyright and Related Rights, Law No. 03-05 of 2003, Article 27.
				Argentina	Legal Intellectual Property Regime, Law No. 11.723 of 1933, as amended by Law No. 26.570 of 2009, Article 2.
Armenia					Copyright and Related Rights, Law No. 3R-142 of 2013, Articles 13 and 19.
		Australia			Copyright Act, Law No. 63 of 1968, as amended by Act No. 80 of 2015, Articles 10 and 31.

Internet Treaties Model		Alternative Language Model		Statutory Silence Model	Reference(s)
Part of the CTTP Right	**Standalone Right Apart from CTTP**	**Part of the CTTP Right**	**Standalone Right Apart from CTTP**		**in National Law**
			Austria		Copyright Act, Law No. 111/1936 of 1936, as amended by Law No. 58/2010 of 2010, Article 18a.
			Azerbaijan		Copyright and Related Rights of 1996, as amended by Law No. 636-IVQD of 2013, Articles 4 and 15.
Bahrain					Protection of Copyright and Neighboring Rights, Law No. 22 of 2006, Articles 1 and 6.
		Belarus			Copyright and Related Rights, Law No. 262-3 of 2011, Articles 4 and 16.
				Belgium	Copyright and Neighboring Rights of 1994, as amended by Law of April 3, 1995, Article 1.

(Continued)

Internet Treaties Model		Alternative Language Model		Statutory Silence Model	Reference(s)
Part of the CTTP Right	Standalone Right Apart from CTTP	Part of the CTTP Right	Standalone Right Apart from CTTP		in National Law
		Benin			Protection of Copyright and Neighboring Rights, Law No. 2005-30, Articles 1, 4, 60, and 65.
		Bosnia and Herzegovina			Copyright and Related Rights Law, 2010, Article 24.
		Botswana			Copyright and Neighboring Rights Act, Act No. 8 of 2000, as amended by Act. No. 6 of 2006, Articles 2, 7, 24, and 25.
	Bulgaria				Copyright and Related Rights, Law No. 56/29 of 1993, as amended by Law No. 25/25 of 2011, Article 18.
		Burkina Faso			Protection of Literary and Artistic Property, Law No. 032-99/AN of 1999, Articles 16, 72, and 76 and the Glossary.

Internet Treaties Model		Alternative Language Model		Statutory Silence Model	Reference(s)
Part of the CTTP Right	Standalone Right Apart from CTTP	Part of the CTTP Right	Standalone Right Apart from CTTP		in National Law
		Burundi			Copyright and Related Rights, Law No. 1/021 of 2005, Articles 1 and 24 (WCT will enter into force on Apr. 12, 2016).
			Canada		Copyright Act, Law No. c. C-42 of 1985, as amended by Economic Action Plan 2015 Act. No. 1, Law No. c. 36 of 2015, Articles 2.2, 2.4, and 3.
		Chile			Intellectual Property Law, Law No. 17.336 of 1970, as amended by Law No. 20750 of 2014, Articles 5 and 18.
			China		Copyright Law, Presidential Order No. 31 of 1990, as amended by Presidential order No. 26 of 2010, Article 10.

(Continued)

Internet Treaties Model		Alternative Language Model		Statutory Silence Model	Reference(s)
Part of the CTTP Right	**Standalone Right Apart from CTTP**	**Part of the CTTP Right**	**Standalone Right Apart from CTTP**		**in National Law**
				Colombia	Copyright Law, Law No. 23 1982, as amended by Law No. 1450 of 2011, Articles 3, 8, and 12.
	Costa Rica				Copyright and Neighboring Rights, Law no. 6683 of 1982, as amended by Law No. 8834 of 2010, Article 16.
			Croatia		Copyright and Related Rights Act, Law No. 167/2003 of 2003, as amended by Law No. 127/2014 of 2014, Article 21.
Cyprus					Copyright Law No. 59 of 1976, as amended by Law No. 181(1)/2007 of 2007, Article 7.
Czech Republic					Copyright and Rights Related to Copyright, Law No. 121/2000 of

Internet Treaties Model		Alternative Language Model		Statutory Silence Model	Reference(s)
Part of the CTTP Right	**Standalone Right Apart from CTTP**	**Part of the CTTP Right**	**Standalone Right Apart from CTTP**		**in National Law**
					2000, as amended by Act No. 168/2008 of 2008, Article 18.
Denmark					Copyright Act, Consolidate Act. No. 1144 of 2014, Article 2.
Dominican Republic					Copyright Law, Law No. 65-00 of 2000, as amended by Law No. 2-07 of 2006, Articles 16 and 19.
		Ecuador			Intellectual Property Law, Law No. 2006-13 of 2006, Articles 19, 20, and 22.
		El Salvador			Promotion of and Protection of Intellectual Property, Decree No. 604 of 1993, as amended by Decree No. 870 of 2009, Articles 7 and 9.
		Estonia			Copyright Act of 1992, as amended in 2014, Articles 10 and 13.

(Continued)

Internet Treaties Model		Alternative Language Model		Statutory Silence Model	Reference(s)
Part of the CTTP Right	**Standalone Right Apart from CTTP**	**Part of the CTTP Right**	**Standalone Right Apart from CTTP**		**in National Law**
European Union					EU Directive 2001/29/EC, Article 3.1.
Finland					Copyright Act, Act No. 404/1961 of 1961, as amended in 2013, Section 2.
				France	Intellectual Property Code, Law No. 92-597 of 1992, as amended by Law No. 2015-195 of 2015, Article L122.
				Gabon	Protection for Copyright and Neighboring Rights, Law No. 1/87 of 1987, Articles 28 and 29.
Georgia					Copyright and Related Rights, Law No. 1585 of 2005, as amended in 2010, Articles 4 and 18.
	Germany				Copyright Act of 1965, as amended in 2013, Articles 15 and 19.

Internet Treaties Model		Alternative Language Model		Statutory Silence Model	Reference(s)
Part of the CTTP Right	Standalone Right Apart from CTTP	Part of the CTTP Right	Standalone Right Apart from CTTP		in National Law
		Ghana			Copyright Act, Law No. 690 of 2005, as amended by Law No. 788 of 2009, Articles 5, 28, and 76.
Greece					Copyright, Related Rights and Cultural Matters, Law No. 2121/1993 of 1993, as amended by Law No. 4281/2014 of 2014, Article 3.
Guatemala					Copyright and Related Rights, Decree No. 33-98 of 1998, as amended by Decree No. 56-2000 of 2000, Articles 4 and 21.
				Guinea	Provisions Relating to Copyright and Neighboring Rights, Act No. 043/APN/CP of 1980, Article 3.
Honduras					Copyright and Related Rights, Law No. 4-99-E of 1999, as amended by

(Continued)

Internet Treaties Model		Alternative Language Model		Statutory Silence Model	Reference(s)
Part of the CTTP Right	**Standalone Right Apart from CTTP**	**Part of the CTTP Right**	**Standalone Right Apart from CTTP**		**in National Law**
					Directive 16-2006 of 2006, Articles 9 and 39.
		Hungary			Copyright Act, Act LXXVI of 1999, as amended by Act CXXIX of 2015, Article 26.
		Indonesia			Copyright Act, Law No. 28 of 2014, Articles 1 and 9.
Ireland					Copyright and Related Rights Act, Law No. 28 of 2000, as amended by S.I. No. 39 of 2007, Article 40.
Italy					Copyright and Neighboring Rights Act, Law No. 22 of 1941, as amended by Decree No. 68 of 2003, Article 16.
	Jamaica				The Copyright Act, Act 5 of 1993, as amended by Act No. 13 of 2015, Section 9(f).

Internet Treaties Model		Alternative Language Model		Statutory Silence Model	Reference(s)
Part of the CTTP Right	Standalone Right Apart from CTTP	Part of the CTTP Right	Standalone Right Apart from CTTP		in National Law
		Japan			Copyright Law, Law No. 48 of 1970, as amended by Law No. 35 of 2014, Articles 2 and 23.
Jordan					Copyright Protection Law, Law No. 22 of 1992, as amended by Law No. 23 of 2014, Article 9.
	Kazakhstan				Copyright and Related Rights, Law No. 6 of 1996, as amended by Annex 3 to Order Number 250 of 2015, Articles 2 and 16.
	Kyrgyz Republic				Copyright and related rights, Law No. 120 of 1999, as amended by Law No. 14 of 2014, Article 16.
	Latvia				Copyright Law of 2000, as amended in 2014, Sections 1 and 15.

(Continued)

Internet Treaties Model		Alternative Language Model		Statutory Silence Model	Reference(s)
Part of the CTTP Right	**Standalone Right Apart from CTTP**	**Part of the CTTP Right**	**Standalone Right Apart from CTTP**		**in National Law**
			Liechtenstein		Copyright and Neighboring Rights, Law No. 160 of 1999, as amended by Law No. 167 of 2014, Article 10.
Lithuania					Copyright and Related Rights, Law No. VIII-1185 of 1999, as amended by Law No. XI-656 of 2010, Articles 2 and 15.
Luxembourg					Copyright, Neighboring Rights and Databases, Law No. 50 of 2001, as amended by Law No. 61 of 2004, Articles 3 and 4.
		Madagascar			Literary and Artistic Property, Law No. 97-036 of 1995, Articles 32-34 and 39.

Internet Treaties Model		Alternative Language Model		Statutory Silence Model	Reference(s)
Part of the CTTP Right	Standalone Right Apart from CTTP	Part of the CTTP Right	Standalone Right Apart from CTTP		in National Law
Malaysia					Copyright Act, Act 332 of 1987, as amended by Act A1420 of 2012, Articles
		Mali			Literary and Artistic Property, Law No. 08-024 of 2008, Articles 1 and 18.
Malta					Copyright Act, Act XIII of 2000, as amended by Act VIII of 2011, Articles 2 and 7.
			Mexico		Federal Law on Copyright, 1996, as amended in 2014, Article 27.
			Mongolia		Copyright and Related Rights, No. 7 of 2006, Articles 3 and 12.
	Montenegro				Copyright and Related Acts, Decree No. 01/933/2 of 2011, Articles 20 and 31.
		Morocco			Copyright and Related Rights, Law No. 2-00 of 2000, as amended by

(Continued)

Internet Treaties Model		Alternative Language Model		Statutory Silence Model	Reference(s)
Part of the CTTP Right	Standalone Right Apart from CTTP	Part of the CTTP Right	Standalone Right Apart from CTTP		in National Law
					Law No. 34-05 of 2006, Articles 1 and 10.
				Netherlands	Copyright Act of 1912, as amended in 2008, Article 12.
Nicaragua					Copyright and Neighboring Rights, Law No. 312 of 1999, as amended by Law No. 577 of 2006, Articles 2 and 23.
Oman					Copyright and Related Rights, Decree No. 65/2008 of 2008, Articles 1 and 6.
Panama					Copyright and Neighboring Rights, Law No. 64 of 2012, Article 55.
		Paraguay			Copyright and Related Rights, Law No. 1328/98 of 1998, Articles 2, 25, and 27.

Internet Treaties Model		Alternative Language Model		Statutory Silence Model	Reference(s)
Part of the CTTP Right	Standalone Right Apart from CTTP	Part of the CTTP Right	Standalone Right Apart from CTTP		in National Law
		Peru			Copyright Law, Decree No. 822 of 1996, as amended by Law No. 30276 of 2014, Articles 2, 31, 33, and 34.
Philippines					Intellectual Property Code, Act No. 8293 of 1997, as amended by Act No. 10372 of 2013, Sections 171 and 177.
	Poland				Copyright and Related Rights, Act No. 83 of 1994, as amended in 2010, Article 50.
	Portugal				Copyright and Related Rights, Law No. 63/85 of 1985, as amended by Law No. 16/2008 of 2008, Articles 67 and 68.
				Qatar	Copyright and Related Rights, Law No. 7 of 2002, Articles 1 and 7.
Republic of Korea					Copyright Act, Law No. 9625 of 2009, as amended by Act No.

(Continued)

Internet Treaties Model		Alternative Language Model		Statutory Silence Model	Reference(s)
Part of the CTTP Right	Standalone Right Apart from CTTP	Part of the CTTP Right	Standalone Right Apart from CTTP		in National Law
					12137 of 2013, Articles 2 and 25.
			Republic of Moldova		Copyright and Related Rights, Law No. 139 of 2010, Articles 3 and 11.
Romania					Copyright and Neighboring Rights, Law No. 8 of 1996, as amended by Law No. 329 of 2006, Articles 13 and 15.
	Russian Federation				Civil Code of the Russian Federation, as amended in 2014, Article 1270.
				St. Lucia	Copyright Act, Law No. 10 of 1995, as amended by Law No. 7 of 2000, Sections 2 and 9.
		Senegal			Copyright and Related Rights, Law No. 2008-09 of 2008, Articles 33 and 34.

Internet Treaties Model		Alternative Language Model		Statutory Silence Model	Reference(s)
Part of the CTTP Right	**Standalone Right Apart from CTTP**	**Part of the CTTP Right**	**Standalone Right Apart from CTTP**		**in National Law**
Serbia					Copyright and Related Rights, Law No. RS 104/2009 of 2009, as amended by Law No. 119/2012 of 2012, Articles 4 and 30.
Singapore					Copyright Act (Chapter 63), Act 2 of 1987, as amended by Act 22 of 2014, Articles 7 and 26.
	Slovakia				Copyright and Related Rights, Act No. 618/2003 of 2003, as amended by Act No. 283/2014 of 2014, Articles 5 and 18.
Slovenia					Copyright and Related Rights Act, Law No. RS 21/95 of 1995, as amended by Law No. 15 of 2006, Articles 22 and 32a.
Spain					Intellectual Property Law, Law No. 1/1996 of 1996, as amended by Law No. 21/2014 of

(Continued)

Internet Treaties Model		Alternative Language Model		Statutory Silence Model	Reference(s)
Part of the CTTP Right	**Standalone Right Apart from CTTP**	**Part of the CTTP Right**	**Standalone Right Apart from CTTP**		**in National Law**
					2014, Articles 20 and 90.
Sweden					Copyright in Literary and Artistic Works, Law No. 1960:729 of 1960, as amended by Act 2011:94 of 2011, Article 2.
			Switzerland		Copyright and Related Rights Law No. 231.1 of 1992, as amended by Annex I No. II 9 of the Civil Procedure Code of 2008, Article 10.
	Tajikistan				Law on Copyright and Related Rights, 1998, as amended in 2009, Articles 3 and 16.
The former Yugoslav Republic of Macedonia					Law on Copyright and Related Rights, Law No. 115/10 of 2010, as amended by Law No. 51 of 2011, Articles 27 and 30.

Internet Treaties Model		Alternative Language Model		Statutory Silence Model	Reference(s)
Part of the CTTP Right	Standalone Right Apart from CTTP	Part of the CTTP Right	Standalone Right Apart from CTTP		in National Law
				Togo	Copyright, Folklore and Related Rights, Law No. 91-92 of 1991, Article 18.
Trinidad and Tobago					Copyright Act, Cap. 82:80, as amended by Act No. 5 of 2008, Articles 3 and 8.
				Turkey	Intellectual and Artistic Works, Law No. 5846 of 1951, as amended by Law No. 5728 of 2008, Articles 20-25.
	Ukraine				Copyright and Related Rights, Law No. 3792-XII of 1993, as amended by Law No. 5460-VI of 2012, Articles 1 and 15.
				United Arab Emirates	Copyright and Related Rights, Law No. 7 of 2002, as amended by Law No. 32 of 2006, Articles 1 and 7.
United Kingdom					Copyright, Designs and Patents Act 1988, as

(Continued)

Internet Treaties Model		Alternative Language Model		Statutory Silence Model	Reference(s)
Part of the CTTP Right	**Standalone Right Apart from CTTP**	**Part of the CTTP Right**	**Standalone Right Apart from CTTP**		**in National Law**
					amended by the Crime and Courts Act 2013, Articles 20 and 20.
				United States of America	Copyright Act of 1976, as amended in 2014, Section 106.
Uruguay					Copyright, Law No. 9.739 of 1937, as amended by Law No. 18.046 of 2006, Article 2.
34	15	21	10	14	
49		31		14	

End Notes

[1] WIPO Copyright Treaty art. 8, Dec. 20, 1996, 36 I.L.M. 65 (1997) ("WCT"); *see also* WIPO Performances and Phonograms Treaty arts. 10, 14, Dec. 20, 1996, 36 I.L.M. 76 (1997) ("WPPT").

[2] *See* Jane C. Ginsburg, Comments Submitted in Response to U.S. Copyright Office's Feb. 25, 2014 Notice of Inquiry at 2 (Apr. 7, 2014) ("Ginsburg Initial Comments") (noting that WCT Article 8 "is designedly 'technology neutral' in order to avoid obsolescence" and that "it does not matter whether the member of the public obtains access to the work via a real-time 'stream' or via the delivery to her computer or other device of a digital copy that she subsequently 'opens' in order to see or hear the work"). As used in this Report, a download is "a transmission of an electronic file containing a digital copy of a . . . work that is sent from an on-line server to a local hard drive," resulting in the creation of a copy of the file at the latter location. *United States v. Am. Soc'y of Composers, Authors and Publishers*, 627 F.3d 64, 69 (2d Cir. 2010) ("*ASCAP*"). A stream is an online transmission that renders a work perceptible by the recipient "as it is received by the client-computer's temporary memory." *Id.* at 74.

[3] *See* WIPO, Diplomatic Conference on Certain Copyright and Neighboring Rights Questions, Geneva, Dec. 2–20, 1996, *Basic Proposal for the Substantive Provisions of the Treaty on Certain Questions Concerning the Protection of Literary and Artistic Works to Be Considered by the Diplomatic Conference*, ¶ 10.10, at 44, WIPO Doc. CRNR/DC/4 (Aug. 30, 1996) ("WIPO Basic Proposal"), *available at* http://www.wipo.int/edocs/mdocs/diplconf/ en/crnr_dc/crnr_dc_4.pdf ("The relevant act is the making available of the work by providing access to it."); *see also* INTERNET POLICY TASK FORCE, U.S. DEP'T OF COMMERCE, COPYRIGHT POLICY, CREATIVITY, AND INNOVATION IN THE DIGITAL ECONOMY 15 (2013) ("GREEN PAPER"), *available at* http://www.uspto.gov/news/publications/copyrightgreenpaper.pdf ("In countries where the 'making available' right has been explicitly adopted, it has been interpreted to cover the placement of a work on the Internet where it can be accessed by individual members of the public.").

[4] *See* JÖRG REINBOTHE AND SILKE VON LEWINSKI, THE WIPO TREATIES ON COPYRIGHT: A COMMENTARY ON THE WCT, THE WPPT, AND THE BTAP ¶ 7.8.33, at 139 (2015) ("Examples of the 'on-demand' situation are websites that offer a choice of musical works, cinematographic works, scientific articles, or other works for access at any time during which the service is offered, to be chosen by the individual members of the public from the place chosen by them.").

[5] WIPO, Diplomatic Conference on Certain Copyright and Neighboring Rights Questions, Geneva, Dec. 2–20, 1996, *Summary Minutes, Main Committee I*, WIPO Doc. CRNR/DC/102 (Aug. 26, 1997) ("WIPO Minutes"), *available at* http://www.wipo.int/ edocs/mdocs/diplconf/en/crnr_dc/crnr_dc_ 102.pdf; *see also* Mihály Ficsor, *The Spring 1997 Horace S. Manges Lecture—Copyright for the Digital Era: The WIPO "Internet" Treaties*, 21 COLUM.-VLA J.L. AND ARTS 197, 211 (1997) ("[W]hen this provision was discussed in Main Committee I, it was stated—and no delegation opposed the statement— that Contracting Parties are free to implement the obligation . . . through the combination of different rights as long as the acts of such 'making available' are fully covered by an exclusive right (with appropriate exceptions).").

[6] *See, e.g.*, *Piracy of Intellectual Property on Peer-to-Peer Networks: Hearing Before the Subcomm. on Courts, the Internet, and Intellectual Prop. of the H. Comm. on the Judiciary*, 107th Cong. 114 (2002) (letter from Marybeth Peters, Register of Copyrights); GREEN PAPER, *supra* note 3, at 15 (noting that at the time of implementation, "both Congress and the Administration concluded that the relevant acts were encompassed within the existing scope of exclusive rights," and concluding that the exclusive right of distribution was intended to include "the mere offering of copies to the public").

[7] *See* Part III.A, *infra*.

[8] See, for example, the district court's one-sentence dismissal of the existence of a "'making available' copyright under § 106" in *Alticor Inc. v. UMG Recordings, Inc.*, No. 6:14-cv-542-Orl-37DAB, 2015 WL 8536571, at *7 (M.D. Fla. Dec. 11, 2015).

[9] *See Diversey v. Schmidly*, 738 F.3d 1196, 1203 (10th Cir. 2013) ("The essence of distribution in the library lending context is the work's availability 'to the borrowing or browsing public.'") (citation omitted); *Hotaling v. Church of Jesus Christ of Latter-Day Saints*, 118 F.3d 199, 203 (4th Cir. 1997) ("When a public library adds a work to its collection, lists the work in its index or catalog system, and makes the work available to the borrowing or browsing public, it has completed all the steps necessary for distribution to the public.").

[10] Letter from Rep. Melvin L. Watt, Ranking Member, Subcomm. on Courts, Intellectual Prop. and the Internet, H. Comm. on the Judiciary, to Maria A. Pallante, Register of Copyrights and Director, U.S. Copyright Office 2 (Dec. 19, 2013) (attached as Appendix A).

[11] WIPO is "the global forum for intellectual property services, policy, information and cooperation," and is "a self- funding agency of the United Nations, with 188 member states." *Inside WIPO*, WIPO, http://www.wipo. int/about- wipo/en/index.html.

[12] WCT, *supra* note 1; WPPT, *supra* note 1. *See* 1 WIPO, RECORDS OF THE DIPLOMATIC CONFERENCE ON CERTAIN COPYRIGHT AND NEIGHBORING RIGHTS QUESTIONS, GENEVA 1996 (WIPO, Publication No. 348(E), 1999), *available at* ftp:// ftp.wipo.int/pub/library/ ebooks/ wipopublications/wipo_pub_348e_v1.pdf.

[13] WCT, *supra* note 1, art. 8.

[14] WPPT, *supra* note 1, arts. 10, 14.

[15] *See* WIPO Basic Proposal, *supra* note 3, ¶¶ 10.10–.11, at 44. For the purposes of this report, the "making available" right refers to the rights set forth in Article 8 of the WCT and Articles 10 and 14 of the WPPT. We do not address herein either the exclusive distribution rights set forth in Article 6 of the WCT and Articles 8 and 12 of the WPPT, or the right of remuneration for performers and producers of phonograms set forth in Article 15 of the WPPT.

[16] Digital Millennium Copyright Act, Pub. L. No. 105-304, §§ 101–105, 112 Stat. 2860, 2861–77 (1998); *see* H.R. REP. NO. 105-796, at 63 (1998) (Conf. Rep.) ("This title implements two new intellectual property treaties, the WIPO Copyright Treaty and the WIPO Performances and Phonograms Treaty, signed in Geneva, Switzerland in December 1996."). The WIPO Internet Treaties were submitted to Congress for advice and consent the previous year, and the Senate voted to approve the Treaties shortly before passage of the DMCA. *See* WIPO Copyright Treaty (1996) and WIPO Performances and Phonograms Treaty (1996), July 28, 1997, S. TREATY DOC. NO. 105-17 (1997); 105 CONG. REC. S12,972 (daily ed. Oct. 21, 1998).

[17] H.R. REP. NO. 105-551, pt. 1, at 9 (1998); *see also WIPO Copyright Treaties Implementation Act; and Online Copyright Liability Limitation Act: Hearing on H.R. 2281 and H.R. 2180 Before the Subcomm. on Courts and Intellectual Prop. of the H. Comm. on the Judiciary*, 105th Cong. 27 (1997) ("*Hearing on H.R. 2281 and H.R. 2180*") (statement of Rep. Howard Coble, Chairman, Subcomm. on Courts and Intellectual Prop.) ("The treaties do not require that the United States change the substance of our domestic copyright rights or exceptions.").

[18] *See Piracy of Intellectual Property on Peer-to-Peer Networks*, *supra* note 6, at 114 (letter from Marybeth Peters, Register of Copyrights); GREEN PAPER, *supra* note 3, at 15; WTO Trade Policy Review Body, *Trade Policy Review, United States, Minutes of Meeting, Addendum 3*, WTO Doc. WT/TPR/M/126/Add.3, at 133–34, 140 (Nov. 22, 2004); WTO Trade Policy Review Body, *Trade Policy Review, United States, Minutes of Meeting, Addendum 2*, WTO Doc. WT/TPR/M/126/Add.2, at 35 (Mar. 25, 2004); WTO Trade Policy Review Body, *Trade Policy Review, United States, Minutes of Meeting, Addendum 1*, WTO Doc. WT/TPR/M/88/Add.1, at 121 (Jan. 8, 2002).

[19] *See* Part III.A, *infra*.

[20] Letter from Rep. Melvin L. Watt, *supra* note 10.

[21] *Id.* at 2.

[22] *Id.*

[23] Study on the Right of Making Available; Comments and Notice of Public Roundtable, 79 Fed. Reg. 10,571 (Feb. 25, 2014). This request and all other Federal Register notices issued in connection with this study are attached as Appendix E. All documents related to this study can be accessed on the Making Available Study webpage on the Copyright Office website, at http:// copyright.gov/docs/making_available/.

[24] The comments received in response to this first request are available on the Copyright Office website at http:// copyright.gov/ docs/ making_available/comments/docket2014_2/. References in this document to these initial comments are by party name (abbreviated where appropriate) followed by "Initial Comments." Complete lists of the parties who submitted written comments in response to the Office's requests are provided in Appendix C.

[25] The agenda for the Office's May 5, 2014 public roundtable is attached as Appendix D, and is also available at http://copyright.gov/docs/making_ available/public-roundtable/Final-Making-Available-Agenda.pdf. The transcript of the roundtable is available at http://copyright.gov/docs/making_ available/public-roundtable/transcript.pdf. References to the transcript in this document are indicated by "Tr.," followed by the page(s) and line(s) of the reference and the speaker's name and affiliation. Videos of the roundtable sessions are available on the Copyright Office website in four parts: Session 1: Existing Rights Under Title 17, Part 1, at http://www.loc.gov/today/cyberlc/ feature_wdesc.php?rec= 6407& loclr=rssloc; Session 2: Existing Rights Under Title 17, Part 2, at http:// www.loc.gov/ today/cyberlc/featurewdesc.php?rec=6408&loclr=rssloc; Session 3: Benefits of Clarification/ Possible Changes to U.S. Law, at http:// www.loc. gov/today/ cyberlc/ feature_wdesc.php?rec=6409 &loclr=rssloc; and Sessions 4/5: Foreign Implementation and Interpretation of the WIPO Treaties, at http://www.loc.gov/today/cyberlc/ feature_wdesc.php? rec=6410&loclr=rssloc.

[26] Study on the Right of Making Available: Request for Additional Comments, 79 Fed. Reg. 41,309 (July 15, 2014); Extension of Comment Period; Study on the Right of Making Available; Request for Additional Comments, 79 Fed. Reg. 44,871 (Aug. 1, 2014). The comments received in response to this second request for comments are available on the Copyright Office website at http://copyright.gov/docs/making_available/ comments/ docket2014_2/reply/. References in this document to these comments are by party name (abbreviated where appropriate) followed by "Additional Comments."

[27] *See, e.g.*, Ass'n of Am. Publishers ("AAP"), Comments Submitted in Response to U.S. Copyright Office's Feb. 25, 2014 Notice of Inquiry at 4 (Apr. 4, 2014) ("AAP Initial Comments") ("Congress's conviction that the existing exclusive rights under Section 106 already provide the 'making available' right in the digital environment has and continues to be clear."); Copyright Alliance, Comments Submitted in Response to U.S. Copyright Office's Feb. 25, 2014 Notice of Inquiry at 2 (Apr. 4, 2014) ("Copyright Alliance Initial Comments") ("[W]e believe the bundle of rights established in § 106, when interpreted as Congress intended and in accordance with international treaty obligations, adequately addresses the making available right. Therefore, we do not believe legislative changes are necessary at this point."); Entm't Software Ass'n ("ESA"), Comments Submitted in Response to U.S. Copyright Office's Feb. 25, 2014 Notice of Inquiry at 1 (Apr. 4, 2014) ("ESA Initial Comments") ("[W]e do not believe that legislative changes are currently warranted. In our view, consistent with the earlier expressed position of the Copyright Office, the bundle of exclusive rights afforded to rights holders by § 106 of the Copyright Act provides protection commensurate to that required by the WIPO Internet Treaties, including the 'making available' and 'communication to the public' rights."); Motion Picture Ass'n of Am., Inc. ("MPAA") and Recording Indus. Ass'n of Am., Inc. ("RIAA"), Comments Submitted in Response to U.S. Copyright Office's Feb. 25, 2014 Notice of

Inquiry at 2 (Apr. 4, 2014) ("MPAA–RIAA Joint Initial Comments") ("Existing U.S. laws fully implement the making available and public communication rights within the framework of the reproduction, distribution, performance and display rights of Section 106 of the Copyright Act."); Software and Info. Indus. Ass'n ("SIIA"), Comments Submitted in Response to U.S. Copyright Office's Feb. 25, 2014 Notice of Inquiry at 3 (Apr. 4, 2014) ("SIIA Initial Comments") ("We do not believe that legislation or any type of further Congressional clarification is needed to provide for a making available right under U.S. law."); U.S. Chamber of Commerce Glob. Intellectual Prop. Ctr. ("GIPC"), Comments Submitted in Response to U.S. Copyright Office's Feb. 25, 2014 Notice of Inquiry at 6 (Apr. 4, 2014) ("The rights of distribution, reproduction, public display and public performance, properly understood, already encompass the act of making available copyrighted works.").

[28] *See* Peter S. Menell, Comments Submitted in Response to U.S. Copyright Office's Feb. 25, 2014 Notice of Inquiry at 2 (Apr. 4, 2014) ("Menell Initial Comments") ("Congress should clarify the scope of the distribution right. The dissensus surrounding the 'making available' issue needlessly creates uncertainty and increases the costs of litigation."); Am. Soc'y of Composers, Authors and Publishers ("ASCAP"), Broadcast Music, Inc. ("BMI"), Songwriters Guild of America ("SGA"), SESAC, Inc., and Nat'l Music Publishers' Ass'n ("NMPA"), Comments Submitted in Response to U.S. Copyright Office's Feb. 25, 2014 Notice of Inquiry at 6 (Apr. 4, 2014) ("Musical Works Organizations Joint Initial Comments") ("To further clarity in the law for all parties, and particularly if the courts cannot straighten the wobbly table, we believe Congress will need to take action by explicitly clarifying the existence of the making available right under Section 106.").

[29] *See, e.g.*, Comput. and Commc'ns Indus. Ass'n ("CCIA"), Comments Submitted in Response to U.S. Copyright Office's Feb. 25, 2014 Notice of Inquiry at 3 (Apr. 4, 2014) ("CCIA Initial Comments") ("[N]o international obligation compels the creation of a new cause of action for attempted distribution or any other right . . . ."); Glynn S. Lunney, Comments Submitted in Response to U.S. Copyright Office's Feb. 25, 2014 Notice of Inquiry at 1 (Apr. 2, 2014) ("Lunney Initial Comments") ("[W]e have satisfied our treaty obligations whether we require proof of a download to establish infringement of the distribution right or not."); Pub. Knowledge ("PK") and Elect. Frontier Found. ("EFF"), Joint Comments Submitted in Response to U.S. Copyright Office's Feb. 25, 2015 Notice of Inquiry at 1–2 (Apr. 4, 2014) ("PK- EFF Joint Initial Comments") ("[O]bligations under the WIPO treaties will be fulfilled even if United States courts conclude that in some situations, merely offering to upload a file does not implicate an exclusive right."); Soc'y of Am. Archivists ("SAA"), Comments Submitted in Response to U.S. Copyright Office's Feb. 25, 2014 Notice of Inquiry at 3 (Apr. 1, 2014) ("SAA Initial Comments") ("[D]istribution requires at least a temporary transfer of custody, such as lending . . . . This interpretation is fully consistent . . . with our international obligations.").

[30] *See, e.g.*, CCIA Initial Comments at 7 ("Adding another exclusive right of 'making available' would further exacerbate problems with overlapping rights, and create another gatekeeper attempting to extract royalties."); Dig. Pub. Library of Am. ("DPLA"), Comments Submitted in Response to U.S. Copyright Office's Feb. 25, 2014 Notice of Inquiry at 1 (Apr. 4, 2014) ("DPLA Initial Comments") ("DPLA has strong reservations about the creation of a broad making available right because we believe such a right would inhibit free and open linking to works that should be legitimately made available online."); Internet Ass'n, Comments Submitted in Response to U.S. Copyright Office's July 15, 2014 Notice of Inquiry at 5 (Aug. 14, 2014) ("Internet Ass'n Additional Comments") ("Commenters warn that a 'making available' right would complicate the current system by presenting problems in existing contracts where new technologies were not considered and would even question the legality of online functions such as linking and embedding."); PK–EFF Joint Initial Comments at 6 ("The United States should not create a new making available right because doing so could risk making a number of desirable behaviors that are currently

lawful, unlawful."); SAA Initial Comments at 3 ("A new explicit right would only lead to further confusion and litigation as to the scope of that right and would reinforce the sometimes overly cautious approach of archivists but with no commensurate benefit to copyright owners.").

[31] *See, e.g.*, CCIA Initial Comments at 2–3 ("[T]he U.S. Copyright Act does not provide a specific 'making available' right in 17 U.S.C. § 106, although it nevertheless provides authors with distribution and performance rights, combined with various doctrines of secondary liability, which are more than adequate to satisfy international obligations."); ESA Initial Comments at 1 ("[T]he bundle of exclusive rights afforded to rights holders by § 106 of the Copyright Act provides protection commensurate to that required by the WIPO Internet Treaties, including the 'making available' and 'communication to the public' rights."); Lunney Initial Comments at 1 ("[O]ur existing structure of rights provides protection equivalent to the 'making available' and 'communication to the public' rights required by the WIPO Copyright Treaty . . . and the WIPO Performance and Phonograms Treaty . . . ."); MPAA–RIAA Joint Initial Comments at 2 ("The Section 106 rights are broad enough to include the rights of making available and communication to the public that were intended by Congress and that the WCT, WPPT, and other international treaties obligate the United States to provide."); PK–EFF Joint Initial Comments at 3 ("[I]t is clear that the United States always intended to fulfill WIPO treaty obligations through existing exclusive rights, and there is no reason to believe that this approach is no longer sufficient to satisfy those obligations.").

[32] SILKE VON LEWINSKI, INTERNATIONAL COPYRIGHT LAW AND POLICY ¶¶ 17.01–.04, at 428–29 (2008).

[33] Between 1971 and 1991, WIPO facilitated a strategy of "guided development" that resulted in "recommendations, guiding principles, . . . model provisions, and . . . studies," rather than preparing for a new revision conference. *Id.* ¶ 17.01, at 428. Expert bodies, convened by WIPO and the United Nations Educational, Scientific and Cultural Organization, focused on photocopying, cable television, computer programs, and other computer-related copyright issues; rental and lending rights; private copying; and direct broadcasting by satellite. *See* MIHÁLY FICSOR, THE LAW OF COPYRIGHT AND THE INTERNET: THE 1996 WIPO TREATIES, THEIR INTERPRETATION AND IMPLEMENTATION ¶¶ 1.03–.10, at 5–8 (2002).

[34] Ficsor, *supra* note 5, at 202.

[35] David Nimmer, *A Tale of Two Treaties–Dateline: Geneva–December 1996*, 22 COLUM.-VLA J.L. AND ARTS 1, 5 (1997).

[36] H.R. REP. NO. 105-551, pt. 1, at 9 (1998).

[37] *See* H.R. REP. NO. 105-551, pt. 1, at 9 (1998) ("With this evolution in technology, the law must adapt in order to make digital networks safe places to disseminate and exploit copyrighted works."); Jane C. Ginsburg, *Global Use/Territorial Rights: Private International Law Questions of the Global Information Infrastructure*, 42 J. COPYRIGHT SOC'Y U.S.A. 318, 319–20 (1995); David R. Johnson and David Post, *Law and Borders—the Rise of Law in Cyberspace*, 48 STAN. L. REV. 1367, 1383–87 (1996); Michael J. O'Sullivan, *International Copyright: Protection for Copyright Holders in the Internet Age*, 13 N.Y. INT'L L. REV. 1, 1, 40 (2000); Julie S. Sheinblatt, *The WIPO Copyright Treaty*, 13 BERKELEY TECH. L.J. 535, 535 (1998) ("The treaties were created in response to the arrival of the digital age, which has made information a key business asset, expanded international commerce, and enabled faster and easier copying of copyrighted work. The value of harmonizing global copyright law has grown accordingly. The Copyright Treaty was formed both to harmonize global copyright law and to extend that law into the digital domain.").

[38] Ficsor, *supra* note 5, at 207.

[39] *See* Berne Convention for the Protection of Literary and Artistic Works art. 11*bis*, Sept. 9, 1886, as revised July 24, 1971, and as amended Sept. 28, 1979, S. Treaty Doc. 99-27, 1161 U.N.T.S. 3 ("Authors of literary and artistic works shall enjoy the exclusive right of

authorizing: (i) the broadcasting of their works or the communication thereof to the public by any other means of wireless diffusion of signs, sounds or images . . . .").

[40] *See* David O. Carson, *Making the Making Available Right Available, 22nd Annual Horace S. Manges Lecture, February 3, 2009*, 33 COLUM. J.L. and ARTS 135, 145 (2010); Pamela Samuelson, *The U.S. Digital Agenda at WIPO*, 37 VA. J. INT'L L. 369, 393–94 (1997) (noting that one possible reason for the divide between the United States and the European Community was rooted in differences in national laws because U.S. copyright law granted authors an exclusive right to distribute copies to the public but not an exclusive right to communicate works to the public, while many European Union member states did not have an exclusive distribution right but did grant authors the right to control communications of works to the public); Thomas D. Sydnor II, *The Making Available Right Under U.S. Law*, 16 PROGRESS ON POINT no. 7, Mar. 2009, at 5–8, 17 (equating the making available right with the right of publication and noting that civil law countries, like most in the European Union, implemented publication rights through the exclusive right to communicate a work to the public).

[41] WIPO, Committee of Experts on a Possible Protocol to the Berne Convention Seventh Session, Committee of Experts on a Possible Instrument for the Protection of the Rights of Performers and Producers of Phonograms Sixth Session Geneva, May 22–24, 1996, *Proposals of the European Community and its Member States*, at 3–4, WIPO Doc. BCP/CE/VII/1- INR/CE/VI/1 (May 20, 1996), *available at* http://www.wipo. int/ mdocsarchives/BCP_CE_VII_1_INR_CE_VI/BCP_CE_VII_1-INR_CE_ VI_ 1_E.PDF; REINBOTHE AND VON LEWINSKI, *supra* note 4, ¶ 7.8.4, at 126; Ficsor, *supra* note 5, at 208–09.

[42] *See* MIHÁLY FICSOR, WIPO, GUIDE TO THE COPYRIGHT AND RELATED RIGHTS TREATIES ADMINISTERED BY WIPO AND GLOSSARY OF COPYRIGHT AND RELATED RIGHTS TERMS ¶¶ CT-8.2–CT-8.9, 207–08 (2003) ("WIPO GUIDE") (discussing the problems associated with adopting either the "distribution" or the "communication to the public" approach to digital distributions of works).

[43] Beyond the disagreement about which exclusive right was preferred, there also was recognition "that the borderlines among the right of reproduction, the right of distribution, and the right of communication to the public are getting blurred." Mihály Ficsor, *International Harmonization of Copyright and Neighboring Rights*, *in* WIPO WORLDWIDE SYMPOSIUM ON COPYRIGHT IN THE GLOBAL INFORMATION INFRASTRUCTURE, 374 (WIPO Pub. No. 746 (E/S), 1995).

[44] WIPO Minutes, *supra* note 5, ¶ 301, at 41. No delegation opposed the statement. *See* Ficsor, *supra* note 5, at 211; REINBOTHE AND VON LEWINSKI, *supra* note 4, ¶ 7.8.24, at 135.

[45] *See* VON LEWINSKI, *supra* note 32, ¶ 17.80, at 458 ("[S]ince the Treaties allow implementation of the making available right by any suitable right . . . its relation to the communication right under the Treaties has no bearing on the choice of its systematic classification under national law."). For a comparison of different implementation models, see the Survey of Foreign Laws Regarding Statutory Approaches to the Right of Making Available, attached as Appendix E.

[46] Ficsor, *supra* note 43, at 139.

[47] FICSOR, *supra* note 33, ¶ C8.06, at 496; *see also* VON LEWINSKI, *supra* note 32, ¶ 17:78, at 458; Tr. at 121:21–122:1 (May 5, 2014) (John C. Beiter, SESAC) (calling technology neutrality "a hallmark of the WIPO Treaties when it comes to [the] making available right").

[48] WCT, *supra* note 1, art. 8; *see* WIPO GUIDE, *supra* note 42, ¶ CT-8.10, at 209 ("[T]he treaty, first, extends the applicability of the right of communication to the public to all categories of works, and then clarifies that the right also covers transmissions in interactive systems described in a legal-characterization-free manner . . . .").

[49] *See* WIPO GUIDE, *supra* note 42, ¶ PPT-10.2, at 247–48; VON LEWINSKI, *supra* note 32, ¶ 17:79, at 458.

[50] WPPT, *supra* note 1, art. 10 ("Performers shall enjoy the exclusive right of authorizing the making available to the public of their performances fixed in phonograms, by wire or wireless means, in such a way that members of the public may access them from a place and at a time individually chosen by them.").

[51] WPPT, *supra* note 1, art. 14 ("Producers of phonograms shall enjoy the exclusive right of authorizing the making available to the public of their phonograms, by wire or wireless means, in such a way that members of the public may access them from a place and at a time individually chosen by them.").

[52] WPPT Article 15 contains a right of equitable remuneration for broadcasting and communication to the public, which is separate from the making available right. *See* REINBOTHE AND VON LEWINSKI, *supra* note 4, ¶ 8.15.32, at 400 ("[T]he right of making available for access as described under Articles 10 and 14 WPPT is not covered by Article 15 WPPT.") (bolding omitted); WIPO GUIDE, *supra* note 42, ¶ PPT-10.4, at 248. In fact, the WPPT contains specific definitions for both "broadcasting" and "communication to the public" as it applies in the WPPT. *See* WPPT, *supra* note 1, art. 2(f), (g).

[53] WIPO Basic Proposal, *supra* note 3, ¶ 10.11, at 44.

[54] *Id.* ¶ 11.03, at 54. The right to authorize physical distribution of copies is covered by Articles 8 (for performers) and 12 (for producers of sound recordings) of the WPPT.

[55] *Id.* ¶ 10.10, at 44.

[56] *Id.*; *see also* Ginsburg Initial Comments at 2 ("[I]t does not matter whether the member of the public obtains access to the work via a real-time 'stream' or via the delivery to her computer or other device of a digital copy that she subsequently 'opens' in order to see or hear the work.").

[57] *See, e.g.*, Case C-306/05, Sociedad General de Autores y Editores de España (SGAE) v. Rafael Hoteles SA, 2006 E.C.R. I- 11519, 2006 EUR-Lex CELEX 62005CJ0306, para. 43 (Dec. 7, 2006) ("*Rafael Hoteles*"); Case C-466/12, Nils Svensson and Others v. Retriever Sverige AB, 2014 EUR-Lex CELEX 62012CJ0466, para. 19 (Feb. 13, 2014) ("*Svensson*") (citing *Rafael Hoteles*, 2006 EUR-Lex CELEX 62005CJ0306, para. 43); Polydor Ltd. v. Brown, [2005] EWHC 3191 (Ch) (Eng.); Landgericht Hamburg [LG Hamburg] [Regional Court of Hamburg] Jan. 25, 2006, MULTIMEDIA UND RECHT [MMR] 2006, 700 (Ger.); Ginsburg Initial Comments at 2 ("The concept of 'making available' set out in WCT article 8 necessarily encompasses not only the actual transmission of a work to members of the public, but especially the offering to the public to access the work on demand."); REINBOTHE AND VON LEWINSKI, *supra* note 4, ¶ 7.8.26, at 137 ("[U]sers do not necessarily need to access the work in order to trigger the making available right. It is sufficient that they have the opportunity to access it as a consequence of the act of making it available so that access is possible."); Brigitte Lindner, *The WIPO Treaties*, *in* COPYRIGHT IN THE INFORMATION SOCIETY 18–19 (Brigitte Lindner and Ted Shapiro eds., 2011) ("First, as far as scope of the right is concerned, it is generally considered that making available covers two connected acts: the offer of the work which may be accessed individually by members of the public and the subsequent transmission of the work to a member of the public at his or her request. However, it is not necessary that such transmission take place: the offer of the content is sufficient for the making available right to come into play whether the user ultimately requests the transmission or not.").

[58] *See* Jane C. Ginsburg, Comments Submitted in Response to U.S. Copyright Office's July 15, 2014 Notice of Inquiry at 2 (Sept. 3, 2014) ("Ginsburg Additional Comments") ("The WCT text is clear that the right covers the offer of individualized access to works, because it specifies the 'making available to the public of [authors'] works in such a way that members of the public *may access* these works from a place *and at a time individually chosen by them*'. . . .") (alteration and emphasis in original); REINBOTHE and VON LEWINSKI, *supra* note 4, § 7.8.26, at 136–37; *Rafael Hoteles*, 2006 EUR-Lex CELEX 62005CJ0306, para. 43 ("It follows from Article 3(1) of Directive 2001/29 and Article 8 of the WIPO Copyright Treaty that for there to be communication to the public it is sufficient

that the work is made available to the public in such a way that the persons forming that public may access it.").

[59] SAM RICKETSON AND JANE C. GINSBURG, INTERNATIONAL COPYRIGHT AND NEIGHBORING RIGHTS: THE BERNE CONVENTION AND BEYOND ¶ 12.58, at 747 (2d ed. 2005).

[60] *See, e.g.*, Am. Ass'n of Indep. Music ("A2IM"), Comments Submitted in Response to U.S. Copyright Office's July 15, 2014 Notice of Inquiry at 2 (Sept. 15, 2014) ("A2IM Additional Comments") ("The concept of 'making available' . . . does not hinge on whether individuals actually receive the delivery of copyrighted material through the broadcast of public performance; rather, it stipulates that the right of distribution inherently belongs to the copyright owner who authorizes and determines how and when a protected work is accessed."); Musical Works Organizations Joint Initial Comments at 4 ("[I]t is necessary to demonstrate only uploading to a public source, and it is not necessary to show transmissions to individual, on-demand recipients."); Ginsburg Initial Comments at 1 ("Compliance with the WCT requires a member state . . . to cover not only actual transmissions of streams and downloads, but also the offering to communicate the work as a stream or a download."); Thomas D. Sydnor II, Comments Submitted in Response to U.S. Copyright Office's Feb. 25, 2014 Notice of Inquiry at 7 (Apr. 4, 2014) ("Sydnor Initial Comments") ("The WIPO Internet Treaties and all recent U.S. Free Trade Agreements inarguably require the U.S. to provide authors with an exclusive right to make copies or performances of their works available over the Internet—regardless of whether the work was made available because it was downloaded or streamed from a website or copied into the 'shared' folder of a file-sharing program like Grokster, KaZaA, LimeWire, or Frostwire."); Tr. at 171:1–3 (Steven Tepp, GIPC) ("[T]he term 'making available' has a plain meaning, and it's making available."); *id.* at 174:12–14 (Joseph DiMona, BMI) ("It is very plain that making available means the offering, not requiring a distribution."). *But see supra* note 29 (comments arguing that Treaties may permit member states to require evidence of dissemination).

[61] 105 CONG. REC. S12,985 (daily ed. Nov. 12, 1998). The resolution provided that "[t]he United States shall not deposit the instruments of ratification for these Treaties until such time as the President signs into law a bill that implements the Treaties." *Id.* The implementing legislation was contained in the DMCA, Title I of which is entitled the WIPO Copyright and Performances and Phonograms Treaties Implementation Act of 1998. H.R. REP. NO. 105-796, at 2 (1998) (Conf. Rep.).

[62] *Hearing on H.R. 2281 and H.R. 2180*, *supra* note 17, at 43 (statement of Marybeth Peters, Register of Copyrights). The two treaty obligations that required implementing legislation were the provisions relating to the circumvention of technological measures used by copyright owners and the alteration or removal of electronic copyright management information, now implemented under 17 U.S.C. §§ 1201 and 1202, respectively.

[63] *Id.* at 37 (statement of Bruce A. Lehman, Assistant Sec'y of Commerce and Comm'r of Patents and Trademarks).

[64] DMCA, Pub. L. No. 105-304, 112 Stat. 2860, 2861 (1998).

[65] H.R. REP. NO. 105-796, at 63 (1998) (Conf. Rep.).

[66] H.R. REP. NO. 105-551, pt. 1, at 9 (1998).

[67] *Piracy of Intellectual Property on Peer-to-Peer Networks*, *supra* note 6, at 114 (letter from Marybeth Peters, Register of Copyrights).

[68] Minutes of Meeting, *United States Trade Policy Review*, at 134, WT/TPR/M/126/Add.3 (Nov. 22, 2004); *see also id.* at 140 ("Copyright owners have a right to communication to the public of their works, by wire or wireless means. This right includes the making available to the public of their works in such a way that members of the public may access these works from a place and at a time individually chosen by them. This obligation is satisfied through sections 106(1), 106(3), 106(4), 106(5) and 106(6) of the U.S. copyright law . . . .").

[69] Minutes of Meeting, *United States Trade Policy Review*, at 121, WT/TPR/M/88/Add.1 (Jan. 8, 2002).

[70] GREEN PAPER, *supra* note 3, at 15. The Task Force's Green Paper also noted that contrary judicial decisions "predate . . . recent academic scholarship" on "previously unanalyzed legislative history." *Id.* at 16.

[71] *See* United States-Korea Free Trade Agreement, U.S.-S. Kor. art. 18.5, June 30, 2007, 46 I.L.M. 642, https://ustr.gov/trade-agreements/free-trade-agreements/korus-fta/final-text; United States-Panama Trade Promotion Agreement, U.S.-Pan., art. 15.6, June 28, 2007, http://www.ustr.gov/trade-agreements/free-trade-agreements/panama- tpa/final-text; United States-Colombia Trade Promotion Agreement, U.S.-Colom., art. 16.5.4, Nov. 22, 2006, http://www.ustr.gov/trade-agreements/free-trade-agreements/colombia-fta/final-text; United States-Peru Trade Promotion Agreement, U.S.-Peru, art. 16.5.4, Apr. 12, 2006, http://www.ustr.gov/trade-agreements/free-trade- agreements/peru-tpa/final-text; United States-Oman Free Trade Agreement, U.S.-Oman, art. 15.5, Jan. 19, 2006, http:// www.ustr.gov/ trade-agreements/ free-trade-agreements/oman-fta/final-text; United States-Bahrain Free Trade Agreement, U.S.-Bahr., art. 14.5, Sept. 14, 2004, 44 I.L.M. 544, http://www.ustr.gov/trade-agreements/free-trade-agreements/bahrain-fta/final-text; Dominican Republic-Central America-United States Free Trade Agreement, U.S.- Costa Rica-Dom. Rep.-El Sal.-Guat.-Hond.-Nicar., art. 15.6, Aug. 5, 2004, 43 I.L.M. 514, https://ustr.gov/trade-agreements/free-trade-agreements/cafta-dr-dominican-republic-central-america-fta/final-text; United States-Morocco Free Trade Agreement, U.S.-Morocco, art. 15.6, June 15, 2004, 44 I.L.M. 544, http:// www.ustr.gov/ trade-agreements/free-trade-agreements/ morocco-fta/final-text; United States-Australia Free Trade Agreement, U.S.-Austl., art. 17.5, May 18, 2004, 43 I.L.M. 1248, http:// www. ustr.gov/trade-agreements/free-trade-agreements/australian-fta/final-text; United States-Chile Free Trade Agreement, U.S.-Chile, art. 17.5.2, June 6, 2003, 42 I.L.M. 1026, http://www.ustr.gov/trade-agreements/free-trade-agreements/chile-fta/final-text; United States-Singapore Free Trade Agreement, U.S.-Sing., art. 16.4.2(a), May 6, 2003, 42 I.L.M. 1026, https://ustr.gov/trade-agreements/free-trade-agreements/singapore-fta/ final-text.

[72] United States-Korea Free Trade Agreement, *supra* note 71, art. 18.5.

[73] *See* United States-Jordan Free Trade Agreement, U.S.-Jordan, art. 4.1(c), (d), Oct. 24, 2000, https://ustr.gov/trade-agreements/free-trade-agreements/jordan-fta/final-text.

[74] *See* 19 U.S.C. § 3805(a)(1)(C).

[75] *See id.* § 3805(a)(1)(C), (2)(A).

[76] Statement of Administrative Action, United States-Panama Trade Promotion Agreement Implementation Act, at 32 (2011), http://waysandmeans.house.gov/ UploadedFiles/ PANAMA_Statement_of_Administrative_Action.pdf; Statement of Administrative Action, United States-Colombia Trade Promotion Agreement Implementation Act, at 30 (2011), http://waysandmeans.house.gov/UploadedFiles/COLOMBIA_Statement_of_Administrative_Action.pdf; Statement of Administrative Action, United States-Korea Free Trade Agreement Implementation Act, at 30 (2011), http:// waysandmeans.house.gov/ UploadedFiles/KOREA_Statement_of_Administrative_Action.pdf; Statement of Administrative Action, United States-Peru Trade Promotion Agreement Implementation Act, at 29 (2007), http://www.finance. senate.gov/imo/ media/doc/Leg% 20110%20100307 peruaction.pdf; Statement of Administrative Action, United States-Oman Free Trade Agreement Implementation Act, H.R. DOC. NO. 109-118, at 288 (2006), https://www.gpo.gov/fdsys/pkg/CDOC-109hdoc118/pdf/CDOC-109hdoc118.pdf; Statement of Administrative Action, United States-Bahrain Free Trade Agreement Implementation Act, at 21 (2005), http://www.finance.senate.gov/ imo/media/doc/ 110805Bahrain%20 FTA%20SAA.pdf; Statement of Administrative Action, Dominican Republic-Central America-United States Free Trade Agreement Implementation Act, at 31 (2005), https://ustr.gov/archive/assets/Trade_Agreements/Regional/CAFTA/ Transmittal/asset_ upload_file816_7815.pdf; Statement of Administrative Action, United States-Morocco Free Trade Agreement Implementation Act, at 23 (2004), http:// waysandmeans.house.gov/

Media/pdf/morocco/hr4842saa.pdf; Statement of Administrative Action, United States-Australia Free Trade Agreement Implementation Act, at 26 (2004), http:// waysandmeans. house.gov/Media/ pdf/australia/australiassa.pdf; Statement of Administrative Action, United States-Singapore Free Trade Agreement Implementation Act, at 34 (2003), http:// waysandmeans.house.gov/Media/pdf/singapore/hr2739SingaporeSAA7-15-03.pdf; Statement of Administrative Action, United States-Chile Free Trade Agreement Implementation Act, at 31 (2003), http://waysandmeans. house.gov/ Media/ pdf/chile/ hr2738ChileSAA7-15-03.pdf.

[77] United States-Panama Trade Promotion Agreement Implementation Act, Pub. L. No. 112-43, § 101(a)(2), 125 Stat. 497, 499 (2011); United States-Colombia Trade Promotion Agreement Implementation Act, Pub. L. No. 112-42, § 101(a)(2), 125 Stat. 462, 464 (2011); United States-Korea Free Trade Agreement Implementation Act, Pub. L. No. 112-41, § 101(a)(2), 125 Stat. 428, 430 (2011); United States-Peru Trade Promotion Agreement Implementation Act, Pub. L. No. 110-138, § 101(a)(2), 121 Stat. 1455, 1457 (2007); United States-Oman Free Trade Agreement Implementation Act, Pub. L. No. 109- 283, § 101(a)(2), 120 Stat. 1191, 1192 (2006); United States-Bahrain Free Trade Agreement Implementation Act, Pub. L. No. 109-169, § 101(a)(2), 119 Stat. 3581, 3582 (2006); Domincan Republic-Central America-United States Free Trade Agreement Implementation Act, Pub. L. No. 109-53, § 101(a)(2), 119 Stat. 462, 464 (2005); United States-Morocco Free Trade Agreement Implementation Act, Pub. L. No. 108-302, § 101(a)(2), 118 Stat. 1103, 1104 (2004); United States- Australia Free Trade Agreement Implementation Act, Pub. L. No. 108-286, § 101(a)(2), 118 Stat. 919, 920 (2004); United States-Singapore Free Trade Agreement Implementation Act, Pub. L. No. 108-78, § 101(a)(2), 117 Stat. 948, 949 (2003); United States-Chile Free Trade Agreement Implementation Act, Pub. L. No. 108-77, § 101(a)(2), 117 Stat. 909, 910 (2003).

[78] In many cases involving online transmissions, the same activity can implicate more than one exclusive right. *See, e.g., Perfect 10, Inc. v. Amazon.com, Inc.*, 508 F.3d 1146, 1161 (9th Cir. 2007) ("Nothing in the Copyright Act prevents the various rights protected in section 106 from overlapping. Indeed, under some circumstances, more than one right must be infringed in order for an infringement claim to arise.").

[79] 17 U.S.C. §§ 106(3), 101 (emphasis added). *See* PK and EFF, Comments Submitted in Response to the U.S. Copyright Office's July 15, 2014 Notice of Inquiry at 2 (Sept. 15, 2014) ("PK–EFF Joint Additional Comments") (arguing that "distributions are not cognizable under section 106 unless they are of 'copies or phonorecords' and 'to the public'"); Andrew P. Bridges, Comments Submitted in Response to U.S. Copyright Office's Feb. 25, 2014 Notice of Inquiry at 4 (Apr. 4, 2014) ("Bridges Initial Comments"); Andrew P. Bridges, Comments Submitted in Response to U.S. Copyright Office's July 15, 2014 Notice of Inquiry at 1–2 (Sept. 15, 2014) ("Bridges Additional Comments"); Tr. 31:7–16 (May 5, 2014) (Andrew P. Bridges).

[80] Bridges Initial Comments at 6; PK–EFF Joint Additional Comments at 6–7; Rick Sanders, Comments Submitted in Response to U.S. Copyright Office's July 15, 2014 Notice of Inquiry at 6–7 (Sept. 15, 2014) ("Sanders Additional Comments").

[81] *See* Bridges Initial Comments at 5 ("Internet transmissions such as email, peer-to-peer transmissions, streaming, and the like do not pass material objects or their ownership from one person to another."); PK–EFF Joint Additional Comments at 6 ("[S]ince the distribution right requires distribution of copies or phonorecords, no infringing distribution can occur without the transfer of possession of a material object."); Tr. at 43:5–7 (Andrew P. Bridges) ("'[T]ransfer of ownership' means, when Person B gets it from Person A, Person A no longer has it.").

[82] *See* Ginsburg Additional Comments at 13 ("Unless Congress thoroughly revisits the distribution and public performance rights, the statutory right 'to distribute copies or phonorecords of the copyrighted work' must include the act of causing copies to be made in

'material objects' including hard drives and servers, lest there be a gap in the rights comprising the U.S. implementation of the making available right."); MPAA and RIAA, Comments Submitted in Response to U.S. Copyright Office's July 15, 2014 Notice of Inquiry at 9 (Sept. 15, 2014) ("MPAA–RIAA Joint Additional Comments") (stating that application of the distribution right in the digital realm is "required for the United States' implementation of the WCT and WPPT treaties, a primary purpose of which was protecting copyrighted works specifically against unauthorized exploitation over the Internet").

[83] *See, e.g.*, *BMG Rights Mgmt. (US) LLC v. Cox Commc'ns, Inc.*, No. 1:14-CV-1611, 2015 WL 7756130, at *26 (E.D. Va. Dec. 1, 2015) ("Not only can electronic files be 'material objects,' but transferring files using a BitTorrent protocol satisfies the transactional element of distribution."); *Capitol Records, LLC v. Re Digi Inc.*, 934 F. Supp. 2d 640, 651 (S.D.N.Y. 2013) ("*ReDigi*") ("[T]he sale of digital music files on ReDigi's website infringes Capitol's exclusive right of distribution."); *Arista Records LLC v. Usenet.com, Inc.*, 633 F. Supp. 2d 124, 147 (S.D.N.Y. 2009) ("*Usenet.com*") ("[T]he delivery of articles and/or content to download at the request of subscribers can be the basis of direct infringement of the distribution right."); *London-Sire Records, Inc. v. Doe 1*, 542 F. Supp. 2d 153, 173 (D. Mass. 2008) ("An electronic file transfer is plainly within the sort of transaction that § 106(3) was intended to reach."); *Arista Records, LLC v. Butler*, No. 8:07-cv-3-T-23EAJ, 2007 WL 4557198, at *2 n.6 (M.D. Fla. Dec. 21, 2007) ("Distributing copyrighted sound recordings without authorization through a peer-to-peer network such as KaZaA is 'distribution' prohibited by the copyright act."); *Arista Records LLC v. Greubel*, 453 F. Supp. 2d 961, 968 (N.D. Tex. 2006) ("*Greubel*") ("[C]ourts have not hesitated to find copyright infringement by distribution in cases of file-sharing or electronic transmission of copyrighted works."); *see also Perfect 10*, 508 F.3d at 1162 ("The Supreme Court has indicated that in the electronic context, copies may be distributed electronically."). Numerous other courts have applied Section 106(3) to such transmissions without expressly addressing the statute's application in the digital context. *See, e.g.*, *New York Times Co. v. Tasini*, 533 U.S. 483, 498 (2001) (stating that selling copies of news articles for download was a violation of the plaintiff's distribution right); *In re Aimster Copyright Litig.*, 334 F.3d 643, 647 (7th Cir. 2003) (stating, in a discussion of sharing copyrighted works as attachments, "such distribution is an infringement unless authorized by the owner of the copyright."); *A&M Records, Inc. v. Napster, Inc.*, 239 F.3d 1004, 1014 (9th Cir. 2001) ("*Napster*") (stating that users who upload files to Napster violated rightsholders' distribution rights); *Lions Gate Films Inc. v. Does*, No. 2:14-cv-06033-MMM-AGRx, 2014 WL 3895240, at *3, *6 (C.D. Cal. Aug. 8, 2014) (finding evidence of plaintiff's movie being shared on a BitTorrent site sufficient to support a claim of infringement of the distribution right); *Call of the Wild Movie, LLC v. Does 1–1,062*, 770 F. Supp. 2d 332, 351–52 (D.D.C. 2011) (stating that claim that the defendants shared, via a BitTorrent swarm, plaintiff's copyrighted works was sufficient to make out *prima facie* claims for reproduction and distributions); *Capitol Records, Inc. v. MP3tunes, LLC*, No. 07 Civ. 9931(WHP), 2009 WL 3364036, at *9–10 (S.D.N.Y. Oct. 16, 2009) (allowing complaint to be amended to add distribution claims for digital copies of CD cover art); *cf.* *MAI Sys. Corp. v. Peak Comput., Inc.*, 991 F.2d 511, 519–20 (9th Cir. 1993) (holding that the defendant infringed the plaintiff's distribution right by offering its copyrighted software for loan).

[84] *Atl. Recording Corp. v. Serrano*, No. 07-CV-1824 W(JMA), 2007 WL 4612921, at *3 (S.D. Cal. Dec. 28, 2007).

[85] 542 F. Supp. 2d 153.

[86] *Id.* at 171. The commenters who argued that the distribution right is inapplicable to digital transmissions did not dispute this conclusion. *See* Bridges Initial Comments at 9 ("It is a well-acknowledged principle that digital file transfers result in a reproduction.").

[87] *London-Sire Records*, 542 F. Supp. 2d at 173–74.

[88] *Id.* at 173.

[89] *Id.* at 174.

[90] *See, e.g.*, Tr. at 38:7–17 (Jane C. Ginsburg, Colum. Law Sch.) (arguing that the repeated use of the phrase "digital phonorecord delivery," defined as a digital transmission, used together with "reproduce and distribute," indicates that a digital file transfer can be a distribution); Tr. at 39:11–40:8, 46:21–47:10 (George Borkowski, RIAA) (stating that Section 115 contains plain language including digital phonorecord delivery as a form of distribution and that "[i]f a digital phonorecord delivery were not a distribution, there would be no need to limit that right through a compulsory license"); MPAA–RIAA Additional Comments at 12 ("Because . . . the Copyright Act gives substantively the same definition to 'phonorecords' and 'copies,' the Section 115(c)(3)(A) compulsory license also demonstrates the existence of a digital distribution right for copies.").

[91] 17 U.S.C. §§ 115(a)(1) ("A person may obtain a compulsory license only if his or her primary purpose in making phonorecords is to distribute them to the public for private use, including by means of a digital phonorecord delivery."), 115(c)(3)(G)(i)(II) (digital phonorecord delivery of sound recording is actionable unless party "has obtained a compulsory license . . . or has otherwise been authorized by the copyright owner of the musical work to distribute or authorize the distribution, by means of a digital phonorecord delivery, of each musical work embodied in the sound recording").

[92] *Id.* § 115(c)(3)(A).

[93] *Id.* § 115(d).

[94] The commenters who argued that the distribution right does not apply in this context further contended that treating digital transfers as distributions requires recognition of a "digital first sale" doctrine. In their view, if an electronic file transfer constitutes a distribution of copies, then the recipient logically should be permitted to transmit the file to another party without the copyright owner's permission, just as the owner of a copy in a physical format (*e.g.*, a used book) may sell or give it away. *See* Bridges Initial Comments at 6–7; PK–EFF Joint Additional Comments at 6; Tr. At 160:9–161:10 (Jonathan Band, Library Copyright Alliance ("LCA")). The Office does not find this construction persuasive because the first sale doctrine "protects only distribution by 'the owner of a *particular* copy or phonorecord . . . of *that* copy or phonorecord.'" *ReDigi*, 934 F. Supp. 2d at 655 (omission and emphases in original) (quoting 17 U.S.C. § 109(a)). By contrast, a digital file transfer creates a new copy or phonorecord on the transferee's computer. *See id.*

[95] *See The Scope of Copyright Protection: Hearing Before the Subcomm. on Courts, Intellectual Prop. and the Internet of the H. Comm. on the Judiciary*, 113th Cong. 13 (2014) (statement of David Nimmer, Professor from Practice, UCLA Sch. of Law, Of Counsel, Irell and Manella, LLP, Los Angeles) ("Both sides of the 'making available' issue recognize that copyright owners enjoy the exclusive right to control distribution of their works; their only point of disagreement concerns the quantum of proof needed to demonstrate that distribution took place (simple uploading for proponents of the right, uploading plus proven downloading for its opponents).").

[96] Several courts, including the Second, Fifth, and Eighth Circuits, have acknowledged the disagreement but have declined on the facts before them to decide whether evidence of an actual download is required. *See, e.g., Capitol Records, Inc. v. Thomas-Rasset*, 692 F.3d 899, 906 (8th Cir. 2012); *Arista Records, LLC v. Doe 3*, 604 F.3d 110, 122 (2d Cir. 2010); *Maverick Recording Co. v. Harper*, 598 F.3d 193, 197 (5th Cir. 2010); *see also Interscope Records v. Leadbetter*, No. C05- 1149-MJP-RSL, 2007 WL 1217705, at *4 (W.D. Wash. Apr. 23, 2007); *Maverick Recording Co. v. Goldshteyn*, No. CV-05-4523 (DGT), 2006 WL 2166870, at *3 (E.D.N.Y. July 31, 2006); *Fonovisa, Inc. v. Alvarez*, No. 1:06-CV-011-C ECF, 2006 WL 5865272, at *2–3 (N.D. Tex. July 24, 2006). The Ninth Circuit, while not directly analyzing the issue, has incorporated language into at least two published opinions that appears to endorse the position that evidence of a download is not required. *See Columbia Pictures Indus, Inc. v. Fung*, 710 F.3d 1020, 1034 (9th Cir. 2013) ("*Fung*") ("Both uploading and downloading copyrighted material are infringing acts. The former

violates the copyright holder's right to distribution, the latter the right to reproduction.'"); *Napster*, 239 F.3d at 1014 (stating in dicta that "Napster users who upload file names to the search index for others to copy violate plaintiffs' distribution rights").

[97] *See, e.g.*, *Atl. Recording Corp. v. Anderson*, No. H-06-3578, 2008 WL 2316551, at *7–8 (S.D. Tex. Mar. 12, 2008) (holding, without analysis, that "placing the Copyrighted Recordings, along with other sound recordings, into a shared folder on his computer while being connected to the media distribution system or peer-to-peer network KaZaA. . . . [and] avail[ing] the 558 digital music files (or sound recordings) in his shared folder at that time, which included the Copyrighted Recordings, for distribution to the vast community of persons also connected to KaZaA" violated plaintiff's right of distribution); *Motown Record Co. v. DePietro*, No. 04-CV-2246, 2007 WL 576284, at *3 (E.D. Pa. Feb. 16, 2007) (stating, without analysis, that "[a] plaintiff claiming infringement of the exclusive-distribution right can establish infringement by proof of actual distribution or by proof of offers to distribute, that is, proof that the defendant 'made available' the copyrighted work"); *Greubel*, 453 F. Supp. 2d at 969–71 (noting, on a motion to dismiss, that "the courts have recognized that making copyrighted works available to others may constitute infringement by distribution in certain circumstances," and finding that plaintiffs had sufficiently alleged distribution to proceed); *Universal City Studios Prods. LLLP v. Bigwood*, 441 F. Supp. 2d 185, 190–91 (D. Me. 2006); *Warner Bros. Records, Inc. v. Payne*, No. W-06- CA-051, 2006 WL 2844415, at *4 (W.D. Tex. July 17, 2006); *Interscope Records v. Duty*, No. 05CV3744-PHX-FJM, 2006 WL 988086, at *2 (D. Ariz. Apr. 14, 2006); *see also Arista Records, Inc. v. Mp3Board, Inc.*, No. 00 CIV. 4660(SHS), 2002 WL 1997918, at *4 (S.D.N.Y. Aug. 29, 2002) (holding that a "copyright holder may not be required to prove particular instances of use by the public when the proof is impossible to produce because the infringer has not kept records of public use," but finding such exception inapplicable to the current case).

[98] *See, e.g.*, *BMG Rights Mgmt.*, 2015 WL 7756130, at *27 ("[T]o establish a direct infringement of its distribution right, BMG must show an actual dissemination of a copyrighted work."); *Atl. Recording Corp. v. Howell*, 554 F. Supp. 2d 976, 981 (D. Ariz. 2008) ("*Howell*") ("The general rule, supported by the great weight of authority, is that 'infringement of [the distribution right] requires an actual dissemination of either copies or phonorecords.'") (alteration in original); *Capitol Records Inc. v. Thomas*, 579 F. Supp. 2d 1210, 1218–19 (D. Minn. 2008) ("*Thomas*") ("[T]he plain meaning of the term 'distribution' does not include making available and, instead, requires actual dissemination."), *vacated on other grounds*, 692 F.3d 899 (8th Cir. 2012). In *London-Sire Records*, the district court required an actual transfer of copies, but found that the plaintiffs need not proffer evidence of such distribution at the pleading stage, so long as it was sufficiently alleged. 542 F. Supp. 2d at 169.

[99] *See BMG Rights Mgmt.*, 2015 WL 7756130, at *21, *27; *Thomas*, 579 F. Supp. 2d at 1225; *London-Sire Records*, 542 F. Supp. 2d at 169, 176–77; *see also Howell*, 554 F. Supp. 2d at 983–84 ("[E]vidence that a defendant made a copy of a work available to the public might, in conjunction with other circumstantial evidence, support an inference that the copy was likely transferred to a member of the public."). *See generally* Robert Kasunic, *Making Circumstantial Proof of Distribution Available*, 18 FORDHAM INTELL. PROP. MEDIA AND ENT. L.J. 1145 (2008).

[100] 17 U.S.C. § 106(3).

[101] 2 MELVILLE B. NIMMER AND DAVID NIMMER, NIMMER ON COPYRIGHT§ 8.11[C][1] (2015) ("NIMMER ON COPYRIGHT").

[102] *Id.*

[103] *The Scope of Copyright Protection*, *supra* note 95, at 10 (statement of David Nimmer, Professor from Practice, UCLA Sch. of Law, Of Counsel, Irell and Manella, LLP, Los Angeles).

[104] 118 F.3d 199, 201 (4th Cir. 1997).

[105] *Id.* at 203.

[106] *See id.*

[107] 738 F.3d 1196 (10th Cir. 2013).

[108] *Id.* at 1203 (quoting *Hotaling*, 118 F.3d at 203).

[109] *Thomas*, 579 F. Supp. 2d at 1217; *see also Howell*, 554 F. Supp. 2d at 981 ("The statute does not define the term 'distribute,' so courts have interpreted the term in light of the statute's plain meaning and legislative history. The general rule, supported by the great weight of authority, is that 'infringement of [the distribution right] requires an actual dissemination of either copies or phonorecords.'") (alteration in original) (quoting *Nat'l Car Rental Sys. v. Comput. Assocs. Int'l, Inc.*, 991 F.2d 426, 434 (8th Cir. 1993)).

[110] *London-Sire Records*, 542 F. Supp. 2d at 168 (citation omitted); *see also Howell*, 554 F. Supp. 2d at 983–84 ("As *Hotaling* seems to suggest, evidence that a defendant made a copy of a work available to the public might, in conjunction with other circumstantial evidence, support an inference that the copy was likely transferred to a member of the public. On its own, however, it does not prove that the copy changed hands. It only shows that the defendant attempted to distribute the copy, and there is no basis for attempt liability in the statute, no matter how desirable such liability may be as a matter of policy.") (citations omitted).

[111] *See, e.g.*, 2 NIMMER ON COPYRIGHT, *supra* note 101, § 8.11[D][3][b] ("*Webster's* second and fourth entries appear the most relevant definitions in the context of copyright: 'to spread out or scatter' as in 'distributing magazines to subscribers' and 'to market (a commodity) under a franchise in a particular area.'") (quoting *Distribute*, WEBSTER'S THIRD NEW INTERNATIONAL DICTIONARY OF THE ENGLISH LANGUAGE, UNABRIDGED 660 (Philip Babcock Gove ed.) (1961 and 1993)); Carson, *supra* note 40, at 151 (citing *Distribute*, CAMBRIDGE ADVANCED LEARNER'S DICTIONARY 362 (3rd ed. 2003) and *Distribute*, WEBSTER'S NEW COLLEGIATE DICTIONARY 333 (1980)); *see also Distribute Definition*, CAMBRIDGE DICTIONARIES ONLINE, http:// dictionary.cambridge.org/ us/ dictionary/ business-english/distribute (defining term to mean "to make a company's goods available to the public, for example, by transporting, storing, and selling them").

[112] Carson, *supra* note 40, at 151.

[113] *FDA v. Brown and Williamson Tobacco Corp.*, 529 U.S. 120, 133 (2000) (citations omitted).

[114] 17 U.S.C. § 506(a)(1)(C).

[115] Pub. L. No. 109-9, § 103(a), 119 Stat. 218, 220 (2005).

[116] *See* Carson, *supra* note 40, at 160 ("It is hard to fathom how this language can be read as anything other than Congress telling us, in the form of an amendment to the copyright statute, that the distribution right includes the act of making copies available on computer networks accessible to members of the public.").

[117] 377 F. Supp. 2d 796, 804–05 (N.D. Cal. 2005).

[118] *Thomas*, 579 F. Supp. 2d at 1218; *accord BMG Rights Mgmt.*, 2015 WL 7756130, at *25.

[119] Carson, *supra* note 40, at 161.

[120] 17 U.S.C. § 506(a)(1)(C); *see* Sydnor Initial Comments at 44 n.163 ("Amendments to § 506(a) *must* 'consider the scope of civil liability for copyright infringement' because infringement is an express prerequisite to *any* violation of § 506(a).") (citation omitted).

[121] *Brown and Williamson*, 529 U.S. at 133 (internal quotation marks and citations omitted).

[122] 17 U.S.C. § 602(a)(1).

[123] H.R. REP. NO. 94-1476, at 169–70 (1976).

[124] Peter S. Menell, *In Search of Copyright's Lost Ark: Interpreting the Right to Distribute in the Internet Age*, 59 J. COPYRIGHT SOC'Y U.S.A. 201, 257 (2011).

[125] 2 NIMMER ON COPYRIGHT, *supra* note 101, § 8.11[B][4][c].

[126] *See BMG Rights Mgmt.*, 2015 WL 7756130, at *24–25; *Thomas*, 579 F. Supp. 2d at 1217; *Howell*, 554 F. Supp. 2d at 983; *see also* Lunney Initial Comments at 2.

[127] 17 U.S.C. § 901(a)(4).

[128] *See Thomas*, 579 F. Supp. 2d at 1217–18.

[129] CCIA Initial Comments at 6; PK–EFF Joint Additional Comments at 8 and n.20; Tr. at 114:6–11 (Matthew Schruers, CCIA).

[130] 2 NIMMER ON COPYRIGHT, *supra* note 101, § 8A.01.

[131] *See* 17 U.S.C. § 902(a); 2 NIMMER ON COPYRIGHT, *supra* note 101, § 8A.02.

[132] For the same reason, the Office is unpersuaded by the *Thomas* court's conclusion that a provision of the Patent Act is indicative of Congress's intent regarding the scope of the distribution right. *See* 579 F. Supp. 2d at 1218–19. That provision, moreover, refers to "offers to *sell*," 35 U.S.C. § 271(a) (emphasis added), not to distribute, further limiting its interpretive value to Section 106(3).

[133] *Hotaling*, 118 F.3d at 203.

[134] *See* SIIA Initial Comments at 31 ("The case law and statute clearly establish that the distribution right in section 106(3) of the U.S. Copyright Act covers the making available of a copyrighted work provided: (i) the transferor has completed all the necessary steps for a public distribution and the only step(s) necessary for a 'transfer in ownership' (as required by the statute) are those that must be undertaken by the transferee or other third party; and (ii) the alleged infringer must have the capacity to transfer a copy of the copyrighted work by possessing a copy of the copyrighted work alleged to be infringed.").

[135] *See* Menell, *supra* note 124, at 257 ("Given the textual ambiguity of Section 106(3) . . . there is good reason to examine the legislative history to understand the broader context and origins of the distribution right."); 2 NIMMER ON COPYRIGHT, *supra* note 101, § 8.11[D][3][b] (concluding that "whether proof of violation of the right to distribute requires actual receipt" is "ambiguous, not susceptible to resolution through dictionary definitions alone"); Tr. at 181:3–6 (Keith Kupferschmid, SIIA) ("We have got ambiguities in our own law in terms of what it means to distribute something, what the right of distribution covers and doesn't cover.").

[136] *See Milner v. Dep't of the Navy*, 562 U.S. 562, 572 (2011) ("Those of us who make use of legislative history believe that clear evidence of congressional intent may illuminate ambiguous text.").

[137] Act of March 4, 1909, Pub. L. No. 60-349, § 1(a), 35 Stat. 1075 (1909).

[138] U.S. COPYRIGHT OFFICE, COPYRIGHT LAW REVISION: REPORT OF THE REGISTER OF COPYRIGHTS ON THE GENERAL REVISION OF THE U.S. COPYRIGHT LAW, 87TH CONG., 21–22 (Comm. Print 1961).

[139] *See* Menell, *supra* note 124, at 241.

[140] STAFF OF H. COMM. ON THE JUDICIARY, 88TH CONG., COPYRIGHT LAW REVISION PART 3: PRELIMINARY DRAFT FOR REVISED U.S. COPYRIGHT LAW AND DISCUSSIONS AND COMMENTS ON THE DRAFT 4 (Comm. Print 1964).

[141] *Id.* at 110.

[142] Menell, *supra* note 124, at 238; *see e.g.*, *Ladd v. Oxnard*, 75 F. 703, 730 (C.C.D. Mass. 1896) ("To constitute publication, it is necessary that the work shall be exposed for sale or offered gratuitously to the general public. . . .") (quoting WALTER A. COPINGER, THE LAW OF COPYRIGHT IN WORKS OF LITERATURE AND ART 119 (1893)); *Nat'l Geographic Soc'y v. Classified Geographic, Inc.*, 27 F. Supp. 655, 659 (D. Mass. 1939) ("In its ordinary acceptation, the word 'publication' means 'the act of publishing a thing or making it public; offering to public notice; or rendering it accessible to public scrutiny.' In copyright law, it is 'the act of making public a book; that is, offering or communicating it to the public by sale or distribution of copies.'") (quoting *D'Ole v. Kansas City Star Co.*, 94 F. 840, 842 (C.C.W.D. Mo. 1899)); *Tiffany Prods., Inc. v. Dewing*, 50 F.2d 911, 914 (D. Md. 1931) ("In its ordinary acceptation the word 'publication' means 'to make public; to make known to people in general * * * to bring before the public as for sale or distribution . . . .' Sale is, of course, not an essential element.") (citation omitted); *William A. Meier Glass Co. v. Anchor Hocking Glass Corp.*, 95 F. Supp. 264, 268 (W.D. Pa. 1951) ("It was offered for sale and constituted a general publication whereby the plaintiff abandoned and surrendered any common law property right it may have had in said design.").

[143] Menell, *supra* note 124, at 238; *see also* Thomas F. Cotter, *Toward a Functional Definition of Publication in Copyright Law*, 92 MINN. L. REV. 1724, 1776 (2008) ("[I]t seems reasonably clear from the [1909 Act] case law that offers for sale to the general public count as publications.").

[144] 1 NIMMER ON COPYRIGHT, *supra* note 101, § 4.02 [B][2].

[145] Menell, *supra* note 124, at 238.

[146] STAFF OF H. COMM. ON THE JUDICIARY, 88TH CONG., COPYRIGHT LAW REVISION PART 3: PRELIMINARY DRAFT FOR REVISED U.S. COPYRIGHT LAW AND DISCUSSIONS AND COMMENTS ON THE DRAFT 128 (Comm. Print 1964).

[147] U.S. COPYRIGHT OFFICE, COPYRIGHT LAW REVISION PART 6: SUPPLEMENTARY REP. OF THE REGISTER OF COPYRIGHTS ON THE GENERAL REVISION OF THE U.S. COPYRIGHT LAW: 1965 REVISION BILL, 89TH CONG., 186 (Comm. Print 1965).

[148] *Id.* at 19. More generally, the Supplementary Report expressed the view that "the author's rights should be stated in the statute in broad terms," in part due to the concern that "the transmission of works by . . . linked computers, and other new media of communication, may soon be among the most important means of disseminating them, and will be capable of reaching vast audiences." *Id.* at 14. "Even when these new media are not operated for profit," the Supplementary Report noted, "they may be expected to displace the demand for authors' works by other users from whom copyright owners derive compensation." *Id.*

[149] H.R. REP. NO. 94-1476, at 61 (emphasis added); S. REP. NO. 94-473, at 57 (1975) (emphasis added).

[150] H.R. REP. No. 94-1476, at 61; S. REP. NO. 94-473, at 57.

[151] S. REP. NO. 94-473, at 58. The House report contains the identical statement, except that the first sentence uses the plural in referring to the right. *See* H.R. REP. NO. 94-1476, at 62 ("Clause (3) of section 106 establishes the exclusive right of publications . . . .").

[152] 2 NIMMER ON COPYRIGHT, *supra* note 101, § 8.11[B][2][c]; *see also Ford Motor Co. v. Summit Motor Prods., Inc.*, 930 F.2d 277, 299 (3d Cir. 1991) ("'Publication' and the exclusive right protected by section 106(3) . . . are for all practical purposes, synonymous. Therefore, any clarification of what is meant by 'publication' would also clarify what is meant by section 106(3) . . . ."); *Elektra Entm't Grp., Inc. v. Barker*, 551 F. Supp. 2d 234, 241 (S.D.N.Y. 2008) ("[T]he House and Senate of the Ninety-Fourth Congress considered the terms 'distribute' and 'publication' to be synonymous."); *In re Napster, Inc. Copyright Litig.*, 377 F. Supp. 2d at 803 ("[T]he [Supreme] Court observed that the legislative history of the 1976 Act equates [distribution] with the right of 'publication' . . . .") (citing *Harper and Row, Publishers, Inc. v. Nation Enters.*, 471 U.S. 539, 552 (1985)).

[153] Menell, *supra* note 124, at 230–51; *see also* GREEN PAPER, *supra* note 3, at 16 (noting that cases construing the distribution right "predate the recent academic scholarship . . . reviewing previously unanalyzed legislative history").

[154] 17 U.S.C. § 101.

[155] *London-Sire Records*, 542 F. Supp. 2d at 169; *accord BMG Rights Mgmt.*, 2015 WL 7756130, at *24; *Thomas*, 579 F. Supp. 2d at 1220; *Howell*, 554 F. Supp. 2d at 984–85.

[156] S. 644, 92d Cong. sec. 101, § 101 ("Publication") (1971).

[157] H.R. REP. NO. 94-1476, at 48.

[158] 1 NIMMER ON COPYRIGHT, *supra* note 101, § 4.03[A] n.25.

[159] STAFF OF H. COMM. ON THE JUDICIARY, 88TH CONG., COPYRIGHT LAW REVISION PART 3: PRELIMINARY DRAFT FOR REVISED U.S. COPYRIGHT LAW AND DISCUSSIONS AND COMMENTS ON THE DRAFT 110 (Comm. Print 1964).

[160] *See* Sydnor Initial Comments at 48 ("That belated and humble origin shows that this sentence was a minor clarification and forecloses serious claims that this sentence could have been intended to retract a publication right.").

[161] As Professors Menell and Nimmer note, the legislative history of the Sound Recording Amendments Act of 1971 ("SRAA") may provide further indication that Congress intended the exclusive right of distribution to cover offers to distribute. The SRRA was passed

shortly before the conclusion of the Convention for the Protection of Producers of Phonograms Against Unauthorized Duplication of their Phonograms, Oct. 29, 1971, 25 U.S.T. 309 ("Geneva Phonogram Convention"). The SRRA amended Section 1 of the Copyright Act of 1909 to add a new exclusive right to "reproduce and distribute to the public by sale or other transfer of ownership, or by rental, lease, or lending, reproductions of the copyrighted work if it be a sound recording." Act of Oct. 15, 1971, Pub. L. No. 92-140, § 1(a), 85 Stat 391. Save for the explicit reference to sound recordings, this text is nearly identical to that of Section 106(3) of the current Copyright Act. The legislative history indicates that the language ultimately enacted in the SRRA was intended to correspond to the text and purpose of the Geneva Phonogram Convention, which defines "distribution to the public" as "any act by which duplicates of a phonogram are offered, directly or indirectly, to the general public or any section thereof." Geneva Phonogram Convention art. 1(d); *see* Menell, *supra* note 124, at 250–51, 259–60; 2 NIMMER ON COPYRIGHT, *supra* note 101, § 8.11[B][4][b]. Thus, both the SRRA and the nearly identical language of Section 106(3) of the current Act should be construed to cover offers to distribute.

[162] *See e.g.*, *Shannon's Rainbow LLC v. Supernova Media, Inc.*, No. 2:08-CV-880 TS, 2011 WL 320905, *4 n.34 (D. Utah Jan. 31, 2011) (citing 2 MELVILLE B. NIMMER and DAVID NIMMER, NIMMER ON COPYRIGHT § 8.11[A] (2007)); *Howell*, 554 F. Supp. 2d at 981 (same); *Leadbetter*, 2007 WL 1217705, at *3 (citing 2 MELVILLE B. NIMMER and DAVID NIMMER, NIMMER ON COPYRIGHT § 8.11[A] (2005); *Perfect 10 v. Google, Inc.*, 416 F. Supp. 2d 828, 841, 844 (C.D. Cal. 2006) (same).

[163] *See* 991 F.2d 426, 434 (8th Cir. 1993). As several commenters noted, however, reliance on *National Car Rental* is misplaced in copyright distribution cases involving "making available" activity. *See, e.g.*, MPAA–RIAA Joint Initial Comments at 13–15; SIIA Initial Comments at 14, 26; Tr. at 206:6–207:11 (Keith Kupferschmid, SIIA). That case involved a software license permitting National Car Rental and its vendor to use computer programs "solely 'to process data of [National] and in no event for the processing of data . . . of any third party.'" *Nat'l Car Rental*, 991 F.2d at 428 (omission in original) (citations omitted). The owner of the software alleged that National breached the license by "using the programs to process the data of third parties." *Id.* The issue was whether that claim was preempted by the Copyright Act. The court held that it was not, holding that the pleadings could not be read to allege a distribution under Section 106(3) because they "did not allege use *by*" the third parties, but only that National and its vendor had used the programs "'for the benefit of'" those parties. *Id.* at 430. There was no allegation that National had offered to distribute copies, and therefore the availability of such a claim was not before the court. *See* Carson, *supra* note 40, at 154 ("Nothing resembling a distribution—or a making available—took place in the National Car Rental case.").

[164] *See, e.g.*, *Thomas*, 579 F. Supp. 2d at 1225 ("*National Car Rental*, not *Hotaling*, is binding upon this Court."); *Howell*, 554 F. Supp. 2d at 981 ("The general rule, supported by the great weight of authority, is that 'infringement of [the distribution right] requires an actual dissemination of either copies or phonorecords.'") (alteration in original) (quoting *Nat'l Car Rental*, 991 F.2d at 434); *London-Sire Records*, 542 F. Supp. 2d at 167 (citing *Nat'l Car Rental* to illustrate the split among courts over the valid reading of Section 106(3)); *In re Napster, Inc. Copyright Litig.*, 377 F. Supp. 2d at 802 ("[A] number of courts, including the Eighth Circuit, have held that 'infringement of the distribution right requires an actual dissemination of either copies or phonorecords.'") (quoting *Nat'l Car Rental*, 991 F.2d at 434).

[165] *See The Scope of Copyright Protection*, *supra* note 95, at 114 (statement of David Nimmer, Professor from Practice, UCLA Sch. of Law, Of Counsel, Irell and Manella, LLP, Los Angeles) ("[Professor Menell's] findings were so important that I invited him to co-author the next treatise revision, in order to include the comprehensive analysis of the proper interpretation of copyright law's distribution right, as set forth in that landmark article.").

[166] 2 NIMMER ON COPYRIGHT, *supra* note 101, § 8.11[B][4][d], [D][4][c]; *see also The Scope of Copyright Protection*, *supra* note 95, at 2 (statement of Rep. Howard Coble, Chairman, Subcomm. on Courts, Intellectual Prop. and the Internet) ("I am pleased to learn that one of our witnesses, Mr. Nimmer, has updated his copyright treatise and made it perfectly clear that making available copyrighted works for others is infringement.").

[167] 2 NIMMER ON COPYRIGHT, *supra* note 101, § 8.11[C][1][a] and n.116 (noting that "actual dissemination" language "simply stated that there is no violation of the distribution right when the substance of the copyrighted work has been *intangibly* dispersed, via performance; to violate the distribution right, instead, *tangible* copies must be at issue").

[168] *Diversey*, 738 F.3d at 1202 and n.7.

[169] *Hotaling*, 118 F.3d at 203.

[170] *See* Part III.C.2, *infra*. As one commenter noted, "It would be awkward, to say the least, were crabbed judicial interpretations of the scope of the right of . . . distribution[] to result in incomplete compliance with the international norms the U.S. purports not only to respect but even to demand that other nations enforce." Ginsburg Initial Comments at 7.

[171] For purposes of the present analysis, we define streaming to include two types of transmissions: (i) real-time multicast streaming, where a server sends out one stream to all users simultaneously in a manner similar to traditional aerial broadcasting (often used for simultaneous Internet transmission by terrestrial radio stations); and (2) unicast streaming, where a session-based one-to-one connection is established between a customer and the server that is used to transmit a video or sound recording over the Internet in response to an individual user's request. *See* Daniel Brenner, *"Gently Down the Stream": When is an Online Performance Public Under Copyright?*, 28 BERKELEY TECH. L.J. 1167, 1175–77 (2013).

[172] 17 U.S.C. § 101.

[173] *Id.* ("To perform or display a work 'publicly' means—(1) to perform or display it at a place open to the public or at any place where a substantial number of persons outside of a normal circle of a family and its social acquaintances is gathered . . . .").

[174] *Id.*

[175] *See supra* notes 57–59 and accompanying text.

[176] 17 U.S.C. § 101.

[177] H.R. REP. NO. 94-1476, at 64–65; *see also* H.R. REP. NO. 90-83, at 29 (1967) ("[A] performance made available by transmission to the public at large is 'public' . . . where the transmission is capable of reaching different recipients at different times, as in the case of sounds or images stored in an information system and capable of being performed or displayed at the initiative of individual members of the public.").

[178] H.R. REP. NO. 94-1476, at 64.

[179] *Cmty. Broad. Serv. v. Time Warner Cable, LLC*, No. 07-139-B-W, 2008 WL 3200661, at *9 (D. Me. Aug. 7, 2008).

[180] *Id.* at *10 (emphasis added).

[181] *On Command Video Corp. v. Columbia Pictures Indus.*, 777 F. Supp. 787, 790 (N.D. Cal. 1991).

[182] *Am. Broad. Cos. v. Aereo, Inc.*, 134 S. Ct. 2498, 2507 (2014) ("*Aereo III*").

[183] *Capitol Records, Inc. v. MP3tunes, LLC*, 48 F. Supp. 3d 703, 719–20 (S.D.N.Y. 2014) ("*MP3tunes*").

[184] No. CV 15-01869 MMM (MRWx), 2015 WL 3649187 (C.D. Cal. June 11, 2015).

[185] *Flava Works, Inc. v. Gunter*, 689 F.3d 754, 761 (7th Cir. 2012).

[186] *Cf. Aereo III*, 134 S. Ct. at 2504 ("Considered alone, the language of the Act does not clearly indicate when an entity 'perform[s]' . . . . But when read in light of its purpose, the Act is unmistakable: An entity that engages in activities like Aereo's performs.").

[187] Ginsburg Additional Comments at 8. As Professor Ginsburg further explained:

> [I]f performances of a work are offered to the public, for example, on a pay-per-view basis, the characterization of the performances as "to the public" should not turn on

> how many members of the public accept the offer and in fact request a transmission of the performance. If one were to understand the [*Aereo*] Court's statement as meaning actual, rather than offered, transmissions, then the "public" nature of a performance could not be ascertained without post-hoc head- counting. Not only does such an interpretation introduce uncertainty for copyright owners and exploiters alike, but it promotes the kinds of baroque copyright-avoiding business models the Court discredited.
>
> *Id.*

[188] *Aereo III*, 134 S. Ct. at 2510 (citing 17 U.S.C. § 101 ("publicly")).

[189] Ginsburg Additional Comments at 8.

[190] H.R. REP. NO. 94-1476, at 64–65.

[191] *Aereo III*, 134 S. Ct. at 2507.

[192] *Id.*

[193] *Cf. id.* at 2509 ("Congress would as much have intended to protect a copyright holder from the unlicensed activities of Aereo as from those of cable companies.").

[194] *Id.* at 2498.

[195] *See supra* note 171.

[196] *Cartoon Network LP v. CSC Holdings, Inc.*, 536 F.3d 121, 134 (2d Cir. 2008) ("*Cablevision*").

[197] *See Twentieth Century Fox Film Corp. v. Cablevision Sys. Corp.,* 478 F. Supp. 2d 607, 622–623 (S.D.N.Y. 2007).

[198] 712 F.3d 676, 686–94 (2d Cir. 2013) ("*Aereo II*").

[199] *Id.* at 689.

[200] *See, e.g.*, *MP3tunes*, 48 F. Supp. 3d at 720 ("Because there was no master copy of the cover art, MP3tunes cannot be directly liable for a public display of cover art."); *Hearst Stations Inc. v. Aereo, Inc.,* 977 F. Supp. 2d 32, 38–39 (D. Mass. 2013) (applying *Cablevision* to hold that transmission of unique copies of a work did not constitute a public performance); *Am. Broad. Cos. v. Aereo, Inc.*, 874 F. Supp. 2d 373, 388 (S.D.N.Y. 2012) ("*Aereo I*") (finding dispositive the defendant's "use of unique copies, accessible only to the users who requested them, and transmitted only to those users"); *ASCAP*, 627 F.3d at 75 ("That same distinction applies here. Just as in *Cablevision*, the Internet Companies transmit a copy of the work to the user, who then plays his unique copy of the song whenever he wants to hear it; because the performance is made by a unique reproduction of the song that was sold to the user, the ultimate performance of the song is not 'to the public.'").

[201] *Cmty. Television of Utah, LLC v. Aereo, Inc.*, 997 F. Supp. 2d 1191, 1200 (D. Utah 2014); *Fox Television Stations, Inc. v. FilmOn X LLC*, 966 F. Supp. 2d 30, 48 (D.D.C. 2013); *Fox Television Stations, Inc. v. BarryDriller Content Sys.*, 915 F. Supp. 2d 1138, 1144 (C.D. Cal. 2012).

[202] *Aereo III*, 134 S. Ct. at 2507.

[203] *Id.* at 2508.

[204] *Id.* at 2509.

[205] *Id.*

[206] 17 U.S.C. § 101 ("publicly").

[207] *Aereo III*, 134 S. Ct. at 2509.

[208] *Id.*; *see also Fox Television Stations, Inc. v. FilmOn X LLC*, No. CV 13-758 (RMC), 2015 WL 7761052, at *22–23 (D.D.C. Dec. 2, 2015) (applying *Aereo* to hold that a service allowing users to record over-the-air television programming and watch the content at a later time performed publicly). The Court in *Aereo* cautioned that its ruling was limited to activities like Aereo's and did not extend to other technologies such as cloud computing and remote storage DVRs. Noting that those services involve content that consumers "'have *already* lawfully acquired,'" the Court stated that it had "not considered whether the public performance right is infringed when the user of a service pays primarily for something other than the transmission of copyrighted works, such as the remote storage of content." 134 S. Ct. at 2511 (quoting Amicus Brief of United States at 31).

[209] *See, e.g.*, Ginsburg Additional Comments at 3.

[210] WCT, *supra* note 1, art. 8; WPPT, *supra* note 1, arts. 10, 14.

[211] *Perfect 10*, 508 F.3d 1146.

[212] *See Fox Broad. Co. v. Dish Network, LLC*, No. CV 12-04529 DMG (SHx), 2015 WL 1137593, at *12 (C.D. Cal. Jan. 20, 2015) ("*Dish Network*").

[213] *See* Ginsburg Additional Comments at 11 ("[A] *Cablevision*-style volition predicate that requires specific agency as to each work transmitted may effectively eviscerate the making available right . . . ."); *see also* ASCAP, BMI, SGA, SESAC and NMPA, Comments Submitted in Response to U.S. Copyright Office's July 15, 2014 Notice of Inquiry at 8 (Sept. 15, 2014) ("Musical Works Organizations Joint Additional Comments") ("Clearly, a volitional conduct test is incompatible with a public performing right that is broadly applicable to on-demand, interactive entertainment technologies. Inventive technicians and software programmers can always engineer transmission systems to have the user initiate the transmission.").

[214] *Milo and Gabby, LLC v. Amazon.com, Inc.*, No. C13-1932RSM, 2015 WL 4394673, at *5 (W.D. Wash. July 16, 2015).

[215] *Cablevision*, 536 F.3d at 133. The *Cablevision* court adopted a test for infringement of the reproduction right that was based on a line of cases beginning with a pre-DMCA opinion from the Northern District of California, looking to "the volitional conduct that causes the copy to be made" to determine whether the defendant should be held liable for direct copyright infringement. *Id.* at 130–31 (citing *Religious Tech. Ctr. v. Netcom On-Line Comms. Servs.*, 907 F. Supp. 1361 (N.D. Cal. 1995) ("*Netcom*")). The courts that have applied the *Cablevision* volitional activity test to govern the outcome in public display and performance cases have done so despite the Second Circuit's warning that "our conclusion in Part II that the customer, not Cablevision, 'does' the copying does not dictate a parallel conclusion that the customer, and not Cablevision, 'performs' the copyrighted work," since "[t]he definitions that delineate the contours of the reproduction and public performance rights vary in significant ways." 536 F.3d at 134. A leading treatise writer has argued that continued reliance on the *Netcom* analysis following passage of the DMCA is misplaced, and that volitional activity should not be used as a threshold test for direct copyright infringement liability outside of the DMCA safe harbors. *See* 4 NIMMER ON COPYRIGHT, *supra* note 101, § 12B.06[B][2][c][ii] ("Looking to *Netcom* rather than the 1998 amendments to the Copyright Act, the *Google* rulings ignore the text and legislative history of those safe harbors. . . . To elevate [the 'automatic technological process'] factor to decisive status fundamentally contradicts the legislative choices that Congress embodied into Section 512. As long as the Online Copyright Infringement Liability Limitation Act remains part and parcel of the Copyright Act, courts cannot simply apply *Netcom*'s volitional rule as the governing standard."). *But see CoStar Grp., Inc. v. LoopNet, Inc.*, 373 F.3d 544, 552 (4th Cir. 2004) ("Given that the statute declares its intent not to 'bear adversely upon' any of the ISP's defenses under law, including the defense that the plaintiff has not made out a prima facie case for infringement, it is difficult to argue, as CoStar does, that the statute in fact precludes ISPs from relying on an entire strain of case law holding that direct infringement must involve conduct having a volitional or causal aspect.").

[216] *See, e.g.*, *Aereo I*, 874 F. Supp. 2d at 386–87 ("To the extent that the Second Circuit's holding in *Cablevision* was premised on an inability to distinguish Cablevision's system from otherwise lawful activities, Aereo's system deserves the same consideration.").

[217] *See, e.g.*, *Arista Records LLC v. Myxer Inc.*, No. CV 08-03935 GAF (JCx), 2011 WL 11660773, at *14 (C.D. Cal. Apr. 1, 2011) ("[I]n light of the fact that copyright infringement is a strict liability offense, the Court is not inclined to adopt a volitional conduct requirement without clear instruction from the Ninth Circuit, and so declines to apply the so-called volitional conduct requirement advocated by [Defendant]."); *Warner Bros. Entm't Inc. v. WTV Sys., Inc.*, 824 F. Supp. 2d 1003, 1011 n.7 (C.D. Cal. 2011) (declining to adopt the *Cablevision* "volitional conduct requirement").

[218] *Aereo III,* 134 S. Ct. at 2506.
[219] *Id.* at 2504–07.
[220] *See id.* at 2512–14 (Scalia, J., dissenting).
[221] *Id.* at 2507.
[222] *Dish Network*, 2015 WL 1137593, at *9–11.
[223] *Id.* at *11.
[224] *Id.*
[225] *Id.* at *12. The court further found DISH could not be secondarily liable, since DISH's subscribers did not transmit the works "to the public," stating that "[w]hen an individual DISH subscriber transmits programming *rightfully in her possession* to another device, that transmission does not travel to 'a large number of people who are unknown to each other.'" *Id.* at *13.
[226] *FilmOn X*, 2015 WL 7761052, at *23.
[227] *Id.*
[228] *Compare* Musical Works Organizations Joint Additional Comments at 8 (arguing that "a volitional conduct test is incompatible with the public performing right" and predicting that lower courts will focus on other factors, such as commercial purpose, "instead of relying on an incomplete and inconsistent 'test' such as the volitional conduct test); MPAA–RIAA Additional Comments at 3 ("Under U.S. copyright law as properly interpreted, proof of 'volitional conduct' is not required to establish a defendant's liability for direct infringement in the context of interactive transmissions of content over the Internet."), *with* Cablevision Sys. Corp., Comments Submitted in Response to U.S. Copyright Office's July 15, 2014 Notice of Inquiry at 13 (Sept. 15, 2014) ("Cablevision Additional Comments") (projecting that, after *Aereo*, "courts will no doubt continue to apply volitional conduct standards in other contexts"); CCIA, Comments Submitted in Response to U.S. Copyright Office's July 15, 2014 Notice of Inquiry at 3 (Sept. 15, 2014) ("CCIA Additional Comments") ("The volitional act doctrine remains valid law; multiple circuits have analyzed the issue and have so held, and *Aereo*'s 'narrow holding' has not changed this."); DISH Network Corp., Comments Submitted in Response to U.S. Copyright Office's July 15, 2014 Notice of Inquiry at 4 (Sept. 15, 2014) ("DISH Additional Comments") ("Nothing the Court said undermines the virtual unanimity among the Courts of Appeals that volitional conduct principles are essential to the copyright balance."); Internet Ass'n Additional Comments at 3 ("In *Aereo*, the Court avoided the issue entirely, deeming a volitional analysis 'not critical' when a platform resembles a cable system. This indicates that the Court does not intend to disturb the line of precedent that has explored how to determine volition when technologies facilitate copying or disseminating protected works."); Internet Commerce Coal., Comments Submitted in Response to U.S. Copyright Office's July 15, 2014 Notice of Inquiry at 4 (undated) ("Internet Commerce Coal. Additional Comments") ("[T]he Court's decision must not be read as altering the requirements to establish copyright infringement, such as volitional conduct . . . ."); PK–EFF Additional Comments at 3–4 (arguing that *Aereo's* reach is narrow and "has little effect on the volitional conduct requirement outside of the context of cable systems").
[229] *See* Ginsburg Additional Comments at 10.
[230] *Id.* at 9.
[231] 17 U.S.C. § 101. The Copyright Act's legislative history shows that the drafters intended the display right to include "[e]ach and every method by which the images . . . comprising a . . . display are picked up and conveyed," including "the projection of an image on a screen or other surface by any method, the transmission of an image by electronic or other means, and the showing of an image on a cathode ray tube, or similar viewing apparatus connected with any sort of information storage and retrieval system." H.R. REP. NO. 94-1476, at 64.
[232] *See, e.g., Capitol Records, LLC v. Vimeo, LLC*, 972 F. Supp. 2d 500 (S.D.N.Y. 2013) (finding the defendant entitled to DMCA safe-harbor protection for certain copyrighted videos uploaded by users); *Io Grp., Inc. v. Veoh Networks, Inc.*, 586 F. Supp. 2d 1132, 1154–55

(N.D. Cal. 2008) (finding the defendant entitled to DMCA safe-harbor protection for copyrighted videos uploaded by users); *Corbis Corp. v. Amazon.com, Inc.*, 351 F. Supp. 2d 1090, 1110–11 (W.D. Wash. 2004) (finding the defendant entitled to DMCA safe-harbor protection for copyrighted images uploaded by third party sellers).

[233] *See, e.g.*, *Soc'y of the Holy Transfiguration Monastery, Inc. v. Gregory*, 689 F.3d 29, 57 (1st Cir. 2012) (holding that a picture uploaded to defendant's website implicated plaintiff's public display right); *BWP Media USA Inc. v. Uropa Media, Inc.*, No. 13 Civ. 7871(JSR)(JCF), 2014 WL 2011775, at *1 (S.D.N.Y. May 16, 2014) ("By posting BWP's copyrighted photographs on its website, Uropa directly infringed BWP's [public display] rights."); *Playboy Enters., Inc. v. Webbworld, Inc.*, 991 F. Supp. 543 (N.D. Tex. 1997) (finding that defendant violated plaintiff's public display right when it "allowed its paying subscribers to view PEI's copyrighted works on their computer monitors while online" through defendant's website).

[234] *See* 17 U.S.C. § 101 ("publicly"). After *Aereo*, one district court applied the "master copy" test from the Second Circuit's *Cablevision* case to find no direct infringement of the public display right where the defendant's software copied cover art from Amazon and saved a copy to a user's individual locker, noting that "[o]nly one user was capable of receiving each copy." *MP3tunes*, 48 F. Supp. 3d at 720. The court concluded that *Aereo*'s holding "was explicitly limited to technologies substantially similar to the one before the Supreme Court." *Id.* at 720–21 (citing *Aereo III*, 134 S. Ct. at 2506, 2510–11).

[235] 508 F.3d 1146 (9th Cir. 2007).

[236] *See* 2-3D COMPUTER LAW § 3D.09[2][g] (2014); Emanuela Arezzo, *Hyperlinks and Making Available Right in the European Union—What Future for the Internet After* Svensson*?*, 45 INT'L REV. INTELL. PROP. AND COMPETITION L. 524, 526 (2015).

[237] *Perfect 10*, 508 F.3d at 1156. For the purposes of this report, we have found useful Professor Emanuela Arezzo's grouping of different types of hyperlinks into four distinct categories: (1) *surface links* direct a user to another website's homepage; (2) *deep links* lead a user past the homepage of the other website directly to a page within it; (3) *framing links* enable a user to see the content of the linked page "framed" by the linking website; and (4) *inline linking*, or embedding, displays digital content within the linking website by serving it up from the original server, giving the impression that the content belongs to the linking website. *See* Arezzo, *supra* note 236, at 526.

[238] The court ultimately concluded that Google's use of the thumbnails constituted fair use. *Perfect 10*, 508 F.3d at 1168.

[239] *Id.* at 1160–61 (quoting 17 U.S.C. § 101).

[240] *Id.* at 1161.

[241] *See, e.g.*, *Leveyfilm, Inc. v. Fox Sports Interactive Media, LLC*, No. 13 C 4664, 2014 WL 3368893, at *5 (N.D. Ill. July 8, 2014) ("Furthermore, Leveyfilm has not submitted any evidence that Wysocki's article or the DVD cover photo were ever saved on Yardbarker's servers. Without such evidence, Leveyfilm cannot show that there is a genuine question of fact regarding whether Yardbarker—and by extension, Fox—copied or displayed the photo."). Some courts, however, have applied the doctrines of contributory and vicarious liability to allow a plaintiff to recover against a defendant engaging in such activity. For example, in *Capitol Records, Inc. v. MP3tunes, LLC*, the defendant ran a website that allowed users to locate and, through a provided browser plugin, "play tracks hosted by third-party websites through the user's browser." 48 F. Supp. 3d at 711, 718. The district court upheld the jury's finding that the defendant was liable for contributory and vicarious copyright infringement based on the public performance of plaintiffs' songs by the third party websites. *Id.* at 718–19.

[242] PACA, Digital Media Licensing Ass'n, Inc. ("PACA"), Nat'l Press Photographers Ass'n ("NPPA"), Am. Soc'y of Media Photographers ("ASMP"), and Graphic Artists Guild ("GAG"), Comments Submitted in Response to U.S. Copyright Office's July 15, 2014 Notice of Inquiry at 4 (capitalization altered) ("Visual Arts Organizations Joint Additional

Comments"); *see also* Tr. at 108:14–21 (Nancy Wolff, PACA) ("[I]f you use clever technology devices, you can essentially cut and paste an image and do inline linking or framing. So that the end-user, the one who is viewing the communication just sees now even a large high-res image which doesn't even now relate back to the original site where it came from."); *id.* at 118:4–7 (Jane C. Ginsburg, Colum. Law Sch.) ("[I]t is not clear that the display right, which is part of the making available right, is fully covered by virtue of decisions like *Perfect 10.*"). Others have noted additional concerns with the practice (also known as "hotlinking"). *See, e.g.*, Abby Ohlheiser, *The Heroic Way One Cartoonist Responded When the Huffington Post Swiped His Art*, WASH. POST (Oct. 28, 2015), https://www.washingtonpost.com/news/the-intersect/wp/2015/10/28/the-heroic-way-one-cartoonist-responded-when- the-huffington-post-swiped-his-art (reporting that inline linking "eats up the bandwidth of the site you took [the image] from, without giving them any of the benefits of actual Web site traffic").

[243] The background summarized here is drawn from the complaint. *See* First Amended Complaint for Injunctive Relief and Damages at 6–12, *Getty Images (US), Inc. v. Microsoft Corp.*, No. 1:14-CV-07114-DLC (S.D.N.Y. Sept. 24, 2014), ECF No. 33.

[244] Plaintiff's Memorandum of Law in Support of Order to Show Cause at 13, *Getty Images (US), Inc. v. Microsoft Corp.*, No. 1:14-CV-07114-DLC (S.D.N.Y. Sept. 5, 2014), ECF No. 6.

[245] *Id.* at 14.

[246] Microsoft Corp.'s Memorandum of Law in Opposition to Plaintiff's Motion for Preliminary Injunction at 16, *Getty Images (US), Inc. v. Microsoft Corp.*, No. 1:14-CV-07114-DLC (S.D.N.Y. Sept. 11, 2014), ECF No. 11.

[247] *Id.* at 15.

[248] *Compare* Internet Ass'n Additional Comments at 5 ("Commenters warn that a 'making available' right . . . would even question the legality of online functions such as linking and embedding."), *with* Visual Arts Organizations Joint Additional Comments at 4 ("Using technology such as in-line linking or framing, a website can easily display high- resolution images without a license and without running afoul of copyright law. . . . With this legal backdrop, websites have no incentive to license images from copyright owners, and visual artists have no incentive to create."), *and* Performance Impressions LLC, Comments Submitted in Response to U.S. Copyright Office's Feb. 25, 2014 Notice of Inquiry at 1 (Mar. 17, 2014) ("Inline linking (hotlinking) of copyrighted works should be proscribed so that third party websites cannot make available copyrighted content without a license from the creators/holders of such works.").

[249] *See supra* note 242.

[250] As discussed below, foreign courts have issued a number of decisions concerning the application of the making available right in this context. *See* Part IV.D, *infra*.

[251] While some plaintiffs have asserted claims against users of file sharing services for violation of the reproduction right, often such claims are treated by the courts as secondary to claims for violation of the distribution right, or are resolved in summary fashion. *See, e.g.*, *Call of the Wild Movie*, 770 F. Supp. 2d at 351–52 (joint discussion of reproduction and distribution rights); *UMG Recordings, Inc. v. Alburger*, No. 07-3705, 2009 WL 3152153, at *4 (E.D. Pa. Sept. 29, 2009) (devoting minimal discussion to reproduction right); *London-Sire Records,* 542 F. Supp. 2d at 165–74 (plaintiffs claimed infringement of the reproduction and distribution rights, but majority of the court's discussion relates to distribution claim); *UMG Recordings, Inc. v. Stewart*, 461 F. Supp. 2d 837, 842 (S.D. Ill. 2006) (recitation of facts and conclusions related to violation of right of reproduction without analysis); *Capitol Records, Inc. v. Mattingley*, 461 F. Supp. 2d 846, 850 (S.D. Ill. 2006) (same). *But see Warner Bros. Records, Inc. v. Walker*, 704 F. Supp. 2d 460, 465–67 (W.D. Pa. 2010) (containing a longer discussion of the claim for violation of the right of reproduction).

[252] A service provider's liability, however, may be significantly limited by its compliance with the relevant safe harbor provisions under Section 512.

[253] In 2001, this Office undertook a study regarding the copyright implications of such "transient" copies, and determined that such files are both "copies" and "fixed" as defined in Section 101, and therefore are potentially actionable under Section 106(1). *See* U.S. COPYRIGHT OFFICE, DMCA SECTION 104 REPORT 109–12 (2001), http://www.copyright.gov/reports/studies/dmca/sec-104-report-vol-1.pdf. Since then, the majority of courts have agreed that, absent an applicable affirmative defense, the creation of temporary copies in RAM constitutes infringement of the reproduction right. *See, e.g., Levey v. Brownstone Inv. Grp., LLC*, 590 Fed. App'x 132, 135-36 (3d Cir. 2014); *Quantum Sys. Integrators, Inc. v. Sprint Nextel Corp.*, 338 Fed. App'x 329, 336–37 (4th Cir. 2009); *Storage Tech. Corp. v. Custom Hardware Eng'g and Consulting, Inc.*, 421 F.3d 1307, 1311 (Fed. Cir. 2005). A few courts, however, have questioned the applicability of the reproduction right to the types of buffer copies created as part of the streaming process. For example, in *Cablevision*, the Second Circuit held that buffer copies created by a remote DVR system were not actionable "copies" under Section 101, where the data resided in the buffer for a "fleeting 1.2 seconds" before being overwritten by new data. *Cablevision*, 536 F.3d at 129–30.

[254] *See, e.g.*, Bridges Initial Comments at 9 (arguing that application of the distribution right to digital file sharing is unnecessary because "[a] person who downloads a file to his own storage media through a peer-to-peer network may . . . violate the reproduction right . . . and the sponsor or 'uploader' of that file may bear secondary liability for the downloader's reproduction"); Tr. at 208:22–209:13 (Jonathan Band, LCA) ("[I]t seems to me . . . that in the kinds of cases that the rights-holders seem to be concerned about, that the reproduction right on its face would take care of the problem. . . . And whether we get to the same result by principles of secondary liability . . . or reproduction right, or whatever, it really doesn't matter . . . as long as there is a way to enforce one's rights."); Tr. at 59:5–9 (Matthew Schruers, CCIA) ("[O]ur broad and often expanding secondary liability doctrines here in the United States are part of our . . . international treaty compliance.").

[255] *See* Carson, *supra* note 40, at 138.

[256] *See id.* ("If I am engaging in file sharing of music that I purchased on iTunes, I may be a copyright infringer, but not by infringing the reproduction right in making the original copy on my computer.").

[257] There are three bases for secondary liability generally recognized by the courts: contributory infringement, vicarious liability, and inducement of infringement. The elements of contributory infringement are generally that the defendant (i) have knowledge of the direct infringement by others (defined as "know[ing] or hav[ing] reason to know"), and (ii) "induce[], cause[], or materially contribute[] to the infringing conduct." *Napster*, 239 F.3d at 1019–20 (citations omitted). The elements of vicarious liability for copyright infringement are that the defendant "has the right and ability to supervise the infringing activity and also has a direct financial interest in such activities." *Id.* at 1022 (citations omitted). The Supreme Court imported the doctrine of inducement of infringement from the patent laws in *Metro-Goldwyn-Mayer Studios Inc. v. Grokster, Ltd.*, holding that "one who distributes a device with the object of promoting its use to infringe copyright, as shown by clear expression or other affirmative steps taken to foster infringement, is liable for the resulting acts of infringement by third parties." 545 U.S. 913, 936–37 (2005).

[258] *See, e.g., Fung*, 710 F.3d 1020 (affirming grant of summary judgment on claims of inducement of infringement against provider of a BitTorrent-based peer-to-peer file sharing network); *Capitol Records, LLC v. Escape Media Grp., Inc.*, No. 12- CV-6646 (AJN), 2015 WL 1402049 (S.D.N.Y. Mar. 25, 2015) (granting summary judgement on claims of contributory infringement and vicarious liability against Grooveshark music streaming service); *Arista Records LLC v. Lime Grp. LLC*, 784 F. Supp. 2d 398 (S.D.N.Y. 2011) (granting summary judgment on claims of inducement of infringement against Gnutella-based peer-to-peer file sharing network, but denying summary judgement on claims for contributory infringement and vicarious liability); *Usenet.com*, 633 F. Supp. 2d 124 (granting summary judgment on claims of inducement, contributory infringement, and

vicarious liability against website that granted access to and allowed digital downloads from Usenet boards); *cf. UMG Recording, Inc. v. Escape Media Grp., Inc.*, No. 11 Civ. 8407, 2014 WL 5089743 (S.D.N.Y. Sept. 29, 2014) (holding for plaintiffs on claims of inducement of infringement, contributory infringement, and vicarious liability violation based on employee uploads of copyrighted music to the Grooveshark music streaming service); *ReDigi*, 934 F. Supp. 2d 640 (granting summary judgment for plaintiffs on claims of contributory infringement and vicarious liability against defendant digital music resale marketplace).

[259] Tr. 79:1–21 (May 5, 2014) (George M. Borkowski, RIAA).

[260] *See, e.g.*, PK–EFF Joint Additional Comments at 5 ("Secondary theories of copyright liability do not directly impact the relationship between the section 106 rights and the requirements of protecting the rights of making available and communication to the public."); GIPC, Comments Submitted in Response to U.S. Copyright Office's July 15, 2014 Notice of Inquiry at 4 (Sept. 15, 2014) ("It is well established that in order for secondary liability to arise, there must be an underlying direct infringement. Thus, secondary liability adds nothing to the analysis, which remains properly focused on the issue of direct liability."); *The Scope of Copyright Protection*, *supra* note 95, at 18 (statement of David Nimmer, Professor from Practice, UCLA Sch. of Law, Of Counsel, Irell and Manella, LLP, Los Angeles) ("The standards adopted for 'making available' are . . . distinct from [indirect liability] doctrines, which remain unaffected by any clarification that the copyright owner's distribution right extends to the unauthorized uploading of protected works.").

[261] *Hearing on H.R. 2281 and H.R. 2180*, *supra* note 17, at 43 (statement of Marybeth Peters, Register of Copyrights).

[262] *Id.* at 37 (statement of Bruce A. Lehman, Assistant Sec'y of Commerce and Comm'r of Patents and Trademarks).

[263] H.R. REP. NO. 105-551, pt. 1, at 9–10 (1998) ("The treaties do not require any change in the substance of copyright rights or exceptions in U.S. law. They do, however, require two technological adjuncts to the copyright law, intended to ensure a thriving electronic marketplace for copyrighted works on the Internet.").

[264] 105 CONG. REC. S12,985 (daily ed. Nov. 12, 1998).

[265] DMCA, Pub. L. No. 105-304, § 101, 112 Stat. 2860, 2861 (1998).

[266] H.R. REP. NO. 105-796, 105th Cong., at 63 (1998).

[267] *United States v. Rutherford*, 442 U.S. 544, 554 n.10 (1979) (quoting *Apex Hosiery v. Leader*, 310 U.S. 469, 488–89 (1940)).

[268] Jane C. Ginsburg, *Recent Developments in US Copyright Law—Part II, Caselaw: Exclusive Rights on the Ebb?* 39 (Colum. Pub. L. and Legal Theory Working Papers, Working Paper No. 08158, 2008), http:// lsr.nellco.org/cgi/ viewcontent.cgi?article=1050&context= columbia_pllt; *see also The Scope of Copyright Protection*, *supra* note 95, at 2 (statement of Rep. John Conyers, Ranking Member, Subcomm. on Courts, Intellectual Prop. and the Internet) ("Congress has repeatedly demonstrated, by ratifying these agreements, that the United States law already includes this right and no change is necessary.").

[269] *Murray v. Schooner Charming Betsy*, 6 U.S. 64, 118 (1804).

[270] RESTATEMENT (THIRD) OF FOREIGN RELATIONS LAW OF UNITED STATES § 114 (AM. LAW INST. 1987). Other formulations of the test have indicated that courts should interpret statutes in a manner consistent with international obligations whenever such interpretation is reasonable. *See* Curtis A. Bradley, *The Charming Betsy Canon and Separation of Powers: Rethinking the Interpretive Role of International Law*, 86 GEO. L.J. 479, 490 (1997) (citing *United States v. Yunis*, 924 F.2d 1086, 1091 (D.C. Cir. 1991); *United States v. Georgescu*, 723 F. Supp. 912, 921 (E.D.N.Y. 1989); *Am. Baptist Churches in the U.S.A. v. Meese*, 712 F. Supp. 756, 771 (N.D. Cal. 1989)).

[271] *See supra* notes 71, 73, and 77 and accompanying text.

[272] *See supra* notes 76–77 and accompanying text.

[273] 579 F. Supp. 2d 1210.

[274] *Id.* at 1226.

[275] 2015 WL 7756130, at *25.

[276] *See Thomas*, 579 F. Supp. 2d at 1217, 1223–25.

[277] Plaintiffs in several cases have advanced an additional argument based on language in Section 106 providing that a copyright owner has the exclusive right "to authorize" the exercise of the enumerated rights. *See* 17 U.S.C. § 106 ("[T]he owner of copyright under this title has the exclusive rights to do *and to authorize* any of the following . . . .") (emphasis added). In their view, this provision gives copyright owners an independent cause of action against persons who authorize infringing activity, including those who make a work available for distribution, performance, display, or reproduction without permission. This argument, however, has been not been embraced by the courts, which have referred to the legislative history to interpret the phrase "to authorize" as only providing a cause of action for secondary liability, meaning there must be direct infringement by a third party for liability to attach to the "authorizing" party. *See Latin Am. Music Co. v. Archdiocese of San Juan of Roman Catholic and Apostolic Church*, 499 F.3d 32, 46 (1st Cir. 2007); *Venegas-Hernández v. Asociación de Compositores y Editores de Música Latinoamericana*, 424 F.3d 50, 57–58 (1st Cir. 2005); *Subafilms, Ltd. v. MGM-Pathe Commc'ns Co.*, 24 F.3d 1088, 1093 (9th Cir. 1994) (en banc); *Howell*, 554 F. Supp. 2d at 987; *Thomas*, 579 F. Supp. 2d at 1220–23; *Elektra Entm't Grp.*, 551 F. Supp. 2d at 245–47; *London-Sire Records*, 542 F. Supp. 2d at 166.

The legislative history relied on for this construction appears in the House Report accompanying the bill that became the 1976 Act:

> Use of the phrase 'to authorize' is intended to avoid any questions as to the liability of contributory infringers. For example, a person who lawfully acquires an authorized copy of a motion picture would be an infringer if he or she engages in the business of renting it to others for purposes of unauthorized public performance.

H.R. REP. NO. 94-1476, at 61. The First Circuit, however, has noted that while the interpretation adopted by courts "appears from legislative history to be closer to congressional intent," the "better bare-language reading would allow the claims in question." *Venegas-Hernández*, 424 F.3d at 58.

[278] *See* Letter from Rep. Melvin L. Watt, *supra* note 10, at 2 (asking the Copyright Office to review and assess "how foreign laws have interpreted and implemented the relevant provisions of the WIPO Internet Treaties").

[279] The cases discussed herein are illustrative of the foreign implementation experiences, but are not exhaustive. The Office surveyed the copyright laws of the 94 contracting parties that have implemented the WCT, and then looked at the available jurisprudence found through our own research and a review of the comments and roundtable discussions received as part of this study. Key challenges faced in compiling this review, however, included a paucity of reported decisions in some jurisdictions, as well as the limited availability of authoritative English translations of decisions in certain countries. Further, because protection under the United States is based on authors and their works (and not on related rights, as used in some international treaties and foreign jurisdictions), we limited our review to cases involving the rights of authors under the "communication to the public" construct as found in WCT Article 8.

[280] For inclusion in this category, the foreign statute contains the WCT phrase (or some close variation thereof): "including the making available to the public of their works in such a way that members of the public may access these works from a place and at a time individually chosen by them." WCT, *supra* note 1, art. 8.

[281] In some Alternative Language Model countries, the statutory language appears to closely track the WCT language but includes additional words or phrases such as "telecommunication" or "information network" that incorporate into the right separate statutory and regulatory schemes. In other Alternative Language Model countries, the language used to provide for

an explicit communication-to-the-public or making available right deviates more significantly from the WIPO Internet Treaties language.

[282] *See* Appendix E.

[283] The WIPO Internet Treaties were signed in 1996 by the European Community, the predecessor to the European Union. In 2001, the EU adopted the Information Society ("InfoSoc") Directive, which includes language identical to Article 8 of the WCT, requiring member states to protect the right of communication to the public, "including the making available to the public of [authors'] works in such a way that members of the public may access them from a place and at a time individually chosen by them." Directive 2001/29/EC, of the European Parliament and of the Council of 22 May 2001 on the Harmonisation of Certain Aspects of Copyright and Related Rights in the Information Society, art. 3(1), 2001 O.J. (L 167) 10, 16. In addition to adopting the language of Article 8 of the WCT, Recital (23) of the InfoSoc Directive preamble states that the "right should be understood in a broad sense covering all communication to the public not present at the place where the communication originates." *Id.*, recital 23, 12. Final implementation of the making available right was left to individual EU member states, though 20 of the 28 have adopted the Internet Treaties language—Bulgaria, Cyprus, the Czech Republic, Denmark, Germany, Greece, Ireland, Italy, Latvia, Lithuania, Luxembourg, Malta, Poland, Portugal, Romania, Slovakia, Slovenia, Spain, Sweden, and the United Kingdom. *See* Appendix E.

[284] *See, e.g.*, Joined Cases C-403/08 and C-429/08, Football Ass'n Premier League Ltd. v. QC Leisure, 2011 E.C.R. I-09083, 2011 EUR-Lex CELEX 62008CJ0403, para. 184 (Oct. 4, 2011) ("It should be noted at the outset that Article 3(1) of the Copyright Directive does not define the concept of 'communication to the public.'") (citing *Rafael Hoteles*, 2006 EUR-Lex CELEX 62005CJ0306, para. 33).

[285] "[A]uthors of literary and artistic works shall enjoy the exclusive right of authorizing any communication to the public of their works, by wire or wireless means, *including the making available to the public of their works in such a way that members of the public may access these works from a place and at a time individually chosen by them*." WCT, *supra* note 1, art. 8 (emphasis added).

[286] This issue is similar to the questions raised by the Aereo technology in the United States, which was the subject of the Supreme Court's decision on the public performance right in *Aereo III*, 134 S. Ct. 2498, discussed in Part III.B.2.b.i, *supra*.

[287] The CJEU has jurisdiction to give preliminary rulings concerning the "validity and interpretation of acts of the institutions, bodies, offices or agencies of the Union." *See* Consolidated Version of the Treaty on the Functioning of the European Union art. 267, Oct. 26, 2012, 2012 O.J. (C 326) 47, 164. Where a question is raised before any member state court or tribunal, the court or tribunal may request a CJEU ruling on that question "if it considers that a decision on the question is necessary to enable it to give judgment." *Id.* Where the CJEU renders a preliminary ruling, it only interprets EU law or rules on its validity. The CJEU does not apply that law to the underlying factual situation. *See Recommendations: Court of Justice of the European Union,* paragraph 7, 2012 O.J. (C 338) 1, 2. A judgment in which the CJEU gives a preliminary ruling on the interpretation or validity of an act of an EU institution "conclusively determines a question or questions of [EU] law and is binding on the national court for the purposes of the decision to be given by it in the main proceedings." Case 69/85, Wünsche Handelsgesellschaft GmbH and Co. v. Fed. Republic of Germany, 1986 E.C.R. 948, 1986 EUR-Lex CELEX 61985CO0069, para. 13 (Mar. 5, 1986).

[288] Case C-607/11, ITV Broad. Ltd. v. TV Catchup, 2013 EUR-Lex CELEX 62011CJ0607, para. 33 (Mar. 7, 2013).

[289] *Id.* at para. 34.

[290] *Rafael Hoteles*, 2006 EUR-Lex CELEX 62005CJ0306. The court reaffirmed that communication to the public requires a communication to an indeterminate but large number of people. Yet, significantly, the court concluded that this number may include both

those viewers who view the content at the same time and those who view it successively, even if those who have access to the communication are in different locations. *Id.* at paras. 37–38. The number constituting the "public" also may include potential viewers; the court concluded that "for there to be communication to the public it is sufficient that the work is made available to the public in such a way that the persons forming that public may access it." *Id.* at para. 43.

291 Singapore's copyright law includes an exclusive right to "communicate [a] work to the public," and defines "communicate" to include "the making available of a work or other subject-matter (on a network or otherwise) in such a way that the work or subject-matter may be accessed by any person from a place and at a time chosen by him." Copyright Act (Cap. 63, 2006 Rev. Ed.), last amended by Act 22 of 2014, ss 7, 26 (Sing.). RecordTV offered registered users a free remote DVR to record MediaCorp's free-to-air broadcasts in Singapore. A registered user logged into RecordTV's DVR service—known as iDVR—using a username and password, and "would select from this database the MediaCorp shows which he wanted to have recorded and enter the selected shows into a playlist" and then would send a request for the iDVR to record those shows; a program in RecordTV's recording computers would monitor for these requests and then instruct the iDVR to record the show. *RecordTV Pte Ltd. v. MediaCorp TV Singapore Pte Ltd.* [2010] SGCA 43 at [6] ("*RecordTV*"), *available at* http://www.singaporelaw.sg/sglaw/laws-of-singapore/case-law/free- law/court-of-appeal-judgments/14385-recordtv-pte-ltd-v-mediacorp-tv-singapore-pte-ltd-and-others-2010-sgca-43. RecordTV operated antennas for each television channel from which it recorded programs, and would record either one or multiple copies and store them on RecordTV's computers, from which the registered user who requested a given program could play it back. *Id.* at [7]. The recording would then be streamed to the registered user. *Id.* at [8].

292 *RecordTV*, [2010] SGCA 43, at [5]–[9]; *see also* Ginsburg Initial Comments, at 6.

293 *RecordTV*, [2010] SGCA 43, at [11].

294 *Id.* at [26]. The appellate court focused particularly on the fact that any user could only access and view "time-shifted" recordings of specific shows requested by that user.

295 *Id.* at [28].

296 *Id.* at [36].

297 The Singapore Copyright Act defines a communication "other than a broadcast" as having "been made by the person responsible for determining the content of the communication at the time the communication is made." Copyright Act (Cap. 63, 2006 Rev. Ed.), last amended by Act 22 of 2014, s 16(6).

298 *RecordTV*, [2010] SGCA 43, at [36].

299 *Id.* at [71]. In reaching this conclusion, the court appears to have been motivated by a desire to avoid constraining the development of what it viewed as socially-useful technologies. *Id.* at [2] ("This appeal raises an important policy issue as to how the courts should interpret copyright legislation in the light of technological advances which have clear legitimate and beneficial uses for the public, but which may be circumscribed or stymied by expansive claims of existing copyright owners. . . . If the law is not clear as to whether the use of improved technology which is beneficial to society constitutes a breach of copyright, should the courts interpret legislative provisions to favour the private rights of the copyright owner or the public's wider interests?").

300 *Id.* at [16]-[19]. *See also* Ginsburg Initial Comments at 6 n.12 (stating that the "appellate court appears to have followed each step of the *Cablevision* reasoning"); Tr. at 327:18–328:06 (Jane C. Ginsburg, Colum. Law Sch.) (noting that "Singapore is the only country that has found that a *Cablevision/Aereo*-type situation engages no right under copyright."); Tr. at 324:20–325:09 (Glynn Lunney, Tul. U. Sch. of Law) ("So, on the *Cablevision* case, for example, where the Second Circuit held that to be not copyright infringement, we have the court in Singapore saying it is not copyright infringement.").

[301] Ginsburg Initial Comments at 3; *see also* VON LEWINSKI, *supra* note 32, ¶ 17.73, at 456–57 ("[T]he covered act already starts prior to the actual transmission, namely with the offering or making available works and phonograms.").

[302] *See* Part III.B.1.b, *supra*.

[303] *See* Tr. at 326:19–22 (Jane C. Ginsburg, Colum. Law Sch.) ("[T]he [phrase] 'may access' makes clear that [the Art. 3(1) communication to the public right] covers not only a completed communication, but the prospect of a communication, the offer of a communication.").

[304] *Rafael Hoteles*, 2006 EUR-Lex CELEX 62005CJ0306, para. 43.

[305] *Id.*

[306] *Svensson*, 2014 EUR-Lex CELEX 62012CJ0466, para. 19 (citing *Rafael Hoteles*, 2006 EUR-Lex CELEX 62005CJ0306, para. 43).

[307] *See e.g.*, Ginsburg Initial Comments at 3 (citing *Svensson* for the proposition that "the 'making available' right covers potential as well as completed access to works of authorship. . . . The act that triggers the making available right is the offer to communicate the work to the public on an on-demand basis."); FICSOR, *supra* note 33, ¶ C8.23, at 508 ("[Under Article 8 of the WCT and Article 3(1) of the Information Society Directive, the concept of 'making available' includes both the element of making on-demand transmission *possible* and the *actual* on-demand transmission carried out on the basis of this possibility . . . . In fact, also under [these provisions], the act of 'communication to the public' in the form of 'making available' is completed by merely making a work available for on-demand transmission."); Rebecca Giblin and Jane C. Ginsburg, *We (Still) Need to Talk About* Aereo*: New Controversies and Unresolved Questions After the Supreme Court's Decision*, 38 COLUM J.L. AND ARTS 109, 121 (2015) ("In Europe, in construing the EU Information Society Directive's identical language, the Court of Justice of the European Union has ruled that the 'public' character of the 'making available' right turns on whether the defendant has *offered* the work to a 'large number of persons'—not whether it has in fact been received.") (emphasis in original).

[308] Musical Works Organizations Joint Initial Comments at 17–18.

[309] *Copyright Act 1968* (Cth) s 10 (Austl.). Note that the term "making available" is also found in the definition of "electronic rights management information" in section 10, as electronic information that appears "in connection with a communication, or the making available, of the work or subject matter."

[310] *See Telstra Corp. Ltd v Australasian Performing Rights Ass'n Ltd* (1997) 191 CLR 140 (Austl.), *available at* http://www.austlii.edu.au/ au/cases/ cth/HCA/1997/41.html ("The transmission may be to individuals in private circumstances but nevertheless be to the public . . . . Lying behind the concept of the copyright owner's public is recognition of the fact that where a work is performed in a commercial setting, the occasion is unlikely to be private or domestic and the audience is more appropriately to be seen as a section of the public."). Australia has had occasion to consider technology similar to that at issue in *Cablevision*. Unlike *Cablevision*, however, the High Court's decision in *National Rugby League v Singtel Optus* involved the exclusive right to make a copy, rather than the public communication right. *See National Rugby League Investments Pty Ltd v Singtel Optus Pty Ltd* [2012] FCAFC 59 (Austl.), *available at* http://www.austlii.edu.au/au/cases/cth/ FCAFC/ 2012/59. html. The technology at issue in *Optus* allowed Optus subscribers to capture and record over-the-air transmissions that the subscriber could then access on demand, via an Internet-connected device. Much of the High Court's decision is devoted to the question of whether the initial copying of the over-the-air programs was made by the subscriber alone, or by either Optus or Optus and the subscriber together. The High Court overturned the lower court's finding that the copy had been made by the subscriber alone, and accordingly ruled that Optus was not entitled to rely on the "time shifting" defense set out in Australian copyright law. *Id.* at [66]–[79]. One issue ruled on by the lower court that was not addressed by the High Court, however, was the question of whether the copies, once made, were

communicated to the public when viewed by the subscriber. The lower court had found that the later playback was a private communication, and thus did not implicate the communication to the public right. *Singtel Optus Pty Ltd v National Rugby League Investments Pty Ltd [No. 2]* [2012] FCA 34 [105] (Austl.).

[311] Copyright Act, R.S.C. 1985, c C-42, s 3(1)(f) (Can.). The Act defines telecommunication as "any transmission of signs, signals, writing, images or sounds or intelligence of any nature by wire, radio, visual, optical or other electromagnetic system." Copyright Act, R.S.C. 1985 c C-42, s 2 (Can.).

[312] Copyright Modernization Act, S.C. 2012, c 20, s 3 (Can.), *available at* http://laws-lois.justice.gc.ca/eng/annualstatutes/2012_20/FullText.html. The Act amended the definition of "communication to the public by telecommunication" to include "making it available to the public by telecommunication in a way that allows a member of the public to have access to it from a place and at a time individually chosen by that member of the public." Copyright Act, R.S.C. 1985, c C-42, s 2.4(1.1) (Can.). Most of the provisions of the Act entered into effect on November 7, 2012.

[313] Rogers Commc'ns Inc. v. Soc'y of Composers, Authors and Music Publishers of Canada ("SOCAN"), [2012] 2 S.C.R. 283, para. 34 (Can.); *see also* CCH Canada Ltd. v. Law Soc'y of Upper Canada, [2004] 1 S.C.R. 339, para. 78 (Can.) (noting that while a single fax transmission to a single individual would not be a communication to the public, repeated transmissions to numerous recipients could be); Jeremy de Beer, Ysolde Gendreau and David Vaver, *Canada*, *in* INTERNATIONAL COPYRIGHT LAW AND PRACTICE CAN-79, § 8[1][b][v] and n.55 (Paul Edward Geller and Lionel Bently eds., 2015).

[314] Chosakuken Hō [Copyright Law], Law No. 48 of 1970, as amended up to Law No. 35 of 2014, art. 23(1) (Japan), *translated at* http:// www.cric.or.jp/ english/clj/doc/ 20151001_October,2015_Copyright_Law_of_Japan.pdf (unofficial translation) ("The author shall have the exclusive right to make the public transmission of his work (including the making transmittable of this work in the case of the interactive transmission).").

[315] Tatsuhiro Ueno and Teruo Doi, *Japan*, *in* INTERNATIONAL COPYRIGHT LAW AND PRACTICE JAP-55, § 8[1][b][v] (Paul Edward Geller and Lionel Bently eds., 2015).

[316] *Id.*

[317] *See* Saikō Saibansho [Sup. Ct.] Jan. 18, 2011, Hei 21 (ju) no. 653, 65 SAIKŌ SAIBANSHO MINJI HANREISHŪ [MINSHŪ] 121 at [5] (Japan) ("*Maneki TV*"), *provisional translation available at* http://www.courts.go.jp/ app/hanrei_en/detail?id=1090; Musical Works Organizations Joint Initial Comments at 22 (citing *Maneki TV* for the premise that the streaming of one- to-one transmissions to individuals were public transmissions infringing transmission rights); Ueno and Doi, *supra* note 315, § 8[1][b][v] and n.29 (noting that Maneki TV's service was one example of an action that violated the rightsholders' public transmission rights).

[318] *Maneki TV*, 65 SAIKŌ SAIBANSHO MINJI HANREISHŪ [MINSHŪ] 121. At issue were the broadcasters' Article 23(1) public transmission rights as well as their Article 99*bis* right to make transmittable. Both articles afford rightsholders the power to transmit their works or broadcasts to the public. The broadcasters alleged violation of their Article 23(1) rights with regard to the broadcast programs they produced and violation of their Article 99*bis* right with regard to the broadcasts they provided.

[319] *Id.* at [6]. Specifically, the Intellectual Property High Court had found that the Location Free service transmitted each digitized broadcast only to a specific computer, and thus the transmission was not to the public. *Id.*

[320] *Id.* at [5].

[321] *Id.*

[322] *Id. See also* Naoya Isoda, *Copyright Infringement Liability of Placeshifting Services in the United States and Japan*, 7 WASH. J.L. TECH. AND ARTS 149, 187 (2011) (discussing the Supreme Court's statement).

[323] *Maneki TV*, 65 SAIKŌ SAIBANSHO MINJI HANREISHŪ [MINSHŪ] 121, at [5]. *Cf.* Saikō Saibansho [Sup. Ct.] Jan. 20, 2011, Hei 21 (ju) no. 788, 65 SAIKŌ SAIBANSHO MINJI HANREISHŪ [MINSHŪ] 399 (Japan) ("*Rokuraku II*"), *summary available at* http://www.courts.go.jp/ app/ hanrei_en/detail?id=1091. The 2011 case of *Rokuraku II* focused on the exclusive right of reproduction instead of the public transmission right, but its outcome was analogous to *Maneki TV*. Similar to *Maneki TV*, the *Rokuraku II* service provider manufactured and sold a product that received terrestrial broadcasts, converted them to digital data, and transmitted the digitized broadcasts via the Internet at the request of a user. The Supreme Court of Japan found the service provider liable for infringing the rightsholders' reproduction right in the broadcasts because, although the copies were made at the user's request, the act of reproduction was under the service provider's management and control. Without the service's involvement, it would have been impossible for users to make reproductions. *Id.* at [4]. While the public transmission right was not at issue in *Rokuraku II*, the court still found the service provider liable for enabling the infringement. This result contrasts with the Second Circuit's findings in *Cablevision* that examined a similar technology—criticized by one commenter in our study as "over-engineered secondary transmissions or offers of video on demand," Ginsburg Initial Comments at 6—and found that the use of individual transmissions rendered Cablevision not liable for violation of the rightsholders' public performance rights. *See id.* at 5–6 and n.11 (pointing to *Maneki TV* as an example, among other international cases, of the making available right correctly reaching on-demand transmissions).

[324] *Roadshow Films Pty Ltd v iiNet Ltd* [2011] FCAFC 23 (Austl.) ("*Roadshow Films I*"), *available at* http://www.austlii.edu.au/au/ cases/cth/ FCAFC/2011/23.html. Note that this was appealed to the High Court on issues of secondary (authorization) liability. *Roadshow Films Pty Ltd v iiNet Ltd* [2012] HCA 16 (Austl.), *available at* http://www.austlii.edu.au/au/cases/ cth/ HCA/2012/16.html.

[325] *Roadshow Films I*, [2011] FCAFC 23 [669]–[670]. While the respondents conceded that infringements were committed by iiNet users, dispute remained as to the number of infringements and how they were to be assessed. *See* Brad Sherman and James Lahore, *Australia*, *in* INTERNATIONAL COPYRIGHT LAW AND PRACTICE AUS-79, § 8[1][b][i][D] (Paul Edward Geller and Lionel Bently eds., 2015).

[326] *Roadshow Films I*, [2011] FCAFC 23 [661].

[327] The right of communication through information network is defined as "the right to make a work available to the public by wire or by wireless means, so that people may have access to the work from a place and at a time individually chosen by them." Zhonghua Rinmin Gongheguo Zhuzuoquan Fa (中华人民共和国著作权法) [Copyright Law of the People's Republic of China ("Copyright Law of China")] (promulgated by the Standing Comm. Nat'l People's Cong., Feb. 26, 2010, effective Apr. 1, 2010), art. 10(12), 2010 FALÜ HUIBIAN 20, 25 (China), *translated at* http://www.wipo. int/wipolex/en/text.jsp?file_id=186569 (unofficial translation). Some other translations call this right the "right of dissemination on information networks."

[328] The term "network service provider" includes both Internet Service Providers (ISPs) and Internet Content Providers (ICPs). *See* Xinxi Wangluo Chuanboquan Baohu Tiaoli (信息网络传播权保护条例) [Regulation on the Protection of the Right of Communication through Information Network] (promulgated by the State Council, May 18, 2006, effective July 1, 2006; rev'd by the State Council, January 30, 2013), art. 14, 20, 22, and 23, ST. COUNCIL GAZ., Feb. 28, 2013, at 12 (China), *version with automatic translation tool available at* http://www.wipo.int/wipolex/en/details.jsp?id=13403) (regulating network service providers who provide information storage, searching, or linking services); *and* Zuigao Renmin Fayuan Guanyu Shenli Sheji Jisuanji Wangluo Zhuzuoquan Jiufen Anjian Shiyong Falü Ruogan Wenti de Jieshi (最高人民法院 关于审理涉及计算机网络著作权纠纷案件适用法律若干问题的解释) [Interpretation of the Supreme People's Court Regarding

Certain Matters of Law Applications to Cases of Computer Net Copyright Disputes] (promulgated by the Supreme People's Court, Nov. 22, 2000, repealed by Zuigao Renmin Fayuan Guanyu Shenli Qinhai Xinxi Wangluo Chuanboquan Minshi Jiufen Anjian Shiyong Falü Ruogan Wenti de Guiding (最高人民法院关于审理侵害信息网络传播 权民事纠纷案件适用法律若干问题的规定) [Supreme People's Court Interpretation on Issues Concerning the Application of Law in the Trial of Civil Cases on the Infringement of Information Network Transmission Right ("Interpretation of Court on Right of Communication through Information Network")] (promulgated by the Supreme People's Court, Nov. 26, 2012, effective Jan. 1, 2013), art. 16, 197 SUP. PEOPLE'S CT. GAZ. 11 (China), *translated at* https://chinacopyrightandmedia.wordpress.com/ 2012/12/17/ regulations-concerning-some-issues-of-applicable-law-in- hearing-civil-dispute-cases-on-infringement-of-the-right-to-dissemination-through-information-networks/), art. 5, 69 SUP. PEOPLE'S CT. GAZ. 26 (China), *a 2006 version with automatic translation tool available at* http://www.wipo.int/ wipolex/en/details.jsp?id=6485 (indicating that "network service providers" encompasses ICP by specifically regulating "network service providers" who provide content services).

[329] Interpretation of Court on Right of Communication through Information Network, *supra* note 328, art. 3.

[330] *See* Appendix E. Even among countries that have adopted the Statutory Silence Model, the U.S. approach to implementation of the making available right is viewed by many commenters as an outlier. *See, e.g.*, Tr. at 329:10–17 (Jane C. Ginsburg, Colum. Law Sch.) ("In the United States our approach, to put some things [in a box] called 'distribution,' including digital, and other things in a box called 'public performance,' is something of an outlier. In most other countries, the concept of communication to the public covers digital communications, whether as a stream or as a download.").

[331] It is possible some cases exist, but upon extensive research and public comments, including a direct request for comments on foreign implementation at the subcommittee hearing, we learned of no cases in the vast majority of countries whose law is silent on the making available right.

[332] *See* Guido Westkamp, *The Implementation of Directive 2001/29/EC in the Member States*, *in* STUDY ON THE IMPLEMENTATION AND EFFECT IN MEMBER STATES' LAWS OF DIRECTIVE 2001/29/EC ON THE HARMONISATION OF CERTAIN ASPECTS OF COPYRIGHT AND RELATED RIGHTS IN THE INFORMATION SOCIETY, Pt. II, p. 120 (Lucie Guibault et al., 2007), *available at* http://ec.europa.eu/internal_market/ copyright/docs/studies/infosoc-study-annex_en.pdf.

[333] Westkamp, *supra* note 332, at 120 (citing Tribunal de première Instance [Civ.] [Court of First Instance] Bruxelles, Oct. 16, 1996, AUTEURS ET MÉDIA [AM] 1996, 426, *confirmé par* Cour d'Appel [CA] [Court of Appeals] Bruxelles, Oct. 28, 1997, AUTEURS ET MÉDIA [AM] 1997, 383 ("*Central Station*") (Belg.)).

[334] *Id.*

[335] For definitions of these terms, see note 237, *supra*.

[336] The "new public" test was first formulated by the CJEU in cases involving television broadcasts, including a case in which television broadcasts were retransmitted to hotel guests. *See, e.g.*, *Rafael Hoteles*, 2006 EUR-Lex CELEX 62005CJ0306, para. 40 ("Thus, such a transmission is made to a public different from the public at which the original act of communication of the work is directed, that is, to a new public.") (discussing the exclusive right of broadcasting and communication to the public under Article 11*bis*(1)(ii) of the Berne Convention).

[337] *See, e.g.*, *Svensson,* 2014 EUR-Lex CELEX 62012CJ0466, at paras. 27–28 (finding that defendant's deep links to content on the plaintiff's website did not violate the plaintiff's right of communication to the public, stating that "where all the users of another site [such

as defendant's] to whom the works at issue have been communicated by means of a clickable link could access those works directly on the site on which they were initially communicated, without the involvement of the manager of that other site, the users of the site managed by the latter must be deemed to be potential recipients of the initial communication and, therefore, as being part of the public taken into account by the copyright holders when they authorised the initial communication"); Case C-348/13, BestWater Int'l GmbH v. Michael Mebes, Stefan Potsch, 2014 EUR-Lex CELEX 62013CB0348 (Oct. 21, 2014) (finding that the use of framing technology to make plaintiff's video available on defendant's website did not violate plaintiff's right of communication to the public, stating "[t]he mere fact that a protected work, freely available on an [I]nternet site, is inserted into another [I]nternet site by means of a link using the 'framing' technique . . . cannot [be] classified as 'communication to the public' . . . since the work at issue is not transmitted to a new public or communicated [via] a specific technical method different from that of the original communication.").

[338] *Svensson*, 2014 EUR-Lex CELEX 62012CJ0466, para. 31 (stating that "where a clickable link makes it possible for users of the site on which that link appears to circumvent restrictions put in place by the site on which the protected work appears in order to restrict public access to that work to the latter site's subscribers only, and the link accordingly constitutes an intervention without which those users would not be able to access the works transmitted, all those users must be deemed to be a new public.").

[339] *See, e.g.*, *Request for a Preliminary Ruling from the Rechtbank Midden-Nederland (Netherlands) Lodged on 5 October 2015— Stichting Brein v Jack Frederik Wullems, Currently Trading Under the Name Filmspeler (Case C-527/15)*, 2016 O.J. (C 27) 6–7 (referring questions regarding the status of "hyperlinks to websites on which copyright-protected works . . . are made directly accessible, without the authorisation of the right holders"); *Request for a Preliminary Ruling From the Hoge Raad der Nederlanden (Netherlands) Lodged on 7 April 2015—GS Media BV v Sanoma Media Netherlands BV and Others (Case C- 160/15)*, 2015 O.J. (C 205) 18-19 (posing the question "[i]f anyone other than the copyright holder refers by means of a hyperlink on a website controlled by him to a website which is managed by a third party and is accessible to the general internet public, on which the work has been made available without the consent of the rightholder, does that constitute a 'communication to the public' within the meaning of Article 3(1) of Directive 2001/29?"). Both cases arose in the Netherlands, which is a Statutory Silence Model country, but is subject to the InfoSoc Directive as a member of the EU. The lower court in *GS Media* had initially found that the defendant violated the plaintiff's right of communication to the public by providing links to otherwise non-indexed pictures on a foreign website. *See* Rb. Amsterdam 12 september 2012, CR 2013/7, m.nt. A.R. Lodder (Sanoma/Geenstijl) (Neth.), *available at* http://www.geenstijl.nl/ archives/ images/vonnisbrittdekkernaakt.pdf, *discussed in Case C-466/12,* Svensson*—hyperlinks and communicating works to the public*, EU Law Radar (Jan. 20, 2013), http://eulawradar.com/case-c-46612-svensson-hyperlinks-and-communicating-works-to-the-public/. The lower court's decision was overturned by the Amsterdam Court of Appeals, and is currently on appeal to the Dutch Supreme Court, which referred the issue above to the CJEU. *Id.* In addition, the Supreme Court of the Netherlands had referred to the CJEU another case raising the question of whether a communication to the public occurs when a website indexes and categorizes meta-data to enable a user to locate and download infringing content, when the content itself is not hosted on the defendant's website. *See* HR 13 november 2015, ECLI:NL:HR:2015:3307 (Stichting Brein/Ziggo B.V. en XS4ALL Internet B.V.) (Neth.), *discussed in Netherlands: Dutch Supreme Court requests ruling on whether The Pirate Bay "makes a communication to the public,"* IRIS MERLIN (Jan. 2016), http://merlin.obs.coe.int/iris/2016/ 1/article22.en.html.

[340] *Compare* Mira Burri, *Permission to Link: Making Available via Hyperlinks in the European Union after* Svensson, 5 J. INTELL. PROP., INFO. TECH. AND ELECTRONIC COM. L. 245, 251

(Dec. 2014) (hailing the new public test as "accommodat[ing] both the essential functions of the Internet as a network of networks in the technical sense, as well as its function as a comprehensive cognitive database with substantial societal implications"), *with* Association Littéraire et Artistique Internationale ("ALAI"), *Opinion Proposed to the Executive Committee and Adopted at its Meeting, 17 September 2014 on the Criterion "New Public", Developed by the Court of Justice of the European Union (CJEU), Put in the Context of Making Available and Communication to the Public* 2 (Oct. 15, 2014, 11:28 AM), http://www.alai.org/assets/files/resolutions/2014-opinion- new-public.pdf (describing the CJEU's application of the "new public" test as "problematic" and "in conflict with international treaties and EU directives," stating that it "has the effect of inappropriate exhaustion of the exclusive right of communication to the public of works which their authors or other rightowners have made available over generally accessible websites").

[341] *See Communication from the Commission to the European Parliament, the Council, the European Economic and Social Committee and the Committee of the Regions: Towards a Modern, More European Copyright Framework*, at 9–10, COM (2015) 626 final (Dec. 9, 2015).

[342] *See supra* note 339.

[343] *See, e.g.*, Paramount Home Entm't Int'l Ltd. v. British Sky Broad. Ltd, [2014] EWHC 937 (Ch) [31]–[35] (Eng.) (finding the *Svensson* "new public test" met where content holder had not authorized the appearance of the content on the linked-to website); 1967 Ltd. v. British Sky Broad. Ltd. [2014] EWHC 3444 (Ch) [20] (Eng.) (same); Bundesgerichtshof [BGH] [Federal Court of Justice] Apr. 29, 2010, NEUE JURISTISCHE WOCHENSCHRIFT [NJW] 2011, 769 (Ger.), *discussed in* Anne Yliniva-Hoffmann, *Germany: BGH Rules on Deep Links Copyright Violation*, IRIS MERLIN (Jan. 2011), http:// merlin.obs.coe.int/iris/ 2011/ 1/ article15.en.html (finding that deep linking would violate the making available right if the link bypassed technical measures taken by the copyright owner to restrict access to certain users, for example, requiring that users could access certain content only after viewing the homepage). *But see* Polymeles Protodikeio [Pol. Pr.] [Multimember Court of First Instance of Athens] 5249/2014 (Greece), *discussed in* Eleonora Rosati, *Greek Court Says that it Doesn't Matter Whether the Content You Link to is Lawful or Unlawful*, IPKAT (Oct. 3, 2015, 1:16 PM), http://ipkitten. blogspot.co.uk/2015/10/greek-court-says-that-it-doesnt-matter.html (holding that defendant's use of deep links to provide access to unauthorized content hosted on a third-party website does not infringe the plaintiff's right of communication to the public unless the defendant directly assisted in the copyright infringement of the initial uploader to the third party website).

[344] *See, e.g.*, Ōsaka Chihō Saibansho [Osaka Dist. Ct.] June 20, 2013, Hei 23 (wa) no. 15245, 2218 HANREI JIHŌ [HANJI] 112 (Japan) ("*Niconico*"), *available at* http:// www. courts.go. jp/app/files/hanrei_jp/364/ 083364_hanrei. pdf (rejecting a claim for violation of the public transmission right based on hyperlinking to unauthorized content hosted by a third party); Shanghai Juli Chuanmei Jishu Youxian Gongsi Su Tianjin Jinbao Chuanmei Wangluo Fazhan Youxian Gongsi, Beijing Ruobobaisi Zixun Youxian GongsiDeng (上海聚力传媒技术有限公司诉天津津报传媒网络发展有限公司、北京若博佰思 咨询有限公司等) [PPLive Inc. v. Tianjin Jinbao Media Network Dev. Inc., Beijing Ruobobaisi Consulting Inc., et al.], 2013-3 RENMIN FAYUAN ANLI XUAN 301, 306–07 (Tianjin Second Interm. People's Ct. Mar. 1, 2013) (China) (providing comment and analysis to the case, in addition to reproducing the court's opinion) (holding that the use of framing links to connect to authorized content on a third party's server did not directly or indirectly infringe the right of communication through information network); Warman v. Fournier, [2012] F.C. 803, para. 37 (Can. Ont.) (rejecting claim for infringement based on an inline link from defendant's website to plaintiff's website, holding that "the [plaintiff] authorized communication of the [work] by posting it on his website and therefore there is no infringement"); *Universal Music Austl. Pty Ltd v Cooper* [2005] FCA 972 [63], [88] (Austl.), *available at*

http://www.austlii. edu.au/au/cases/cth/FCA/2005/972.html (finding no direct liability where defendant made works available through hyperlinks to unauthorized content on third parties' servers, on the grounds that the act of making available was performed by "the [third party] remote websites which make available the sound recordings and from which the digital music files are downloaded as a result of a request transmitted to the remote website," but finding secondary liability).

[345] *See supra* note 98 and accompanying text.

[346] *See RecordTV*, [2010] SGCA 43, at [5]–[9], [28].

[347] *See, e.g.*, *Svensson*, 2014 EUR-Lex CELEX 62012CJ0466; *BestWater*, 2014 EUR-Lex CELEX 62013CB0348.

[348] *See, e.g.*, Tr. at 324:10–325:14 (Lunney, Tul. U. Sch. of Law) (noting that various foreign jurisdictions had come to differing conclusions with regard to one-to-one transmissions, and concluding that "they have come to some different outcomes in some areas, but, on the whole, it is hard to see where their law is in any sense preferable on these issues or clearer on these issues than ours").

[349] Letter from Rep. Melvin L. Watt, *supra* note 10, at 2.

[350] *See supra* notes 57–60 and accompanying text.

[351] WCT, *supra* note 1, art. 8; WPPT, *supra* note 1, arts. 10, 14.

[352] *See* 17 U.S.C. §§ 107–122.

[353] *Id.* § 506(a)(1)(C).

[354] As discussed, *see supra* note 163, the *National Car Rental* case before the Eighth Circuit did not involve an offer to distribute copies of a work.

[355] *Diversey*, 738 F.3d at 1202 n.7.

[356] MPAA–RIAA Joint Initial Comments at 25 ("[T]he MPAA and RIAA do not believe it is necessary, at this time, to change U.S. laws to implement U.S. obligations under the WCT and WPPT, including the obligations to provide rights of making available and communication to the public."); AAP Initial Comments at 5 ("If further clarification is needed in the absence of additional wayward court decisions, AAP believes that Congress should simply reaffirm the existence of the right within the current set of exclusive rights provided in Section 106 without amending the Copyright Act to create an explicit, stand-alone 'making available' right.") (citations omitted); Copyright Alliance Initial Comments at 2 ("[W]e believe the bundle of rights established in §106, when interpreted as Congress intended and in accordance with international treaty obligations, adequately addresses the making available right. Therefore, we do not believe legislative changes are necessary at this point."); SIIA Initial Comments at 33 ("Based on our analysis, SIIA strongly believes that, at this time, neither legislation nor any type of further Congressional clarification is needed to provide for a making available right under U.S. law.").

[357] MPAA–RIAA Joint Initial Comments at 25 ("The Office and Congress should closely monitor developments in this area and if other courts adopt the flawed analysis requiring proof of actual dissemination or otherwise impose additional requirements inconsistent with the Copyright Act and U.S. international obligations, action should be taken to remedy any such misinterpretation of United States law."); AAP Initial Comments at 4 ([W]e ask the Copyright Office and Congress to closely monitor court decisions regarding the practical application of this right in physical and digital scenarios and to consider appropriate legislative action should barriers to effective online enforcement persist because some courts continue to require proof of actual distribution (*i.e.*, the downloading of a file by a specific user) in order to support a claim of violation of the 'making available' right."); Copyright Alliance Initial Comments at 2 ("We . . . encourage the U.S. Copyright Office and Congress to remain watchful and ready to address judicial erosion of the right, should it occur, in order to ensure continued compliance with Congress' intent and U.S. international obligations.").

[358] The Office notes, however, a disturbing trend in some recent district court decisions that have rejected the existence of a making available right out of hand, or with only cursory analysis.

See, e.g., *Alticor*, 2015 WL 8536571, at *7 ("[T]he court agrees that the Act does not confer a 'making available' copyright under § 106."); *Dish Network*, 2015 WL 1137593, at *21 ("While neither the Ninth Circuit nor any other circuit court has addressed the 'make available' theory of distribution under the Copyright Act, it has been considered by a number of courts, and '[t]he great majority of courts that have considered the question . . . have stopped short of fully endorsing the 'make available' right.'") (citations omitted). If district courts continue to take this approach to the issue, without correction or further guidance from the circuit courts, there may be a need for Congress to step in to clarify the law.

[359] PK–EFF Joint Additional Comments at 8.

[360] *See* Tr. at 320:13–16 (Jane C. Ginsburg, Colum. Law Sch.) ("[W]hether or not it is a prima facie violation, it is not necessarily an infringement because of the fair use doctrine and other exceptions.").

[361] *See supra* note 99 and accompanying text.

[362] *See The Scope of Copyright Protection*, *supra* note 95, at 13–16 (statement of David Nimmer, Professor from Practice, UCLA Sch. of Law, Of Counsel, Irell and Manella, LLP, Los Angeles).

[363] *Id.* at 13.

[364] *Id.* at 15–16.

[365] 17 U.S.C. § 101 ("publicly").

[366] *See* Part III.B.1.a, *supra*.

[367] *Aereo III*, 134 S. Ct. at 2509.

[368] *See* Ginsburg Additional Comments at 2 ("The *Aereo* decision clearly establishes that the public performance right extends to asynchronous transmissions."); Musical Works Organizations Joint Additional Comments at 6 ("The Court's decision in *Aereo* is on point with the technology-neutral emphasis of the WIPO Internet Treaties in correctly rejecting any notion that technological engineering can somehow limit the broad rights granted by the Copyright Act to copyright holders.").

[369] 134 S. Ct. at 2507.

[370] *Dish Network*, 2015 WL 1137593, at *10–12.

[371] 134 S. Ct. at 2510.

[372] *Id.* at 2511.

[373] *See, e.g.*, *Dish Network*, 2015 WL 1137593, at *13 (holding that DISH subscriber did not perform publicly by transmitting programming rightfully in her possession to another device).

[374] *See* CCIA Initial Comments at 5 ("That there is litigation over the reach of the 106 rights says nothing about those rights' adequacy; the limits of any right are bound to be tested by litigants.").

[375] 17 U.S.C. § 901(a)(4).

[376] *See id.* § 101 ("publicly").

[377] Under another approach, Congress could consider giving copyright owners an independent cause of action for "authorizing" infringing conduct based on the introductory clause of Section 106. *See id.* § 106 ("the owner of copyright under this title has the exclusive right to do *and to authorize* any of the following") (emphasis added). As noted, courts have rejected the argument that the "to authorize" language establishes direct liability for making works available for infringement, holding that it provides only for secondary liability. *See supra* note 277. Congress could overturn those decisions by adding a definition to Section 101 providing that the right to "authorize" the exercise of an exclusive right is independent of the right to "do" those activities. However, this approach could be considered overbroad because, for example, it would permit claims for authorizing the preparation of derivative works. *See* 17 U.S.C. § 106(2).

[378] WIPO Basic Proposal, *supra* note 3, ¶ 10.14, at 44; *see also* REINBOTHE and VON LEWINSKI, *supra* note 4, ¶¶ 7.8.13 (arguing that WCT uses the term "communication to the public" in the same sense as under the Berne Convention, meaning that it "excludes forms of direct presentation" that "do not involve any transmission to a remote place"), 7.8.30 (WCT communication-to-the-public right "is limited to remote transmissions").

[379] *See* PK–EFF Joint Initial Comments at 9 ("An explicit making available right would most likely overlap extensively with currently existing exclusive rights, and thus Congress may have to consider eliminating some of those rights in the event it elects to create a making available right.").

[380] *See* Bridges Initial Comments at 12 ("Undue expansion of the Section 106(3) right, through a broad conception of 'making available,' would also disturb settled expectations in transactions and legal relationships that rest upon existing classifications of rights in Section 106."); CCIA Initial Comments at 7 ("Creating or redefining exclusive rights also causes problems for existing contracts under which rights were properly licensed yet newer technologies weren't anticipated."); ESA Initial Comments at 3 ("Adjustments to the scope of existing rights, or the introduction of new exclusive rights, can be disruptive to existing licensing practices.").

[381] PK–EFF Joint Initial Comments at 10.

[382] Case C-607/11, ITV Broad. v. TV Catch Up, 2013 EUR-Lex CELEX 62011CJ0607, para. 34 (Mar. 7, 2013).

[383] *RecordTV*, [2010] SGCA 43, at [26].

[384] WCT, *supra* note 1, pmbl.; *see also* WPPT, *supra* note 1, pmbl. ("*Recognizing* the profound impact of the development and convergence of information and communication technologies on the production and use of performances and phonograms . . . .").

[385] WIPO Copyright Treaty art. 8, Dec. 20, 1996, 36 I.L.M. 65 (''Without prejudice to the provisions of Articles 11(1)(ii), 11*bis*(1)(i) and (ii), 11*ter*(1)(ii), 14(1)(ii) and 14*bis*(1) of the Berne Convention, authors of literary and artistic works shall enjoy the exclusive right of authorizing any communication to the public of their works, by wire or wireless means, including the making available to the public of their works in such a way that members of the public may access these works from a place and at a time individually chosen by them.'') (text of Agreed Statement omitted). WCT Article 8 is entitled ''Right of Communication to the Public.''

[386] WIPO Performances and Phonograms Treaty arts. 10, 14, Dec. 20, 1996, 36 I.L.M. 76. Articles 10 and 14 provide the making available right to performers whose performances are fixed in sound recordings (phonograms) and to producers of sound recordings. The separate ''communication to the public'' provision in the WPPT (Article 15) involves a right of remuneration, and is not the same ''communication to the public'' right found in the Berne Convention and WCT Article 8.

[387] This flexible approach is known as the ''umbrella solution.'' *See* Miha´ ly Ficsor, World Intellectual Property Organization, Guide to the Copyright and Related Rights Treaties Administered by WIPO and Glossary of Copyright and Related Rights Terms 209 (2003) (WCT Article 8's umbrella solution allows treaty members to implement the making available right through ''a right other than the right of communication to the public or through the combination of different rights''); *id.* at 247–48 (WPPT Articles 10 and 14 apply umbrella solution ''in a fully fledged manner incorporating the neutral description of interactive digital transmissions directly'').

[388] Public Law 105–304, 112 Stat. 2860 (1998).

[389] *See* H.R. Rep. No. 105–551, at 9 (1998) (''The treaties do not require any change in the substance of copyright rights or exceptions in U.S. law.''); *see also WIPO Copyright Treaties Implementation Act and Online Copyright Liability Limitation Act: Hearing on H.R. 2281 and H.R. 2180 Before the H.R. Subcomm. on Courts and Intellectual Property of*

the Comm. on the Judiciary, 105th Cong. 43 (1997) (Register of Copyrights advised Congress that there was ''no need to alter the nature and scope of the copyrights and exceptions, or change the substantive balance of rights embodied in the Copyright Act''). More recent research into the legislative history of U.S. law by Professor David Nimmer and Professor Peter Menell has provided additional textual support regarding Congress's views on the breadth of existing U.S. law and the broad scope of the making available right. *See Melville B. Nimmer and David Nimmer,* 2 Nimmer On Copyright § 8.11 (2012); Peter S. Menell, *In Search of Copyright's Lost Ark: Interpreting the Right to Distribute in the Internet Age,* 59 J. Copyright Soc'y U.S.A. 1, 50–51 (2011).

[390] *Piracy of Intellectual Property on Peer-to-Peer Networks: Hearing Before the Subcomm. on Courts, the Internet, and Intellectual Property of the H. Comm. on the Judiciary,* 107th Cong. 114 (2002) (letter from Marybeth Peters, Register of Copyrights, United States Copyright Office).

[391] *See* Internet Policy Task Force, U.S. Dep't of Commerce, Copyright Policy, Creativity, and Innovation in the Digital Economy 15–16 (2013), *available at http://www.uspto.gov/news/publications/copyrightgreenpaper.pdf* (noting that Copyright Act's distribution right was intended to include ''the mere offering of copies to the public'' and that contrary judicial decisions ''predate . . . recent academic scholarship'' on ''previously unanalyzed legislative history'').

[392] The Section 106 distribution right is far broader than the new distribution right afforded under the WIPO Treaties (WCT art. 6 and WPPT arts. 8, 12).

[393] 991 F.2d 426, 430 (8th Cir. 1993) (''[W]e cannot conclude that an allegation that National 'permitted the use' necessarily amounts to an allegation of the actual distribution of a copy of the program.'').

[394] 118 F.3d 199, 202 (4th Cir. 1997).

[395] *Id.* at 203.

[396] *Id.*

[397] *Diversey* v. *Schmidly,* No. 13–2058, 2013 U.S. App. LEXIS 25506, at *12–13 (10th Cir. Dec. 23, 2013).

[398] *Id.* at *13–14 n.7.

[399] *A&M Records, Inc.* v. *Napster, Inc.,* 239 F.3d 1004, 1014 (9th Cir. 2001); *see also Universal City Studios Prods. LLLP* v. *Bigwood,* 441 F. Supp. 2d 185, 190 (D. Me. 2006) (''[B]y using KaZaA to make copies of the Motion Pictures available to thousands of people over the internet, Defendant violated Plaintiffs' exclusive right to distribute the Motion Pictures.''); *Warner Bros. Records, Inc.* v. *Payne,* 2006 U.S. Dist. LEXIS 65765, at *8 (W.D. Tex. 2006) (''Listing unauthorized copies of sound recordings using an online file-sharing system constitutes an offer to distribute those works, thereby violating a copyright owner's exclusive right of distribution.'').

[400] 542 F. Supp. 2d 153, 168 (D. Mass. 2008) (quoting *Hotaling,* 118 F.3d at 203).

[401] *Id.* at 169.

[402] *See Capitol Records, Inc.* v. *Thomas,* 579 F. Supp. 2d 1210, 1218 (D. Minn. 2008) (concluding it was bound by the holding in *National Car* and stating that although ''the Copyright Act does not offer a uniform definition of 'distribution' . . . Congress's choice to not include offers to do the enumerated acts or the making available of the work indicates its intent that an actual distribution or dissemination is required in § 106(3)''); *Atlantic Recording Corp.* v. *Howell,* 554 F. Supp. 2d 976, 983 (D. Ariz. 2008) (''The statute provides copyright holders with the exclusive right to distribute 'copies' of their works to the public 'by sale or other transfer of ownership, or by rental, lease, or lending.' Unless a copy of the work changes hands in one of the designated ways, a 'distribution' under § 106(3) has not taken place. Merely making an unauthorized copy of a copyrighted work available to the public does not violate a copyright holder's exclusive right of distribution.'').

[403] As noted, in addition to the distribution right, the right of making available also implicates the rights of reproduction, public performance, and public display. The Supreme Court recently grated certiorari in a case involving the scope of the public performance right in the context of online streaming of broadcast television programs. *See Am. Broad. Cos., Inc.* v. *Aereo, Inc.*, 82 U.S.L.W. 3241 (U.S. Jan. 10, 2014) (No. 13–461). Oral argument is scheduled for April 22, 2014.

[404] *See The Scope of Copyright Protection: Hearing Before the Subcomm. on Intellectual Property, Courts, and the Internet of the H. Comm. on the Judiciary,* 113th Cong. (2014), available at http:// judiciary.house.gov/index.cfm/2014/1/the-scope-of- copyright-protection.

[405] *See* Statement of David Nimmer, Professor, UCLA School of Law, *The Scope of Copyright Protection, supra* note 20 (''Nimmer Statement''); Statement of Glynn S. Lunney, Jr., Professor, Tulane University School of Law, *The Scope of Copyright Protection, supra* note 20 (''Lunney Statement''). These witness statements are available at *http:// docs.house.gov/ Committee/Calendar/ ByEvent.aspx?EventID=101642*.

[406] *See* Nimmer Statement at 2–3; Lunney Statement at 1–4.

[407] Study on the Right of Making Available; Comments and Public Roundtable, 79 FR 10571 (Feb. 25, 2014).

[408] WIPO Copyright Treaty art. 8, Dec. 20, 1996, 36 I.L.M. 65; WIPO Performances and Phonograms Treaty arts. 10, 14, Dec. 20, 1996, 36 I.L.M. 76.

[409] *See Making Available Study,* U.S. Copyright Office, *http://www. copyright.gov/docs/ making_available/.*

[410] *See* 17 U.S.C. 101.

[411] 573 U.S., No. 13–461, 2014 U.S. LEXIS 4496 (June 25, 2014).

[412] *See* 17 U.S.C. 106(4).

[413] *Id.* section 101 (definition of ''To perform . . . a work 'publicly' '').

[414] *Aereo,* 2014 U.S. LEXIS 4496, at *19 (alterations added). *See* 17 U.S.C. 101 (''To 'transmit' a performance or display is to communicate it by any device or process whereby images or sounds are received beyond the place from which they are sent.'').

[415] *Aereo,* 2014 U.S. LEXIS 4496, at *28.

[416] *Id.* at *42 (Scalia, J., dissenting).

[417] Study on the Right of Making Available; Request for Additional Comments, 79 FR 41309 (July 15, 2014).

[418] The national laws reviewed are identified in the last column of the chart. In some cases, official English translations of foreign laws were not available and informal translations were used to evaluate the statutory provisions at issue and place them in the appropriate category. Furthermore, this chart represents a snapshot in time; copyright law reform was under consideration in several countries at the time this Report was issued in February 2016, and proposed legislation is not reflected in this chart.

[419] For inclusion in this category, the foreign statute contains the WCT phrase (or some close variation thereof): "including the making available to the public of their works in such a way that members of the public may access these works from a place and at a time individually chosen by them." In a few instances, a European county had a law where the communication-to-the-public right is part of, or a subset of, a larger making available right. In that case, these countries (specifically Denmark, Finland, Ireland, and Sweden) have been categorized as Internet Treaties Model/Part of the CTTP Right because the right of making available, as expressed statutorily there, appears to be intertwined with the communication-to-the-public right.

[420] In some Alternative Language Model countries, the statutory language appears to closely track the WCT language but includes additional words or phrases such as "telecommunication" or "information network" that may reflect influences from other legal and regulatory schemes of that country. In other Alternative Language Model countries, the language used to

provide for an explicit communication-to-the-public or making available right deviates more significantly from the WIPO Internet Treaties language.

In: Creative Works …
Editor: Brandon S. Casey
ISBN: 978-1-63485-522-8

Chapter 2

STATEMENT OF DAVID NIMMER, PROFESSOR, UCLA SCHOOL OF LAW. HEARING ON "THE SCOPE OF COPYRIGHT PROTECTION"*

POLICY CONSIDERATIONS RELATING TO COPYRIGHT LAW'S "MAKING AVAILABLE" RIGHT

I. Framing the Issue

I thank the House Judiciary Committee for inviting me to address a critical question that goes to the essential functioning of copyright protection in the modern age—whether the act of placing (or "uploading") a digital file containing a copyrighted work into an Internet-accessible resource, such as a filesharing folder, violates copyright law. More precisely, the issue at hand is whether that act of uploading should itself be considered to violate the copyright owner's exclusive rights or, alternatively, whether the copyright owner should be required to shoulder the burden of proving, in addition, that a third party downloaded that particular digital file, before the person who uploaded it can be held responsible.

To confront the matter in a concrete posture, let us imagine that a user uploads a full copy of the motion picture *Avatar* to a share folder operated by a

* This is an edited, reformatted and augmented version of a statement presented January 14, 2014 before the House Judiciary Committee, Subcommittee on Courts, Intellectual Property and the Internet.

peer-to-peer (P2P) service. The consequence is that anyone else on that P2P network can watch *Avatar* at no charge. The issue under examination is whether the copyright owner should be able to state a claim for infringement against that individual by showing proof of the unauthorized upload—or conversely, should be forced to prove, as part of its case in chief, that other third parties subsequently downloaded that particular copy of *Avatar*.

To be clear at the outset, there is no stand-alone "making available" right. Instead, current copyright law accords proprietors various exclusive rights, including the right to distribute their works to the public. The item currently on the table is whether the activity of making a work available is one means by which a plaintiff can demonstrate that its existing distribution rights have been violated.

In resolving such matters posing the "making available" question as the above *Avatar* hypothetical, courts have ruled on both sides and there is no clear path towards resolution of this split of authority. The matter therefore becomes ripe for clarification by Congress. For the reasons set forth below, I respectfully suggest that the better course of congressional action is to reaffirm the existence of a "making available" right. That course of action streamlines judicial procedures, comports with our treaty obligations, and continues the sound policy adopted by Congress in past copyright enactments.

II. The Historic Basis for the "Making Available" Right

Before turning to the core policy analysis, I note that this issue arises largely as the result of an arcane jurisprudential twist that was long submerged in the 1976 Copyright Act's turgid history, and only recently excavated. The matter has been the subject of confusion and controversy in the federal courts, the legal academy, the press, and among the public since it first rose to the fore more than a decade ago.

From the passage of the first federal copyright law in 1790 through the 1909 Act that governed throughout most of the twentieth century, copyright law recognized the "twofold right to make and to *publish* copies" as the "historic basis of copyright."[1] Had the 1976 Act retained the terminology of "right to publish," the "making available" question likely never would have arisen, given that the act of "publication" entails no requirement that a copyrighted work be received by a third person. Merely making a copyrighted work available to the public without authorization would have violated the copyright owner's right to "publish" under the old regime.

In fact, though, the actual language adopted in the Copyright Act of 1976 rendered the issue murky. That Act recast the historic right to publish as the right "to distribute."[2] Nonetheless, until the advent of file-sharing technology at the turn of the millennium, whether actual receipt of a copy formulated an element of proof was of little significance. Most copyright enforcement actions were premised on violations of the *reproduction* right;[3] the relatively rare cases invoking the *distribution* right involved unusual scenarios, such as placing a copyrighted work in a library that was open to the public. NIMMER ON COPYRIGHT, along with other treatises, reported on the sparse interpretations of the distribution right, but did not delve into the legislative history that might reveal why Congress shifted from a right to "publish" to a right to "distribute." (More on that score is explicated in Appendix 1 to this statement.)

It was only after record companies began suing music file-sharers en masse a decade ago that this theoretical puzzle assumed salience. Lacking compelling guidance, some courts construed the language of the 1976 Act to afford copyright owners the right to make their works available as a construction of the statute's distribution right, others reached the opposite conclusion.[4]

In response to those divided rulings, Prof. Peter Menell (with whom I had coauthored several past copyright articles) mined the legislative history of the 1976 Act to develop insight into this fundamental question of how to construe the copyright owner's distribution right.[5] As Prof. Menell's exegesis details, the change in terminology from the right to "publish" to the right to "distribute" in the 1976 Copyright Act stemmed not from any legislative intention to narrow the historic publication right, but rather out of concern over the confusing jurisprudence surrounding technical details inherent in the law of "publication" (namely, the distinction between *investive* and *divestive* publication). Examined closely, the legislative history of the 1976 Copyright Act confirmed that the drafters intended to *broaden* protection beyond the historic publication right, in order "to avoid any questions as to whether 'publish' or 'vend' is used in such a narrow sense that there might be forms of distribution not covered."[6]

That voluminous history affords no indication that Congress intended to impose an "actual receipt" requirement on the exercise of the distribution right. To the contrary, the general legislative history reveals that Congress drafted the Copyright Act's exclusive rights in broad terms so that authors' rights would not lose their value because of "unforeseen technical advances" that might unfold "10, 20 or 50 years" in the future.[7] The particular legislative history looking "50 years" into the future actually was articulated 49 years ago[8]— making return to it particularly timely today.[9]

After examining the contemporaneous explanation behind the shift in terminology during the revision process of the Copyright Act that took place from the 1950s through 1971, as illuminated in Prof. Menell's article, I invited him to collaborate in redrafting the sections of NIMMER ON COPYRIGHT devoted to that subject matter. The revised treatise now reflects the conclusion—as a matter of statutory interpretation—that a prima facie case of infringing a copyright owner's distribution right does not require proof of "actual distribution," namely someone downloading a concrete file that another previously uploaded.

III. The Policy Underlying the "Making Available" Right

That history serves as prologue. The focus of today's hearing is not on the proper interpretation of the words that were enacted as part of the 1976 Act, but instead on the optimal policy for Congress to adopt going forward with respect to this thorny and highstakes question of copyright law.

A. The Need to Act

As noted above, district courts have reached conflicting rulings regarding the existence of a "making available" aspect of the copyright owner's distribution right. As a result, both copyright holders and potential target defendants have been left wondering what the precise extent of their rights and liabilities might be. Last month, the first appellate court to confront the scope of the distribution right since the publication of Prof. Menell's research endorsing the "making available" theory handed down its ruling. The Tenth Circuit agreed with both that article and the discussion of that issue in NIMMER ON COPYRIGHT, relying on both sources.[10]

In doing so, however, the court recognized the "dissensus, particularly among district courts," regarding this issue.[11] Other circuit courts may follow the Tenth Circuit's lead—or may decline to do so. At the present time, uncertainty continues to cloud the legal rights and liabilities fundamental to the recording, motion picture, and publishing industries As such, legislative clarification of the "making available" right is appropriate, if not imperative.

The Register of Copyrights has issued a clarion call for legislative reform.[12]Attentive to that suggestion, this committee has scheduled a number of hearings.[13] For today's hearing, the committee specifically has asked for my views on the "making available" component of the copyright owner's distribution right.

B. Defining the "Making Available" Right to Serve Copyright Law's Goals

The premise of our copyright law is that enforcement of the Act's exclusive rights generally promotes progress in the creative arts. Those considerations lead organically to recognition of the "making available" right. When a studio releases a current picture such as *The Wolf of Wall Street* in theaters, or an older film such as *Avatar* in Blu-ray, there is simply no valid reason for a P2P user to place the entirety of that work in a share folder accessible to the world-at-large. The issue is not "remixing" or generating other "user generated content," as those aspects are inapplicable to the hypothesized upload of an entire motion picture. Neither is the issue the facilitation of third-party "sampling"—interested fans enjoy many legal avenues to view trailers for that film (or, in the case of music, to listen to a segment on iTunes, for example) without the work's entirety being uploaded to a share folder.

Both sides of the "making available" issue recognize that copyright owners enjoy the exclusive right to control distribution of their works; their only point of disagreement concerns the quantum of proof needed to demonstrate that distribution took place (simple uploading for proponents of the right, uploading plus proven downloading for its opponents). Thus, both should agree that deterring unauthorized distribution (properly defined) promotes progress in the creative arts by empowering creators to determine when and how to commercialize their works. To proponents of the "making available" right, its creation of effective enforcement against uploaders of entire films "will channel consumers into the marketplace for copyrighted works—increasing the ability of creators to appropriate a return to their efforts, competition, and incentives to develop improved dissemination technologies and platforms."[14]

To be sure, even for opponents of the "making available" aspect of the distribution right, the same consequences flow. The difference is that, under their scheme, there is much less certainty of reaching those consequences, and the need to slog through cumbersome legal maneuvering before reaching them. For the reasons set forth in the next subsection, that maneuvering carries heavy burdens without any corresponding gain that might justify its adoption.

C. Streamlining Judicial Proceedings

The salient difference between recognizing or denying the existence of a "making available" component as part of the copyright owner's distribution right inheres in how P2P cases unfold in the courts. If that right is recognized, then proof of the plaintiff's case becomes extremely straightforward: Once evidence has been presented that the plaintiff uploaded the totality of the copyrighted work in question, the plaintiff's case in chief is complete. At that point, expeditious procedures, such as summary judgment, can quickly resolve the entire matter. Indeed, if Congress were to couple recognition of the "making available" right with the adjunct amendments offered below—tightening up damage awards and furnishing a "small claims" tribunal for resolution of P2P claims—the amount of judicial time saved in these matters promises to be immense.

By contrast, if the "making available" right is denied, then essentially every P2P upload case becomes a trying exercise in laborious discovery. The copyright owner, after identifying the uploader in question, would need to issue subpoenas to Internet Service Providers in order to furnish the identity of the subscribers behind the Internet Protocol addresses that have engaged in downloading from that user. Extensive monitoring would be required, in order to generate that list. After the subpoenas have issued, the copyright owners would still need to slog through the type of extensive discovery disputes that have punctuated these proceedings in the past. Among the issues that judges across the country have confronted in P2P proceedings are the following: improper joinder and severance in the context of "swarms" from which a given copyrighted work is accessed by numerous users; whether personal jurisdiction and venue are properly asserted in the district in question against numerous downloaders scattered across the country; the need for specially tailored protective orders; when intervention is permissive to challenge the scope of the copyright owners' subpoenas; whether those subpoenas compromise their targets' rights of due process; and a hornet's nest of other procedural pitfalls (including the ones detailed in the next section).[15]

D. Protecting User Privacy

Additional defenses have arisen in the raft of P2P cases just mentioned that implicate user privacy. Some challenge those subpoenas as a statutory matter under the Electronic Communications Privacy Act.[16] Others, more broadly, invoke the Constitution to protect the anonymity interests of those targeted by subpoenas.[17] As a matter of First Amendment doctrine, those challenges have proven largely unsuccessful in the past.[18] Nonetheless, the broader policy implications of those challenges remain of the utmost concern at present and for the future.

History affords invaluable perspective here. Let us revert to the world of 1955, when Congress first embarked on the copyright reform that ultimately culminated in adoption of the 1976 Act. At that time, the copyright owner enjoyed the exclusive right to "publish, copy, [or] vend the copyrighted work."[19] Someone who published the work without authorization was therefore an infringer (absent affirmative defenses); likewise the vendor who purveyed a work produced by another. Accordingly, if we imagine a bookstore in 1955 featuring numerous copies of *The Good Shepherd* by C.S. Forester stacked up on a table near the front door, the case against the store owner was complete. In other words, copyright law at that time imposed no obligation to place undercover agents near the cash register to develop evidence that third-party customers actually walked out with copies of the book in hand.

Still, if such evidence had been affirmatively required in that era, the exercise at least could have been performed—it simply would have been a needless waste, and for that reason never formed part of the copyright owner's case for copyright infringement. By contrast, if Congress were to adopt a new regime defining the distribution right not to incorporate the right of "making available," the result would be to saddle copyright owners with the burden of developing evidence regarding third party downloads. Unlike the hypothesized investigator standing unobtrusively in the corner of a 1955 store, the consequences in 2014 would be far more intrusive—and troubling. On the one hand, the exercise might require the type of after-the-fact investigation just described, of massive subpoenas served on ISPs to disclose subscriber identities. Alternatively, it could necessitate even more invasive measures—one can imagine systematic dragnets placed in advance on P2P systems, in order to identify everyone who is undertaking every transaction there, such that they can be identified later and charged with facilitating infringement. Given how unpopular and contentious this type of comprehensive electronic data-vacuuming has proven of late, we should powerfully disfavor "potentially offensive strategies that have deleterious implications for privacy, anonymity, and freedom of expression."[20]

One attempt to avoid this dilemma that prospective plaintiffs have employed in the past is to send their investigators to download copyrighted works directly from the defendant who uploaded it. If the opponents of a "making available" right would concede the adequacy of that procedure, it could at least be performed without engendering the invasion of numerous third parties' privacy interests. Yet that expedient itself has been rejected by those defending P2P uploading cases, who have interposed the defense that the investigator's conduct on behalf of the copyright owner "ratifies" the distribution in question, thus rendering it unable to sustain an infringement claim.[21] The important point for the present is that the entire problem can be avoided simply by confirming the existence of the "making available" aspect of the copyright owner's distribution right.

The Supreme Court has called the probable scope of P2P infringement "staggering,"[22] and even those courts that construe the statutory language of the 1976 Act not to include a "making available" right agree with the proposition that "continuous, highvolume file sharing—offering exact duplicates to millions of peer-to-peer users for free— would negatively affect the market for these copyrighted works."[23] When vacating the damages component of that last ruling, the Court of Appeals added, "Between 1999 and 2008, the recording industry as a whole suffered a fifty percent drop in both sales and revenues, a figure plaintiffs attribute to the rise of illegal downloading."[24] Under those circumstances, it is difficult to imagine how sound policy could favor solicitude to filesharers, allowing them to evade liability depending on the vicissitudes of evidence-gathering from third parties.

In sum, the only effect of rejecting "making available" is to unduly raise the costs of enforcing the copyright owner's distribution right, with the unfortunate concomitant of reducing the deterrent effects of copyright enforcement. The better path of the law is to discourage unauthorized filesharing of copyrighted works, channeling fans of such works into the marketplace, which thereby increases the rewards available to creators.[25]

E. Complying with Treaty Obligations

The foregoing considerations have focused on domestic concerns. When we broaden our perspective to encompass the requirements of international law, additional reasons emerge for Congress to adopt an explicit "making available" right into our copyright laws.

The U.S. adheres to several multilateral copyright treaties, which require all adherents (such as the United States) to embody such a provision. Indeed, the precise phrase of "making available" entered the copyright lexicon from the two WIPO Internet Treaties, which the United States was instrumental in formulating.[26]

The first treaty accords copyright owners a general "right of communication," which includes "the exclusive right of … the making available to the public of their works in such a way that members of the public may access these works from a place and at a time individually chosen by them."[27] The other treaty incorporates articles captioned "Right of Making Available of Fixed Performances" and "Right of Making Available of Phonograms."[28]

Since those two treaties were formulated in 1996, the United States government has consistently taken the position that our domestic copyright law already includes the "making available" right within the existing distribution right.[29] By the same token, the Register of Copyrights has stated to Congress that "making [a work] available for other users of [a] peer to peer network to download ... constitutes an infringement of the exclusive distribution right…."[30]

Moving backwards and forwards in time from those 1996 treaties strengthens the treaty rationale for recognizing the "making available" right. Back in 1971, the United States ratified the Geneva Convention for the Protection of Producers of Phonograms Against Unauthorized Duplication of Their Phonograms.[31] That treaty obligates member states to "protect the producers of phonograms . . . against the making of duplicates without the consent of the producer . . . and against the distribution of such duplicates to the public."[32] The last clause, in turn, is defined as "any act by which duplicates of a phonogram are *offered*, directly or indirectly, to the general public or any section thereof."[33] Thus, in substance if not by name, the "making available" right of international copyright law dates back over forty years.

More recently, the United States has entered into free trade agreements (FTAs) with twenty other countries,[34] obligating this nation to provide a "making available" right tracking the language of the WIPO Internet Treaties.[35] Based on all the extensive history noted above, the General Counsel of the United States Copyright Office concluded that "the United States is obligated by a number of treaties and trade agreements to provide a making available right."[36]

F. Separating Out Issues that Do Not Bear on "Making Available"

To avoid confusion, it is essential not to be sidetracked by collateral issues that exert no effect on the current investigation. A number of hot-button issues can arise in the context of peer-to-peer services that, by themselves, may warrant redress—but because they do not bear on the "making available" right, they fall outside today's scope.

For instance, a given individual might use only 15 seconds out of *Avatar* for the purpose of engaging in her own remix. If sued, she could defend herself by asserting the fair use doctrine. Although all the circumstances would need to be ventilated to determine the robustness of that defense, in the abstract, it seems likely to prevail. That fair use doctrine arises as an affirmative defense asserted by the defendant. The matter at hand, by contrast, concerns only the plaintiff's prima facie case of infringement. If the "making available" right is recognized as part of the copyright owner's distribution right, then the plaintiff's case is complete once proof is tendered that the defendant uploaded the file in question; at that point, the case can revolve around her fair use defense of remixing, which she remains free to develop in full. Conversely, if the "making available" right is not recognized, the plaintiff will have to separately prove the existence of a downloader; at that juncture, the case will still proceed to the fair use defense of remixing. Thus, remixing has nothing to do with the instant policy determination regarding the "making available" right.

The same considerations apply across the board to all other affirmative defenses. Let us imagine that a different user buys a DVD of *Avatar* and then uploads it to a P2P service, ostensibly in order to watch it at his vacation home. If sued, that hypothetical defendant might defend himself by asserting that his "space shifting" amounts to fair use or is otherwise defensible under the "first sale" doctrine. Again, all the circumstances would need to be ventilated to determine the robustness of those defenses but, in the abstract, they seem unlikely to prevail; after all, that individual could easily watch the movie at his vacation home without making it accessible to millions of others through a P2P network. The important point, once again, is that those putative defenses will arise regardless of whether the law recognizes a "making available" right.

In short, the question on the table is how much proof to require of a plaintiff whose works have been uploaded without permission, which is a matter of calibrating the case in chief. Affirmative defenses are, by definition, wholly independent of the case in chief. Therefore, the matter at hand should not be clouded with such distractions as fair use and the "first sale" doctrine, as they raise affirmative defenses that do not affect the "making available" right.

By the same token, the current investigation focuses on the case in chief for *direct* liability; it is not concerned with *indirect* liability, whether denominated vicarious liability, contributory infringement, or inducing infringement. The standards adopted for "making available" are therefore distinct from those doctrines, which remain unaffected by any clarification that the copyright owner's distribution right extends to the unauthorized uploading of protected works. One may add that online services that are sought to be held accountable for works made available through their instrumentality enjoy an additional statutory safe harbor from liability.[37] As yet another affirmative defense, that aspect falls outside the current investigation, for the reasons already articulated.

To belabor what is *not* at issue in the current investigation, there should be no relitigation of any copyright cases posing issues other than proof of the copyright owner's distribution right. As already noted, there is no stand-alone "making available" right. Therefore, no new causes of action should be permitted under the self-standing rubric of making works available; neither individual users of copyrighted works nor online service providers should be concerned about facing new-fangled theories of liability. Instead, the only matter under scrutiny at present is how a copyright owner can prove violation of its distribution right—proponents of the "making available" right believe that proof of that violation occurs by showing that the subject work has been uploaded; opponents maintain that additional proof is required that the copy in question was subsequently downloaded. Anything beyond that question falls outside the scope of today's hearing.

Another aspect that should not be conflated with the current inquiry arises out of the large number of P2P suits that have arisen against those who obtain access to pornographic material. A flood of such complaints has been filed; individual cases often target thousands of individual defendants in a single pleading.[38] Typically, those cases arise in the mirrorimage of such cases as our *Avatar* hypothetical above, in which the copyright owner files suit against an uploader for unauthorized exploitation of its distribution right through making the work available. In the pornography context, by contrast, it is usually the copyright owner itself who uploads the work in question, in the hopes of ensnaring numerous parties as downloaders who have engaged in unauthorized exploitation of its distribution right.[39]

The vice of those pornography cases is that, after a particular downloader has been identified by his ISP, "To save himself from embarrassment, even if he is not the infringer, the subscriber will very likely pay the settlement price. And if the subscriber is a business, it will likely pay the settlement to save itself from the hassle and cost of complying with discovery—even though one of its customers or employees is the actual infringer."[40]

One judge has condemned the filing of those sort of P2P complaints as "essentially an extortion scheme" in which "many Does will send back a nuisance-value check to the plaintiff."[41] For current purpose, the vital feature is that each John Doe who sends back a check has already been identified through discovery as a downloader of the particular file in question. Therefore, even if the law were modified to eliminate any "making available" right, that unfortunate spate of pornography cases would continue unabated. In other words, the same mischief would continue to unfold in those cases, which arise only after the plaintiff has issued subpoenas to "the ISPs to obtain the identities of these Does."[42] Therefore, imposing a burden on the plaintiffs beyond proof of the "making available" of its works cannot shut down any of those "extortion schemes."

But the cost of imposing that burden on non-pornography copyright plaintiffs in general would be to make enforcement geometrically more complicated in their non-extortionate cases. In a universe containing no "making available" aspect of the distribution right, the complaint filed against those who upload *Avatar* to P2P sites for no legitimate reason would be transmuted into an inherently complex proceeding. That change represents a loss with no corresponding gain. For all these reasons, the best policy is for Congress to recognize that the copyright owner's distribution right includes a "making available" component.

IV. Changes Adjunct to Clarification of the "Making Available" Right

Of course, any amendment to the Copyright Act must fit into its larger fabric. In that spirit, I would like to broaden our current focus, to consider alterations to other aspects of copyright law that fit naturally with a recognition of the "making available" right.

A. Rationalization of Statutory Damages

In the case of the "making available" right, the same district judges who rejected that doctrine also systematically overturned the jury verdicts rendered against file-sharers as unconscionably large.[43] The affected trial judges viewed the conduct of file-sharing as wrongful, but nonetheless "fairly low on the totem pole of reprehensible conduct"[44] such that defendants who made no personal profit from such file-sharing should not saddled with multi-million dollar judgments. The dilemma that those judges faced is that Congress set the level of statutory damages in 1999—prior to the full onslaught of the P2P era—to allow recovery of up to $150,000 per infringed work. Given that one individual may share many thousand files, the theoretical multiplication of damages becomes astronomical.

The potential of such stratospheric statutory damages seems to have functioned as the proverbial "elephant in the room" when it came time for those district judges to construe whether the 1976 Act incorporates a "making available" component of the distribution right.[45] The unpalatability of those mega-awards may have influenced them to deny the existence of a "making available" right, whereas they very well may have recognized the existence of that same right, had it been prone to give rise to more reasonable recoveries.

The time is ripe for Congress to confront the appropriate level of statutory damages for the digital age. An individual file-sharer should face meaningful recovery, far more than the amount that could have been paid at the outset to obey the law or a slap on the wrist reflecting a modest increase over that amount. Sitting as a district judge, Justice Sotomayor captured the essential features that a sensible law must embody: Statutory damages "serve the dual purposes of the Copyright Act—compensation and deterrence."[46] At the same time that the amount of statutory damages "should bear some relationship to the actual damages suffered,"[47] they must not be "calibrated to favor a defendant by merely awarding minimum estimated losses to a plaintiff."[48]

On the other hand, statutory damages against an individual file-sharer should not ramify to the level of a small nation's gross national product. It is not necessary for a Jamie Thomas-Rassett to face a multi-billion dollar award in order to deter her infringement and provide just compensation to the plaintiffs. In sum, at the same time that Congress reassesses the "making available" right, it should appropriately calibrate recovery of statutory damages.

B. Institution of Small Claims Courts for Routine P2P Cases

Some years ago, the Copyright Office reported to this committee, "we believe that consideration of new procedures, such as establishment of a 'small claims' or other inexpensive dispute resolution procedure, would be an important issue for further study by Congress."[49] In 2012, the Office completed two series of hearings on the subject. Its report should be issued in the near future.

The raft of P2P cases in which no cognizable affirmative defense is presented seems ideal for summary disposition. If the range of available damages is limited, as proposed above, then there should be little impediment to their orderly resolution. Therefore, as part of the full parcel of reforms, Congress may wish to consider the appropriate shuttling of those cases to a newly established tribunal for resolution by a type of copyright "small claims" court.

C. Attention to Other Aspects of the Distribution Right

Today's hearing is devoted to the "making available" right, which is a subspecies of the copyright owner's distribution right. In the context of fine-tuning the distribution right, it only makes sense to examine all of its components. That exercise could reasonably lead, in turn, to at least two other contested aspects of the distribution right, apart from its "making available" component.

The first concerns the interplay between the copyright owner's distribution right (insofar as it is incorporated into a coordinate importation right[50]) and the exception to the distribution right for particular copies that have been lawfully made, colloquially called the "first sale" doctrine.[51] In short, the question arises whether "gray market" goods lawfully manufactured abroad may be imported into the United States, or conversely may be excluded at the border. After decades of divided rulings on the subject from lower tribunals, the United States Supreme Court last year adopted a scheme of "international exhaustion," effectively allowing such importations.[52] The dissent complained that the Court's ruling placed the United States in derogation of our treaty obligations, as well as out of sync with our trading partners.[53] The majority responded that the determination whether copyright owners should have the "commercial power to divide international markets is a matter for Congress to decide."[54] This issue forms part of the constellation of the copyright owner's distribution right, and hence is live for review in the broader context of the matters at issue in today's hearing.

The second also concerns the reach of the "first sale" doctrine, but this time solely in the domestic context. The flash point in past cases has arisen with regard to software. In 1980, Congress defined computer programs as a type of "literary work" in the eyes of the Copyright Act. Just as old novels and textbooks can be freely sold at second-hand shops or lent out by libraries, the same status applies to old diskettes, CD-ROMs, and the like. But Congress tweaked that treatment in 1990, by prohibiting the *rental* of copies of computer programs, at the same time continuing to allow their untrammeled *sale*.[55]

The legal consequence of that progression is that extant law allows resale equally of old books and old CD-ROMs. In practice, nonetheless, most courts have drawn a line between those two domains. The majority rule has banned copies of computer programs from resale on the secondary market, with some decisions ruling to the contrary.[56] At present, Congress therefore has the option of clarifying its intent: barring resale of books and ROMs alike;

allowing their resale alike; or constructing one rule for "literary works" in the nature of software and another for literary works that more traditionally fit that moniker. The matter obviously requires considerable finesse, to formulate the optimal resolution.

Taking the matter one step further, we stand at the cusp of a major paradigm-shift today. The advent of "cloud computing" portends a world in which books, records, videos, ROMs, and other physical media are no longer sold. Instead, users will be able to obtain temporary access via their computer screens to the bestsellers they wish to read, the hits they wish to hear, the blockbusters they wish to watch, and the software they wish to run.[57] In that world of The Cloud, there is no "owner of a particular copy" able to assert a "first sale" defense.[58] Notwithstanding that "United States copyright law historically has carved out important exceptions to the rights of copyright owners,"[59] that history faces its potential end in the storm of The Cloud. Fair use could be rendered into "fare" use, as every private utilization of protected expression becomes transformed into a revenue-generating opportunity.[60]

Confronting these questions, Congress could determine, at one extreme, that the "first sale" doctrine was only needed ancillary to the legal doctrine of alienation of physical chattels, and therefore has no purchase in the world of The Cloud. Or it could determine, at the opposite end, that the "first sale" doctrine has served as an essential counterbalance to proprietors' rights since it was articulated in 1908 and remains necessary even today and tomorrow to guard against "a 'pay per use' society."[61] It could also choose an intermediate point on the spectrum as the ideal compromise. As deep waters swirl here whose depths have not been remotely plumbed, the matter can only be identified at present as a fitting item for further study.[62]

V. Possible Alternative Directions

The subject matter of today's hearing is recognition of the copyright owner's distribution right as including the right of "making available." Nonetheless, because we stand at the very start of the process of copyright reform, it is possible that new directions will emerge with the passage of time. When Congress started to consider reform of the 1909 Act, it took more than two decades to reach fruition. Many changes of directions are therefore possible, as Congress grapples with the best avenues to reform the 1976 Act.

A. *Defining Rights More Broadly than "Distribution"*

One possibility is to carve up rights differently. At its adoption in1976, the Act accorded five exclusive rights to copyright owners. Dissension has arisen over all five of those rights, not solely as to *distribution*—witness Circuit Judge Chin's scathing critique of a recent Second Circuit construction of the *performance* right not to apply to a service offering its subscribers the ability to view over-the-air shows on demand.[63] One can find equal dissension concerning the other rights of the copyright owner.

In 1995, Congress added a sixth right, in an amendment designed to accommodate the digital age—the Digital Performance Right in Sound Recordings Act of 1995.[64] Unfortunately, technology moves quickly, often faster than lawmaking. In fact, the hermetic boundaries separating distribution from performance and from reproduction had already broken down by the time that amendment was adopted, rendering suspect much of that 1995 handiwork.[65] Accordingly, the question arises whether the unitary flow of digits in the current world would be better suited by one omnibus right under copyright, as opposed to the five-fold division adopted a half-century ago (or its six-fold enumeration elaborated two decades ago).

The 1996 WIPO Copyright Treaty takes a step in that direction. One of its articles accords a "right of communication to the public."[66] It is possible that variations on that wording could set the framework for a better scheme than attempting artificial separation between the current six-fold enumeration of rights. But it is important to realize that even that Treaty provision is drafted to explicitly "includ[e] the making available to the public of their works in such a way that members of the public may access these works from a place and at a time individually chosen by them."[67] Thus, even with a reformulation of rights, it appears likely that any well-drafted copyright law will include a "making available" right as part of the copyright owner's arsenal. Without prejudging the issue, it would therefore appear that the subject matter of today's hearing will continue to form part of the backbone of any revised Copyright Act.

B. *Defining Distribution as Other Than a "Right"*

Of course, even more radical revisions to the Copyright Act are conceivable. Rather than according copyright owners the legal right to control unauthorized distribution of their works, the concept of *superdistribution* turns the legal scheme on its head by making all works of authorship made publicly available in encrypted form and encouraging their widespread dissemination.[68] Besides that strategy, other commentators have proposed a variety of new approaches to solve the P2P phenomenon, ranging from imposition of levies to "entertainment taxes" to governmental subventions of the arts.[69]

These proposals face obstacles in terms of both feasibility and treaty incompatibility.[70] None has gained sufficient traction to make it an obvious candidate for legislative reform. Nonetheless, it is impossible at present to predict what twists and turns the future legislative process may assume. In the event that one of those options were to gain consideration, its effect on copyright law's "making available" right would need to be evaluated.

APPENDIX 1.

The bulk of my written statement confronts the policy implications of the "making available" right. In the past, I have written up the doctrinal basis for that right under the language adopted as part of the Copyright Act of 1976. The additional considerations set forth below flesh out that aspect of the matter.

1. A number of cases have construed the Copyright Act of 1976 not to include any "making available" component of the distribution right, and have cited my writings to support that proposition. Illustrative is a 2008 case so holding:

> The general rule, supported by the great weight of authority, is that "infringement of [the distribution right] requires an actual dissemination of either copies or phonorecords." * * * 2 DAVID NIMMER and MELVILLE B. NIMMER, NIMMER ON COPYRIGHT § 8.11[A], at 8-149 (2007) ("Infringement of [the distribution right] requires an actual dissemination of either copies or phonorecords.").[71]

That analysis in NIMMER ON COPYRIGHT § 8.11[A] attempts to vindicate the language of the distribution right as enacted in the 1976 Act. By contrast, the instant written statement focuses on the policy implications of a prospective amendment to the 1976 Act. The two tasks are distinct. Nonetheless, it is worth sketching the genesis of the sentence as quoted from the treatise. Its background arose out of a suit that was filed two decades ago.

In the early 1990s, a man named Michael Agee contended that Paramount violated the distribution right in his Laurel and Hardy sound recordings by transmitting those works. The Southern District of New York issued a tortured opinion about the performance right that threatened to set the law on the wrong path.[72] The Second Circuit stopped that approach in its tracks, as can be observed from the following excerpt:

> 3. *Distribution Right.* Agee contends that Paramount infringed his exclusive right to distribute his sound recording when it transmitted Hard Copy, including his work, by satellite to the TV stations because such a transmission constituted a distribution of one or more copies of his recording "to the public" under 17 U.S.C. § 106(3). His contention is meritless.
>
> * * *
>
> We find no basis for concluding that Paramount's transmission of Agee's recording to viewers via the TV stations, rather than directly, was a "distribution." In a slightly different context, a number of courts have held that "transmissions by a cable network or service to local cable companies who in turn transmit to individual cable subscribers constitute 'public performances' by the network under [the Copyright Act]."
>
> * * *
>
> It is clear that merely transmitting a sound recording to the public on the airwaves does not constitute a "distribution"; otherwise, sound recording copyright owners would have the performance rights expressly denied to them under the statute. For this reason, distribution is generally thought to require transmission of a "material object" in which the sound recording is fixed: a work that is of "more than transitory duration." *See* 17 U.S.C. § 101 (defining "copy"); David Nimmer and Melville B. Nimmer, 2 NIMMER ON COPYRIGHT, § 8.11[A] (1993) (distribution right is right "publicly to sell, give away, rent or lend any material embodiment of copyrighted work"). *See also* House Report at 138 ("any form or dissemination in which a material object does not change hands—performances or displays on television, for example—is not a publication no matter how many people are exposed").
>
> Although we are unwilling to say that disseminations must always be in physical form to constitute "distributions," *see, e.g., Playboy Enterprises, Inc. v. Frena*, 839 F. Supp. 1552 (M.D. Fla. 1993) (unauthorized uploading of copyrighted images onto computer bulletin board with knowledge that images would be downloaded by other bulletin board subscribers), in the broadcasting context, the distinction between material and non-material embodiments, and the fact that Paramount, like most television and radio broadcasting networks, transmitted its program for broadcast to the public, are relevant factors in

> determining whether Paramount engaged in broadcasting rather than distribution. We conclude that Paramount's transmission of Agee's recording constituted a performance of that recording and not a distribution.[73]

After that decision was handed down, I revised the text and footnotes of § 8.11[A], as cited by the Second Circuit, to reflect the developments of that case. The 1996 edition of NIMMER ON COPYRIGHT therefore included a paragraph as follows:

> Infringement of this right requires an actual dissemination of either copies or phonorecords. A public performance of a work is not a publication and hence, even if unauthorized does not infringe the distribution right. Given that transmissions qualify as public performances, liability for that conduct lies outside the distribution right.[74]

The footnote accompanying that text cited *Agee*. It is the first sentence of that excerpt that is quoted out of context by decisions such as the one noted above.

To appreciate what that excerpt conveyed and did not convey, it is useful to posit two propositions of law:

- *Proposition 1:* To violate the copyright owner's distribution right, plaintiff must show that a tangible copy of the work passed hands, rather than to show the existence of a volatile instantiation by which the public got to experience the work. In other words, there had to be "actual distribution" of the work, not its constructive "distribution" over the airwaves.
- *Proposition 2:* To violate the copyright owner's distribution right, plaintiff must show not only that the subject work was offered to the public, but also that the transaction was consummated. In other words, there had to be an "actual distribution" of a given copy to a proven individual.

These propositions are wholly distinct. The former contrasts 17 U.S.C. §106(3) with 106(4). The latter, solely within the ambit of 17 U.S.C. §106(3), makes an evidentiary point about how much proof is required.

The 1996 write-up of *Agree* contained in NIMMER ON COPYRIGHT purported to address only Proposition 1. It had nothing to do with Proposition

2. Indeed, at that juncture, the phrase "actual distribution" only had the sense of Proposition 1, and it did not occur to me at that time that there could be a distinct evidentiary point using the same nomenclature.

Let us imagine a case arising in 1997 in which the treatise language became operative. It could not have been a peer-to-peer case, as Napster (the first P2P service) still lay another two years in the future. But one could imagine a publisher suing a bookstore for violating the public distribution right by having 20 piratical copies of *Into Thin Air* offered for sale on a table near the front window. The defendant could thereupon remonstrate,

> "I can't be held culpable for infringing the copyright, as the proof shows only that I was offering those copies for sale to the public. Notably absent is any proof that a customer actually came in and plopped down $15.00 to purchase one of the infringing copies. As NIMMER ON COPYRIGHT clearly indicates, 'Infringement of this right requires an actual dissemination of either copies or phonorecords.' There is no such evidence here, so I deserve summary judgment."

If a court had adopted that proposition, I would have written up the decision as conflating two different propositions. In actuality, though, the issue did not arise until much later, when the P2P cases came down. At that point, many of those cases quoted the one treatise sentence above in isolation. They did so for the analytically incorrect proposition just ventilated.

When the treatise wrote up those cases in 2011, it made exactly that point. More specifically, newly revised NIMMER ON COPYRIGHT § 8.11 embodied the comprehensive research undertaken in the interim by Prof. Peter Menell.[75] His article amply proved that the correct resolution of Proposition 2 is to reject the heightened evidentiary burden. At the same time that the revision set forth the research uncovered by that outstanding article, it preserved the old paragraph from the treatise, to show how courts in the interim had taken that simple proposition out of context. *See* 2 NIMMER ON COPYRIGHT § 8.11[C][1][a] n.116 (Release 85).

2. Four months later, the treatise turned to another aspect of the distribution right. Again, its concern was to vindicate the language of the 1976 Act, not to advocate optimal policy resolutions for future possible amendments to the statute. Specifically, the treatise discussed three decisions from a Ninth Circuit panel, which construed the distribution right in the context of the "first sale" defense. *See* 2 NIMMER ON COPYRIGHT § 8.12[B][1][d][i][III] (Release 86).

In that section, the treatise offered its view on each of those cases. One Ninth Circuit ruling upheld the defense and ruled against the copyright owner. The treatise agreed with its statutory construction. The other two Ninth Circuit decisions rejected the defense and ruled in favor of the copyright owners as to the distribution right. The treatise registered its respectful disagreement with those rulings. Thus, in all three instances, the treatise construed the 1976 Act to "limit" the distribution right of the copyright owner. That stance marks a counterpoint with the foregoing discussion of the "making available" aspect, in which the treatise construed the 1976 Act to "expand" the distribution right of the copyright owner.

The overarching lesson is that each domain must be treated on its own merits. The treatise has no *a priori* stance towards expanding or limiting the distribution right. It attempts to interpret the Copyright Act faithfully and independently as to each case it considers.

3. During the interval noted above (1996-2011), I represented a variety of clients, ranging from Verizon to Disney to Amazon.com to numerous individuals. I did not spend any significant amount of time during those decades representing any record company or other entities in the music business.

The work noted above in Releases 85 and 86 was performed in my scholarly role. By the same token, Prof. Menell's composition of *In Search of Copyright's Lost Ark: Interpreting the Right to Distribute in the Internet Age*, which furnished the backbone for the treatise's discussion of the "making available right" in Release 85, likewise took place in his scholarly role. Neither he nor I ran the contents by any client or industry representative for approval. Indeed, during that general time-frame, Prof. Menell consulted for the plaintiff in a case adverse to a subsidiary of Universal Music Group,[76] as he discusses in his BraceLecture.[77]

4. Supplementing my Disclosure Form to the Committee, I would like to add that my receipt of federal funds has occurred exclusively for participation in the Federal Judicial Center's Intellectual Property in the New Technological seminar, which has taken place annually over the past two decades in Berkeley, California. For lecturing about copyright law to federal judges, I have received reimbursement of my travel expenses from Los Angeles.

APPENDIX 2.

Excerpt from 1965 Report of the Register of Copyrights[78]

The basic legislative problem is to insure that the copyright law provides the necessary monetary incentive to write, produce, publish, and disseminate creative works, while at the same time guarding against the danger that these works will not be disseminated and used as fully as they should because of copyright restrictions. The problem of balancing existing interests is delicate enough, but the bill must do something even more difficult. It must try to foresee and take account of changes in the forms of use and the relative importance of the competing interests in the years to come, and it must attempt to balance them fairly in a way that carries out the basic constitutional purpose of the copyright law.

Obviously no one can foresee accurately and in detail the evolving patterns in the ways author's works will reach the public 10, 20, or 50 years from now. Lacking that kind of foresight, the bill should, we believe, adopt a general approach aimed at providing compensation to the author for future as well as present uses of his work that materially affect the value of his copyright. As shown by the jukebox exemption in the present law, a particular use which may seem to have little or no economic impact on the author's rights today can assume tremendous importance in times to come. A real danger to be guarded against is that of confining the scope of an author's rights on the basis of the present technology so that, as the years go by, his copyright loses much of its value because of unforeseen technical advances.

For these reasons, we believe that the author's rights should be stated in the statute in broad terms, and that the specific limitations on them should not go any further than is shown to be necessary in the public interest. In our opinion it is generally true, as the authors and other copyright owners argue, that if an exclusive right exists under the statute a reasonable bargain for its use will be reached; copyright owners do not seek to price themselves out of a market. But if the right is denied by the statute, the result in many cases would simply be a free ride at the author's expense.

We are entirely sympathetic with the aims of nonprofit users, such as teachers, librarians, and educational broadcasters, who seek to advance learning and culture by bringing the works of authors to students, scholars, and the general public. Their use of new devices for this purpose should be encouraged. It has already become clear, however, that the unrestrained use of photocopying, recording, and other devices for the reproduction of authors' works, going far beyond the recognized limits of "fair use," may severely curtail the copyright owner's market for copies of his work. Likewise, it is becoming increasingly apparent that the transmission of works by nonprofit broadcasting, linked computers, and other new media of communication, may soon be among the most important means of disseminating them, and will be capable of reaching vast audiences. Even when these new media are not operated for profit, they may be expected to displace the demand for authors' works by other users from whom copyright owners derive compensation. Reasonable adjustments between the legitimate interests of copyright owners and those of certain nonprofit users are no doubt necessary, but we believe the day is past when any particular use of works should be exempted for the sole reason that it is "not for profit."

End Notes

[1] U.S. Copyright Office, *Report of the Register of Copyrights on the General Revision of the U.S. Copyright Law* 22 (July 1961) (emphasis added).

[2] 17 U.S.C. § 106(3) (1976 Act, which took effect on January 1, 1978).

[3] 17 U.S.C. § 106(1).

[4] *Compare Universal City Studios Prods. LLP v. Bigwood*, 441 F. Supp. 2d 185 (D. Me. 2006), *with Atlantic Recording Corp. v. Brennan*, 534 F. Supp. 2d 278 (D. Conn. 2008).

[5] *See* Peter S. Menell, *In Search of Copyright's Lost Ark: Interpreting the Right to Distribute in the Internet Age*, 59 J. COPR. SOC'Y 1 (2011).

[6] *Id.* at 57.

[7] *See* Appendix 2 to this statement, for the lengthy excerpt by the Register of Copyrights, from which that language was drawn.

[8] For another expression that same year of the sentiment that "we must be prepared to live with any new copyright law for 50 years or more," *see Copyright Law Revision: Hearings on H.R. 4347, H.R. 5680, H.R. 6831 and H.R. 6835 Before Subcomm. No. 3 of the House Comm. on the Judiciary,* 89th Cong (1965) (statement of Prof. Melville B. Nimmer, School of Law, University of California, Los Angeles), 7 OMNIBUS COPYRIGHT REVISION LEGISLATIVE HISTORY 1809-12 (George S. Grossman, ed., Wiilliam Hein and Co., Inc. 2001).

[9] It took over two decades of study until the Copyright Act was enacted in 1976. The final contours of most issues—including the distribution right here at issue—were reached in 1965. The succeeding 11 years were spent working out ongoing disagreements about jukebox compulsory licenses, cable television, and other matters not relating to the core rights of the copyright owner.

[10] "No consummated act of actual distribution need be demonstrated . . . to implicate the copyright owner's distribution right." *Diversey v. Schmidly*, 2013 U.S. App. LEXIS 25506, 2013 WL 6727517, at *4 10th Cir. Dec. 23, 2013) (quoting NIMMER ON COPYRIGHT § 8.11[B][4][d]).

[11] *Id.* n.7 .

[12] *The Register's Call for Updates to U.S. Copyright Law. Before the Subcomm. on Courts, Intellectual Property and the Internet of the H. Comm. on the Judiciary*, 113th Cong. 6-38

(2013) (statement of Maria A. Pallante, Register of Copyrights of the United States); *see* Maria A. Pallante, *The Next Great Copyright Act*, 36 COLUM. J.L. and ARTS 315 (2013).

[13] *Press Release, U.S. House of Representatives, Comm. on the Judiciary, Chairman Goodlatte Announces Comprehensive Review of Copyright Law* (Apr. 24, 2013), http://judiciary.house.gov/news/2013/04242013_2.html (visited January 9, 2014).

[14] Peter S. Menell, 59 J. COPR. SOC'Y at 64-65. In addition, discouraging infringement at the end-user level reduces the pressure to enforce copyright protection at the distribution level, thus relieving potential chilling effects on software developers. *Id.* at 65 (citing Mark A. Lemley and R. Anthony Reese, *Reducing Digital Copyright Infringement Without Restricting Innovation*, 56 STAN. L. REV. 1345 (2004)).

[15] A rundown of many such cases, and their conflicting rulings, is set forth in 4 NIMMER ON COPYRIGHT § 12B.09[A][4].

[16] *See First Time Videos, LLC v. Does 1-500*, 276 F.R.D. 241 (N.D.Ill. 2011).

[17] Again, a rundown of many such cases is set forth in 4 NIMMER ON COPYRIGHT § 12B.09[A][3].

[18] Still, courts have recognized that there is "some limited First Amendment protection" associated with making files available to others via P2P networks, which "subject[s] the plaintiff's subpoenas to somewhat heightened scrutiny." *London-Sire Records, Inc. v. Doe 1*, 542 F.Supp. 2d 153, 162-63 (D.Mass. 2008).

[19] 17 U.S.C. § 1(a) (1909 Act).

[20] Sonia K. Kaytal, *Privacy vs. Piracy*, 7 YALE J.L. AND TECH. 222, 224 (2005).

[21] *See* 2 NIMMER ON COPYRIGHT § 8.11[D][5][a] (collecting cases); Robert Kasunic, *Making Circumstantial Proof of Distribution Available*, 18 FORDHAM INTELL. PROP. MEDIA AND ENT. L.J. 1145, 1157-60 (2008).

[22] *Metro-Goldwyn-Mayer Studios, Inc. v. Grokster Ltd.*, 545 U.S. 913, 923 (2005).

[23] *Sony BMG Music Entm't v. Tenenbaum*, 672 F. Supp. 2d 217, 222 (D. Mass. 2009).

[24] *Sony BMG Music Entm't v. Tenenbaum*, 660 F.3d 487, 492 (1st Cir. 2011).

[25] *See* Peter S. Menell, *This American Copyright Life: Reflections on Re- Equilibrating Copyright for the Internet Age*, J. COPR. SOC'Y (forthcoming 2014) (42nd Donald C. Brace Memorial Lecture).

[26] *See* David O. Carson, *Making the Making Available Right Available*, 33 COLUM. J.L. and ARTS 135, 140-41 (2010).

[27] WIPO Copyright Treaty, art. 8, Dec. 20, 1996, 2186 U.N.T.S. 121, S. Treaty Doc. No. 105-17.

[28] WIPO Performances and Phonograms Treaty, arts. 10, 14, Dec. 20, 1996, 2186 U.N.T.S. 203, S. Treaty Doc. No. 105-17.

[29] 33 COLUM. J.L. and ARTS at 146 (reflecting "consensus within the Copyright Office and the Patent and Trademark Office, the two expert agencies involved in the negotiations and the formulation of implementing legislation").

[30] *Piracy of Intellectual Property on Peer-to-Peer Networks: Before the Subcomm. on Courts, the Internet and Intellectual Property of the H. Comm. on the Judiciary*, 107th Cong. 1 (2002) (letter from Marybeth Peters, Register of Copyrights, to Rep. Howard L. Berman, Subcomm. on Courts, the Internet and Intellectual Prop.).

[31] 25 U.S.T. 309, 888 U.N.T.S. 67 (Oct. 29, 1971).

[32] *Id.*, art. 2.

[33] *Id.*, art. 1(d) (emphasis added).

[34] *See Free Trade Agreements*, OFFICE OF THE U.S. TRADE REPRESENTATIVE, http://www.ustr.gov/trade-agreements/free-trade-agreements (last visited Jan. 9, 2014).

[35] 33 COLUM. J.L. AND ARTS at 148-49. Carson quotes the FTA with Australia as typical—its Article 17.5 mandates that "each Party shall provide to authors the exclusive right to authorise or prohibit the communication to the public of their works, by wire or wireless means, including the making available to the public of their works in such a way that

members of the public may access these works from a place and at a time individually chosen by them." *Id.*

[36] *Id.* at 150.

[37] *See* 17 U.S.C. § 512.

[38] *See West Coast Prods., Inc. v. Does 1-5829*, 275 F.R.D. 9 (D.D.C. 2011).

[39] The issue of what might be called "attempted copyright entrapment" sweeps far more broadly than P2P exploitation and affects works across the board, not only pornography. *See Field v. Google Inc.*, 412 F. Supp. 2d 1106 (D. Nev. 2006). Nonetheless, any necessary redress for those problems occupies its own domain, far afield from today's "making available" investigation.

[40] *Malibu Media, LLC v. Does 1 through 10*, No. 2:12-cv-3623, 2012 U.S. Dist. LEXIS 892862012 WL 5382304, at *2 (C.D. Cal. June 27, 2012).

[41] *Id.* at *3.

[42] *Id.*

[43] *See Capitol Records Inc. v. Thomas-Rasset*, 799 F. Supp. 2d 999, 1001 (D. Minn. 2011), *vacated*, 692 F.3d 899 (8th Cir. 2012); *Sony BMG Music Entm't v. Tenenbaum*, 721 F.Supp.2d 85, 121 (D.Mass. 2010), *vacated in part*, 660 F.3d 487 (1st Cir. 2011).

[44] *Tenenbaum*, 721 F. Supp. 2d at 116.

[45] Menell, 59 J. COPR. SOC'Y at 19.

[46] *Peer Int'l Corp. v. Luna Records*, 887 F. Supp. 560, 568 (S.D.N.Y. 1995).

[47] *Id.*

[48] *Top Rank, Inc. v. Allerton Lounge, Inc.*, No. 96 Civ. 7864, 1998 U.S. Dist. LEXIS 2267, 11998 WL 35152791, at *1 (S.D.N.Y. Mar. 25, 1998). In this instance, Judge Sotomayor rejected the magistrate's lenient recommendation corresponding to "estimated losses to the plaintiff," and instead imposed larger awards of statutory damages. *Id.*

[49] *Remedies for Small Copyright Claims: Before the Subcomm. on Courts, the Internet, and Intellectual Property of the H. Comm. on the Judiciary*, 109th Cong. 45-48 (2006) (statement of the U.S. Copyright Office).

[50] Pursuant to the 1976 Act, "Importation into the United States or exportation from the United States, without the authority of the owner of copyright under this title, of copies or phonorecords … is an infringement of the exclusive right to distribute copies or phonorecords…." 17 U.S.C. § 602(a).

[51] Notwithstanding that label, the doctrine applies not only to first "sales" but also other authorized transfers. *See* 17 U.S.C. § 109(a).

[52] *See Kirtsaeng v. John Wiley and Sons, Inc.*, 133 S. Ct. 1351 (2013).

[53] *Id.* at 1385 (Ginsburg, J., dissenting).

[54] *Id.* at 1375 (majority opinion of Breyer, J.).

[55] *See* Computer Software Rental Amendments Act of 1990, Act of Dec. 1, 1990, Pub. L. 101-650, 104 Stat. 5089, tit. VIII.

[56] *Compare Adobe Sys. Inc. v. One Stop Micro, Inc.*,84 F. Supp. 2d 1086 (N.D. Cal. 2000), *with Softman Prods. Co., LLC v. Adobe Sys., Inc.*, 171 F. Supp. 2d 1075 (C.D. Cal. 2001).

[57] *See* DEPT. OF COMMERCE INTERNET POLICY TASK FORCE, COPYRIGHT POLICY, CREATIVITY, AND INNOVATION IN THE DIGITAL ECONOMY 79-80 (July 2013).

[58] 17 U.S.C. § 109(a).

[59] The full quotation, made in the context of the Digital Millennium Copyright Act (DMCA), is as follows:

> As copyrighted works are afforded more protection, they will be encrypted in "digital wrappers" that make them impenetrable to anyone other than those who are willing to pay the going rate. While that may sound like the American way, it is not. United States copyright law historically has carved out important exceptions to the rights of copyright owners.

144 Cong. Rec. H7099 (daily ed. Aug. 4, 1998) (remarks of Rep. Dingell).

[60] *See* Tom W. Bell, *Fair Use vs. Fared Use: The Impact of Automated Rights Management on Copyright's Fair Use Doctrine*, 76 N.C. L. REV. 557, 580-81 (1998).

[61] One of the flashpoints in congressional deliberations over the DMCA was "the specter of moving our Nation towards a 'pay-per-use' society." 144 Cong. Rec. S11887 (daily ed. Oct. 8, 1998) (statement of Sen. Ashcroft). Speakers from both sides of the aisle and in both chambers unanimously denounced that specter. *See* 144 Cong. Rec. H7101 (daily ed. Aug. 4, 1998) (remarks of Rep. Stearns) (noting the inclusion of language to "protect consumers from a 'pay-per-view' world in the digital area"); 144 Cong. Rec. E2144 (daily ed. Oct.13, 1998) (remarks of Rep. Tauzin) (describing pay-per-view as "profoundly antithetical to our long tradition of the exchange of free ideas and information").

[62] At passage of the DMCA, the committees charged with formulating the bill incorporated into it various safeguards designed to mitigate "the risk that enactment of the bill could establish the legal framework that would inexorably create a 'pay-per-use' society." H.R. Rep. No. 105-551, Part 2, 105th Cong., 2d Sess. 25 (1998). Nonetheless, their handiwork fell short of its goal, as the actual safeguards incorporated into the law do little to guard against that specter. *See* 4 NIMMER ON COPYRIGHT § 12A.06[B][3]. The advent of The Cloud brings new threats of creating "a 'pay-per-use' society." Thus, the matter with which Congress grappled in 1998 now returns to the fore.

[63] *WNET, Thirteen v. Aereo, Inc.*, 712 F.3d 676, 697 (2d Cir. 2013) (Chin, J., dissenting) ("the system is a Rube Goldberg-like contrivance, over-engineered in an attempt to avoid the reach of the Copyright Act and to take advantage of a perceived loophole in the law"); *WNET, Thirteen v. Aereo, Inc.*, 722 F.3d 500 (2d Cir. 2013) (Chin and Wesley, JJ., dissenting from the denial of rehearing *en banc*).

[64] *See* Act of Nov. 1, 1995, Pub. L. 104-39, 109 Stat. 336.

[65] Consider that amendment's definition of one type of *distribution*:

> A "digital phonorecord delivery" is each individual *delivery* of a phonorecord by digital *transmission* of a sound recording which results in a specifically identifiable *reproduction* by or for any transmission recipient of a phonorecord of that sound recording, regardless of whether the transmission is also a public performance of the sound recording or any nondramatic musical work embodied therein.

17 U.S.C. § 115(d) (emphasis added). That definition contemplates that a "delivery" (seemingly implicating copyright law's distribution right) will be accomplished via "transmission" (a species of copyright law's performance right) resulting in a "reproduction" (the essence of copyright law's reproduction right). It thus promiscuously crosses three barriers in the course of a single sentence. Such confusion is part and parcel of the digital world, in which the division between separate rights is often difficult to discern.

[66] WIPO Copyright Treaty, art. 8.

[67] *Id.*

[68] *See* Ryoichi Mori and Masaji Kawahara, *Superdistribution: The Concept and the Architecture*, TRANSACTIONS OF THE INSTITUTE OF ELECTRONICS, INFORMATION, AND COMMUNICATION ENGINEERS, vol. E73 #7 (1990).

[69] *See* WILLIAM W. FISHER III, PROMISES TO KEEP (2004); Neil Weinstock Netanel, *Impose a Noncommercial Use Levy to Allow Free Peer-to-Peer File Sharing*, 17 HARV. J.L. AND TECH. 1 (2003). OTHER ARTICLES ARE CITED IN DEPT. OF COMMERCE INTERNET POLICY TASK FORCE, COPYRIGHT POLICY, CREATIVITY, AND INNOVATION IN THE DIGITAL ECONOMY 41 n.212. (July 2013).

[70] *Id.*

[71] *Atlantic Recording Corp. v. Howell*, 554 F. Supp. 2d 976, 981 (D. Ariz. 2008).

[72] *See Agee v. Paramount Commc's, Inc.*, 853 F. Supp. 778 (S.D.N.Y. 1994).

[73] *Agee v. Paramount Commc'ns, Inc.*, 59 F.3d 317, 324-27 (2d Cir. 1995).

[74] 2 NIMMER ON COPYRIGHT § 8.11[A] (1996).

[75] *See* Peter S. Menell, *In Search of Copyright's Lost Ark: Interpreting the Right toDistribute in the Internet Age*, 59 J. COPR. SOC'Y 1 (2011).

[76] *F.B.T. Prods., LLC v. Aftermath Records*, 621 F.3d 958 (9th Cir. 2010).

[77] See *This American Copyright Life*, *supra*.

[78] SUPPLEMENTARY REPORT OF THE REGISTER OF COPYRIGHTS ON THE GENERAL REVISION OF THE U.S. COPYRIGHT LAW, 89TH CONG, 1965 REVISION BILL 13-14 (Comm. Print 1965).

In: Creative Works …
Editor: Brandon S. Casey
ISBN: 978-1-63485-522-8

Chapter 3

STATEMENT OF GLYNN S. LUNNEY, JR., MCGLINCHEY STAFFORD PROFESSOR OF LAW, TULANE UNIVERSITY SCHOOL OF LAW. HEARING ON "THE SCOPE OF COPYRIGHT PROTECTION"*

AGAINST THE 'MAKING AVAILABLE' RIGHT

Introduction

Committee Chairman Goodlatte, Subcommittee Chairman Coble and Ranking Member Conyers, and members of the subcommittee, thank you for the opportunity to speak to you today. I am Glynn Lunney, the McGlinchey Stafford Professor of Law at Tulane University in New Orleans. I am an engineer, a lawyer, and an economist, and I have been writing, teaching, and practicing in the field of copyright for over twenty years.

I appreciate the opportunity to address whether Congress should give copyright owners the exclusive right to make their works available to the public. As a general rule, I believe that copyright for the economy is like sugar for my coffee: a little bit is a good thing, but too much is worse than none at all. While giving copyright owners the exclusive right to make their works available to the public would probably not change existing law very

* This is an edited, reformatted and augmented version of a statement presented January 14, 2014 before the House Judiciary Committee, Subcommittee on Courts, Intellectual Property and the Internet.

much, I oppose the addition of the making available right to the copyright statute for three reasons. First, there is no need to add such a right expressly to the Act in order to satisfy our international treaty obligations. The combination of the reproduction, distribution, public performance, and public display rights under current United States law, together with principles of secondary liability, provides protection effectively equivalent to a "making available" right and thus fully satisfies our obligations under the WIPO Copyright Treaty and the WIPO Performances and Phonograms Treaty.

Second, there would be no benefit from adding such a right. Although giving copyright owners the exclusive right to make their work available to the public might make it slightly easier to pursue file sharers, it would not put the proverbial file-sharing genie back in the bottle, nor is file sharing the problem that the copyright industries would have us believe. Rather than help legitimate businesses control the unauthorized copying and distribution of their works through file sharing networks, giving copyright owners the exclusive right to make their works available to the public would more likely contribute instead to the growing problem of copyright trolls.

Third, adding the right would cause very real harm to the economy. Whether intended to displace or merely supplement the existing framework of public performance, public display, and distribution rights, adding a making available right to the act would create substantial and undesirable uncertainty. Although the existing legal framework is far from perfect, we have spent the last twenty years litigating whether, and if so, when various uses of the Internet, and digital networks more generally, infringe the existing legal rules. If Congress were to give copyright owners a new making available right, this relatively predictable legal framework, and the resulting certainty, would be gone. It would be gone not because Congress decided, as a policy matter, that some of the existing rules were wrong. Rather, it would be gone because the linguistic scope of a "making available" right is sufficiently vague and ambiguous that it would give parties a perfectly plausible excuse to re-litigate cases they lost under the existing statutory language. As a result, we would have to re-litigate previously-settled areas of law; legitimate businesses would, once again, be forced to close in the face of ruinous litigation expense; and investment in new business models and technological innovation would be stifled.

Thus, we have little to gain and much to lose if Congress were to give copyright owners the exclusive right to make their works available to the public. As a result, I oppose the addition of a making available right to the act.

To assist the Subcommittee in its deliberations, I will further develop each of these three concerns.

Discussion

1. There Is No Need to Add a Making Available Right

There is no need to give copyright owners the exclusive right to make their works available to the public. The existing rights of reproduction, distribution, public performance, and public display, together with secondary liability doctrines, already provide effectively equivalent protection, and fully satisfy our obligation to provide such a right under the WIPO Copyright Treaty and the WIPO Performances and Phonograms Treaty.

Under the heading "Right of Distribution," article 6(1) of the WIPO Copyright Treaty provides:

> Authors of literary and artistic works shall enjoy the exclusive right of authorizing the making available to the public of the original and copies of their work through sale or other transfer of ownership.[1]

Also under the heading "Right of Distribution," article 12(1) of the WIPO Performances and Phonograms Treaty provides an identical "making available" right for the distribution of "phonograms" to the "[p]roducers of phonograms."[2]

In addition, both Treaties require a further making available right. The Copyright Treaty, under the heading "Right of Communication to the Public," provides in Article 8:

> . . .[A]uthors of literary and artistic works shall enjoy the exclusive right of authorizing any communication to the public of their work, by wire or wireless means, including the making available to the public of their works in such a way that members of the public may access these works from a place and at a time individually chosen by them.[3]

Similarly, the Performances and Phonograms Treaty, under the heading "Right of Making Available of Phonograms," provides in Article 14:

> Producers of phonograms shall enjoy the exclusive right of authorizing the making available to the public of their phonograms, by

wire or wireless means, in such a way that members of the public may access them from a place and at a time individually chosen by them.[4]

The United States is a signatory to, and in 1999, ratified, both treaties.

In negotiating these Treaties, the United States delegation was well aware that our Copyright Act did not provide an express right to communicate or otherwise make available a work to the public. To ensure that our existing law would satisfy our obligations to provide for a making available right, during the Diplomatic Conference associated with these Treaties, the United States stated, and no delegation opposed the statement, that each Contracting Party would be free to satisfy the obligation to provide the "making available" right through the application of some other right or through a combination of different rights.[5] A similar approach has long been followed by member countries under the Berne Convention.[6] It recognizes that the legal characterization of a right may differ from country to country. The United States is therefore free to provide equivalent protection through our existing structure of rights, rather than through a separate "making available" right.

This is precisely what we have done. During the ratification process for these Treaties, both the Administration and the Register of Copyrights at the time, Marybeth Peters, stated that we did not need to add a separate making available right to our Copyright Act in order to satisfy our treaty obligation. Our existing structure of rights, including the reproduction, distribution, public performance, and public display rights, provided protection essentially equivalent to the making available right.[7] As a result, an express making available right was unnecessary.

We continue to provide essentially equivalent protection under our law today. The United States pushed for these treaties in order to address two issues. The first was the streaming of works on the Internet, and the second was the digital distribution of works on the Internet. Both at the time of ratification, and today, streaming a work across the Internet would, absent a license, violate the public performance right for, literary and artistic works, as well as both musical works and sound recordings. Although the United States provides for statutory licensing for certain public performances of sound recordings,[8] the Performances and Phonograms Treaty expressly leaves room for such statutory licensing.[9] Similarly, both at the time of ratification, and today, the digital distribution of copies or phonograms, through sale or other transfer of ownership, would violate the distribution right.[10] Although the United States limits the distribution right when a first sale has occurred, both Treaties expressly leave room for Contracting Parties to limit the "making available" right when a first sale, or exhaustion, has occurred.[11]

Thus, both at the time of ratification and today, existing U.S. law provides protection equivalent to the "making available" provisions of these two Treaties. There is therefore no need to add a separate "making available" right to our Copyright Act.

2. There Is No Benefit from Adding a Making Available Right

There would be no benefit from giving copyright owners the exclusive right to make their works available to the public. Although adding the right might make it slightly easier to pursue file sharers, file sharing is not the problem copyright owners would have us believe, and even if it were, a making available right would not solve it. Rather than help legitimate businesses control the unauthorized copying and distribution of their works through file sharing networks, adding a making available right would instead contribute to the growing problem of copyright trolls.

As discussed, the making available right is intended to ensure that copyright owners have the exclusive right to stream and distribute their works digitally over the Internet. Existing United States law already provides such protection. Adding a making available right would not materially improve copyright owners' ability to seek legal relief against either: (i) so-called "rogue" sites, often located in foreign jurisdictions, which offer to stream copyrighted works to American consumers; or (ii) file sharing.

With respect to streaming, as the *iCraveTV* litigation[12] demonstrates, a foreign website that offers streaming of copyrighted works to American consumers violates the public performance right under our existing Copyright Act. In the *iCraveTV* litigation, a Canadian website was retransmitting American and Canadian television broadcasts over the Internet. Although its actions were legal under Canadian law, American copyright owners sued the website in Pennsylvania, alleging copyright infringement under United States law. In deciding whether to grant a preliminary injunction against the website, the district court found that many of the retransmission streams were going to United States residents. It therefore held that such streams, although originating in Canada, violated the copyright owners' public performance right under United States law, and granted the injunction.[13]

As this case reflects, existing United States law already addresses streaming from foreign sites to United States residents. In some instances, pursuing foreign sites has proven difficult, but the difficulties do not arise from some deficiency in copyright's existing scope. Rather, the difficulties arise from limitations on our ability to enforce a United States judgment in a foreign jurisdiction. Even if we were to add a making available right to the Act, these difficulties would remain.

With respect to file sharing, as the $222,000 and $675,000 statutory damages judgments in the *Thomas-Rasset* and *Tenenbaum* cases demonstrate, an individual who engages in file sharing violates the existing rights of reproduction and distribution.[14] To be perfectly fair, file sharing is the issue on which adding a making available right expressly to the statute would most clearly change existing law, at least as a formal matter. It would not, however, change existing law very much, and as a practical matter, perhaps not at all. Under existing law, to establish infringement under the reproduction or distribution right, a majority of the district courts that have addressed the issue have required a copyright owner to prove not only that an individual made a copyrighted work available for sharing through a peer-to-peer service or cyber-locker, but that the copyrighted work was, in fact, shared.[15] If Congress were to give copyright owners the exclusive right to make their works available to the public, then a copyright owner could establish a *prima facie* case of infringement by showing simply that the copyrighted work was made available for sharing. No proof that the file was, in fact, shared, or that another user actually downloaded the work would be required, at least as a matter of formal law.

Yet, as a practical matter, adding a making available right would make essentially no difference in the sort of evidence a copyright owner would need in order to show infringement in the file sharing context. To find infringing file sharers, copyright owner typically retain investigators who use file sharing programs to browse the files made available. While browsing, the investigator identifies IP addresses at which copyrighted works are available for sharing, and uses that information to begin the subpoena process to identify the individual who owns the associated account. Under existing law, the copyright owner must show a download to establish an infringing distribution, but can do so simply by having its investigator download a copy of each of the works made available.[16] If Congress adds a making available right, it would not change things. The investigator would still need to download the works listed as available. The investigator would need to do so, not to satisfy a specific element of the making available right, but to verify that the listed work was, in fact, the copyrighted work at issue. Things on the Internet are not always what they say they are. A work listed as available on a file sharing program could as readily be a spoof file, or malware, or mislabeled. The only way to prove that the file listed as available was in fact the copyrighted work at issue would be to download the file and check. As a practical matter, then, there is no material difference between the evidentiary burden to establish infringement under a making available right, and the burden to establish infringement under the existing distribution right. In either case, the investigator will need to download the work, and by doing so, can establish infringement. It is hard therefore to see how giving copyright owners the exclusive right to make their works available would facilitate legal action against file sharing.

Moreover, when measured against copyright's constitutionally-delimited purpose, the unauthorized copying, distribution, and streaming of copyrighted works across the Internet are not the problem that copyright owners would have us believe. Copyright owners complain that file sharing has significantly reduced their revenue, especially in the music industry. Yet, the purpose of copyright is not to maximize the revenue of the music industry, or copyright owners, more generally. Copyright owners argue that the loss of this revenue has reduced employment in the copyright industries. Although this argument represents a well-known fallacy,[17] the purpose of copyright is also not to provide more employment in the copyright industries.

The Constitution authorizes Congress to enact copyright for a sole purpose: "to promote the Progress of Science."[18] The Supreme Court has defined this standard to encompass two legitimate ends: (i) encouraging the creation of new works; and (ii) encouraging the dissemination of existing works.[19] When we measure file sharing against these ends, it is undeniable that file sharing promotes the dissemination of existing works. Even while formally illegal, file sharing has provided much broader access to existing works than the preexisting market mechanisms had accomplished.[20] Yet, even as it promotes broader dissemination, the concern has been that because file sharing is unauthorized and unpaid, it will reduce the revenue authors, artists, and copyright owners will receive for any given work and hence lead to fewer new works.

To the question, "How will file sharing affect the creation of new works?," there would seem to be a simple answer. If consumers can obtain a copy of a work for free, why would anyone bother to pay? And if no one bothers to pay, why would anyone bother to create new works? Despite the attraction of this neat and plausible reasoning, the answer to whether file sharing reduces creative output turns out to be not quite so straightforward. In both theory and practice, the relationship between revenues and marginal output in the field of creative authorship is more complex than "more incentives equals more works." In the end, the only way to know whether any given increase or decrease in revenues will lead to more or fewer new original works is to allow the increase or decrease to occur and then see what happens.

Opportunities to test copyright's fundamental premise in this way do not arise very often. Understandably, Congress does not and should not arbitrarily change the copyright laws just to see what will happen. Nevertheless, the rise of file sharing has presented us with a rare opportunity to explore the essential relationship between copyright protection, revenue, and creative output. We are all familiar with file sharing's basic story. Since Napster opened its virtual doors in 1999, widespread consumer copying and distribution of copyrighted works through file sharing services has become the new reality. While copyright has formally defined file sharing as infringement, file sharing has nonetheless become commonplace. To illustrate the growth in file sharing, Figure 1 presents an estimate of the file sharing traffic on the Internet in North America, from Cisco's Visual Networking Index for 2008 and 2012.[21]

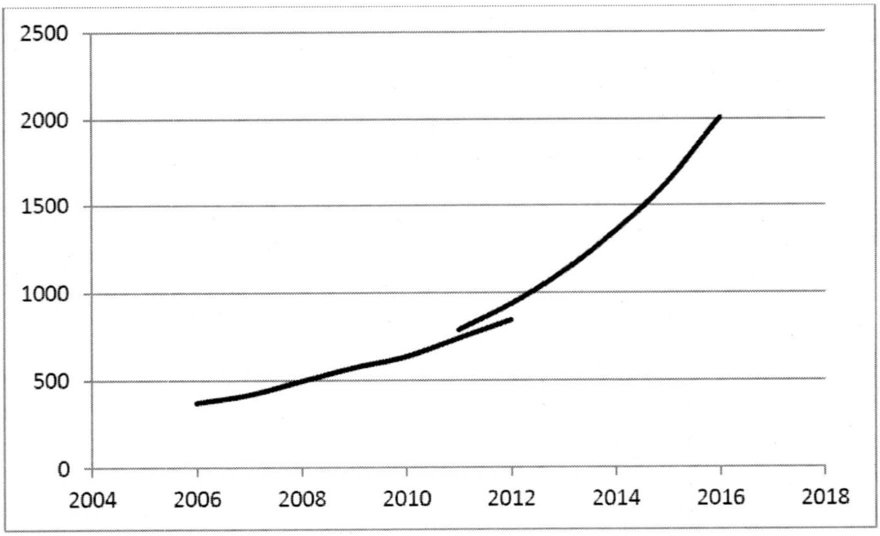

Source: Cisco, Visual Networking Index for 2008 and 2012.

Figure 1. File Sharing Traffic on the Internet: North America (in petabytes/month).

As Figure 1 reflects, file sharing traffic in North America presently amounts to just under one thousand petabytes per month, and, as of the 2012 index, that traffic was expected to double over the next three years, reaching two thousand petabytes a month by 2016.[22] Just to give a sense of scale to this issue, the typical music CD contains 800 megabytes of data. One step up from a megabyte is a gigabyte. A gigabyte is one thousand megabytes, and a typical DVD contains 4 gigabytes of data. At one thousand petabytes per month, the current rate of file sharing traffic represents approximately 250 million DVDs or 1.25 billion CDs, copied each month. Compare that to the roughly 70 million albums that I estimated U.S. consumers made through file sharing on Napster in September 2000,[23] and we can see that, despite the copyright industries' "victories" over file sharing, file sharing has increased by a factor of nearly twenty over the past twelve years. While not all of this traffic represents the unauthorized copying and distribution of copyrighted works, estimates suggest that the vast majority of it does.[24]

Unable to stop consumer copying, the effective level of copyright protection provided to original works has fallen dramatically since 1999. As file sharing has grown and the *de facto* level of copyright protection provided has fallen, the music industry, in particular, has been hard hit. With the rise of file sharing, the music industry has seen revenue from record sales decline steadily and sharply. To illustrate this, Figure 2 presents the total dollar value for music shipments, in all formats, whether physical or electronic, from 1973 to 2012.[25] In order to account for inflation, shipments are in constant 2012 dollars.

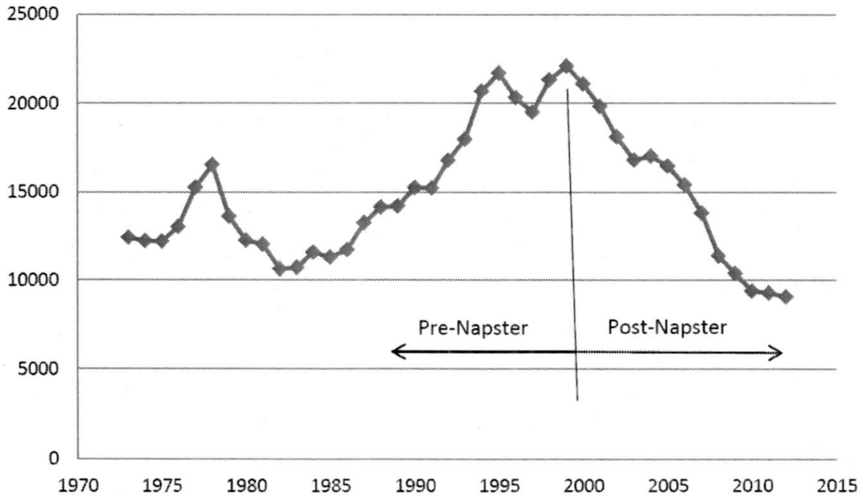

Source: RIAA.

Figure 2. Dollar Value of Music Sales (All Formats) in the United States (Constant 2012 Dollars, in Millions): 1973-2012.

As Figure 2 reflects, since Napster opened its doors, the RIAA reports that shipments of music have fallen from a peak of $22.1 billion in 1999 to only $9.1 billion in 2012. This is a fall of some $13 billion, or 58.9 percent. Such a fall is not entirely unprecedented. A similar peak and fall occurred from 1978 through 1982, when shipments peaked at $16.5 billion (in constant 2012 dollars) before falling to $10.6 billion in 1982 – a fall of some $6 billion or 35.8 percent. Presumably, not even the music industry would contend that file sharing caused this initial fall in music sales. Rather, this initial fall was likely due to difficulties in the economy generally from 1980 through 1982. Because music is a luxury good, spending on it can fall quite rapidly when unemployment rates rise or per capita income falls.

Yet, even if not entirely unprecedented, the decline in music shipments that follows Napster and parallels the rise of file sharing is both sharper and lasts longer than the decline during the early 1980s. Undoubtedly, difficulties in the economy generally, particularly after the start of the Great Recession in 2008, contribute to the post-Napster decline in music shipments. But file sharing may also have played a role. Existing economic studies disagree as to whether, and if so, to what extent, file sharing may have contributed to this decline.[26] Yet, I am perfectly prepared to accept that file sharing is responsible, directly or indirectly, for some part of this decline.

The relevant question, however, is not whether file sharing caused this decline in record sales, but how this decline in record sales affected the creation of new music. Before examining how this decline in revenue from record sales affected the creation of new music, I should acknowledge that record sales are not the only source of revenue that supports the creation of new music. Sync licenses,[27] endorsement deals, concert ticket sales and associated merchandising, and public performance royalties, just to name a few, provide revenue streams that support the creation of new music, as well. Many of these are complements to the sale of recorded music, and so may serve as a means for recapturing part of the revenue lost as a result of declining music sales.

While possible in theory, in reality, growth in the revenues associated with complementary products, such as live performances, has not done much to mitigate the decline in music sales. While we do not have data on all of the revenue sources available to artists and songwriters, two of the main alternative revenue sources, concert revenue and public performances royalties, are available, and they have not grown sufficiently to offset the revenues lost from falling record sales. As reported by Pollstar, revenue from the top 200 concerts grew from $2.07 billion in 1999 (adjusted to 2012 dollars) to $2.52 billion in 2012. Similarly, royalties paid by ASCAP and BMI for the public performance of musical works grew from $1.29 billion in 1999 (again, adjusted to 2012 dollars) to $1.58 billion in 2012. Since 2003, SoundExchange has also begun paying royalties for the public performance of sound recordings, and paid out approximately $426 million in 2012. While these revenue sources grew faster than the rate of inflation, the total increase in revenue available from these two sources from 1999 to 2012, at roughly $1.166 billion, is not enough to offset the $13 billion decline in revenue from record sales over that same period.[28]

This brings us to the heart of the matter: how has this decline in revenue affected creative output in the music industry? We begin with industry data. Figure 3 presents data from SoundScan on the number of new albums released in the United States each year since 1996.

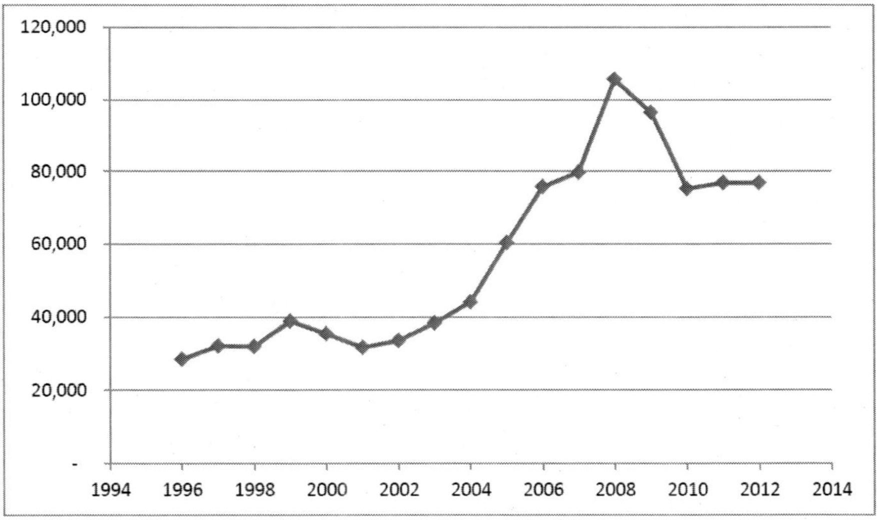

Source: Nielsen SoundScan.

Figure 3. New Albums Released in the United States: 1996-2012.

As Figure 3 illustrates, the quantity of new music released in the United States is up substantially since Napster's debut. Using a consistent methodology, SoundScan estimates that the number of new albums released increased from just under forty thousand albums in 1999 to a peak of over one hundred thousand albums in 2008. With the onset of the recession in 2008, the number of new albums fell back in 2009-2012, but even so, the number of new albums released in 2012, at just under eighty thousand, nearly doubles the pre-Napster output.

While the increasing number of albums released suggests that the revenue decline has not affected music output in terms of quantity, it does not account for a possible decline in quality, nor does it foreclose the possibility that even more albums might have been released but-for the decline in revenue. In a just completed empirical study,[29] I have attempted to account for these possibilities. In the study, I treat the rise of file sharing and the parallel fall in music industry revenue as a natural experiment in radically reduced copyright protection. To explore the relationship between copyright protection, revenue, and high quality creative output, I created a hand-coded data set for the songs that appeared in the top fifty of the Billboard Hot 100 in the first week of each month for each year from 1985 through 2013. I focused on songs that appeared in the top fifty of the Hot 100 as a proxy for, and in order to control for, quality.[30] Both before and after file sharing, a radio station maximizes its advertising revenue by playing those songs that best satisfy the musical preferences of its listeners. A new song will hit the top fifty of the Hot 100 only if it receives repeated radio airplay. It will receive repeated radio airplay only if it satisfies the preferences of the radio station's listeners better than the preexisting songs that a radio station could have played instead.[31] Appearance in the top fifty thus provides a reasonable proxy for quality that should be consistent across the pre- and post-file sharing eras.

Using regression analysis, I show that the sharp decline in music industry revenue that paralleled the rise of file sharing was associated, if we hold all else constant: (i) with fewer new artists entering the market; but (ii) also with more hit songs, on average, by those new artists who did enter. Moreover, because the second marginal effect was larger than the first, the decline in revenue since file sharing began was associated with a net increase in the number of new hit songs, holding all else constant. Thus, for the music industry, the rise of file sharing and the parallel decline in revenue has meant the creation of more new music.[32]

If copyright really intends, then, to promote "the Progress of Science," file sharing, at least for the music industry, is not the problem copyright owners would have us believe. While this is only one study and it focuses on only one industry, it strongly suggests that, with file sharing, we may be able to have both broader dissemination and vibrant creative output. Giving copyright owners the exclusive right to make their works available to the public would not therefore be desirable even if adding that right proved to be the silver bullet that could solve the supposed problem of file sharing.

Unfortunately, even if we wanted to end file sharing, adding a making available right is not the proverbial silver bullet. From 2003 through 2008, the music industry threatened or filed copyright lawsuits against more than thirty-five thousand Americans for file sharing. As discussed, file sharing constitutes copyright infringement under existing law. In the end, the music industry abandoned this approach as a viable means for controlling file sharing. It did so not, however, because it was too difficult to prove a download and thus establish copyright infringement under existing law. Rather, it abandoned this approach for three reasons. First, there are tens of millions of file sharers in the United States alone.[33] Suing all of them was never a practical approach, whether the copyright owner had to establish a download as part of its *prima facie* case or not. Second, these file sharers were also the music industry's customers. Suing them was bad for business. Third, suing file sharers directly did not work. As Figure 1 illustrates, file sharing continued to grow unabated.

Even if we assume, merely for the sake of argument, that a making available right would make it much easier to establish copyright infringement by individual file sharers, it is far from clear that the music industry, or any other legitimate business, would resume, or begin, filing mass lawsuits against individual file sharers. Given that threatening tens of thousands of Americans with lawsuits was not sufficient to stop, or even slow, file sharing, copyright owners might have to sue hundreds of thousands, perhaps millions, to make this approach work. Even if a making available right would make such lawsuits cost effective, suing millions of Americans for file sharing would not stop file sharing. Instead, accusing so many Americans of violating the law would more likely create a political firestorm that would lead Congress to change the law.[34]

As a result, even if file sharing were the problem that copyright owners would have us believe and even if a making available right would facilitate mass filings against individual file sharers, the addition of a making available right would not solve the file sharing "problem" for legitimate businesses. Instead, the addition of a making available right would more likely exacerbate the growing problem of copyright trolls. Unlike a legitimate business, the business model of a copyright troll is to make money by threatening to sue a file sharer for copyright infringement. A troll creates its own customers (or victims) by planting its copyrighted work on a file sharing system.[35] Then when the work is downloaded, the troll uses the subpoena power of the federal courts to identify the owner of the downloading account in order to begin a campaign to extort a "settlement" payment from the owner. In its campaign, the troll may use the threat of embarrassing exposure, litigation costs, or statutory damages to persuade the file sharer to settle for a small fee in order to avoid a lawsuit.[36] Unlike a legitimate business, the troll is not trying to slow or stop file sharing in order to promote legitimate sales of its work. In some cases, the work at issue is not available through legitimate distribution channels. Rather, the troll aims to make money by suing or threatening to sue file sharers. It does not therefore want to stop file sharing. For the troll, more file sharers means more money. Moreover, the troll is not using copyright "to promote the Progress of Science." Whatever original work the troll may create, or in which the troll may claim copyright, is simply bait.

While facilitating lawsuits against individual file sharers may not help legitimate businesses much, it is likely to advance the business model for copyright trolls a great deal. As a result, rather than legitimate copyright owners, copyright trolls are likely to be the real beneficiaries were Congress to give copyright owners the exclusive right to make their works available to the public. Thus, adding a making available right to the Act would not generate any real benefit.

3. There is Real Harm from Adding a Making Available Right

Adding a making available right to the Copyright Act would cause real harm to the economy by creating uncertainty as to when, and under what circumstances, particular uses of copyrighted works on the Internet and digital networks more generally, create a substantial risk of copyright liability. While it is relatively clear that a making available right would ease the evidentiary burden on copyright owners in the file sharing context, for a wide variety of other uses, it is entirely unclear both whether, and if so, how, a making available right would change the law. In contrast, litigation over the last twenty years has gone a long ways towards resolving whether certain uses on the Internet create a risk of liability under our existing statutory language.

For example, in *Perfect 10, Inc. v. Amazon.com, Inc.*[37] the Ninth Circuit addressed whether framing and inline linking[38] of a copyrighted photograph constituted direct infringement of the public display right, or alternatively, whether such linking could serve as a basis for secondary liability. In the case, when a user searched on Google[39] for images, Google would display reduced resolution thumbnails of the responsive images, and also would display a linked image of the full-size image directly from the website where the image was found. As a result of such displays, Perfect 10 sued alleging copyright infringement, claiming that the images Google found and displayed were unauthorized copies and public displays of its work. In resolving the case, the Ninth Circuit applied the so-called "server" test on the issue of direct infringement. Under the "server" test, Google itself was liable for direct infringement of the public display right only for those images Google displayed from its own servers.[40] If, instead, Google used a link that displayed an image from the server of another website, then Google was not liable for direct infringement of the public display right. Applying this test, the Ninth Circuit held that Google could be directly liable for the thumbnail image, because it was displayed directly from Google's own servers. However, the Ninth Circuit further held that the thumbnail was a fair, and therefore, non-infringing use.[41] With respect to the link, which displayed the full-size image, Google did not display the full-sized image from its own servers but rather provided instructions or code that caused the consumer's browser to display the image directly from the servers for the website where the image had been found. As a result, the Ninth Circuit held that Google was not liable for direct infringement of the public display right.[42] Although not directly liable, the court held that Google could be liable for the display of the full-sized image under the doctrine of contributory liability. On that issue, the Ninth Circuit remanded for further proceedings to determine whether Google had the requisite knowledge that the image was infringing.[43]

By so ruling, the Ninth Circuit reinforced the notice-and-takedown approach to copyright infringement on the Internet. Rather than place the burden on a search engine to police the Internet for infringing content and subject the search engine to potentially astronomical statutory damages under a strict liability regime when it failed, the Ninth Circuit's approach placed the burden of policing infringements on the copyright owner. Google, and other search engines, are required to cooperate with a copyright owner's efforts to police its copyrights, by complying with proper takedown requests. They are not, however, required to guess: (i) the ownership of the copyright on any given image, and (ii) whether the copyright owner has authorized, or in any event, objects to a given use of its work, on the Internet.

It is not clear whether adding a making available right to the Copyright Act would change the applicable legal rules on these issues. With respect to the reduced resolution thumbnail, presumably fair use would still apply. With respect to the inline link to the full image, it is possible that such a link would infringe the making available right directly. Indeed, I have heard some suggest that the "making available" right would impose strict liability on a search engine if it merely provided a hyperlink to the website where an infringing image appeared, or perhaps even if the search engine provided a hyperlink to an authorized copy of the image posted on the copyright owner's own website. Whether, in the end, the legal rules governing linking would or would not differ under a making available right is simply unclear. In Europe, where many states provide an express making available right, European courts are struggling to resolve these issues under their own "making available" and "communication to the public" statutory provisions.[44]

Re-opening the question whether hyperlinking, and other forms of linking, constitutes direct copyright infringement would be exceedingly dangerous. The European Copyright Society, for example, has asked the European Court of Justice to conclude, in a case now pending, that hyperlinking does not constitute a "communication to the public." In its opinion on the issue, the European Copyright Society warned the Court of the essential role hyperlinking plays on the Internet:

> Although hyperlinking takes many forms and has multiple functions, there can be no doubt that it is the single most important feature that differentiates the Internet from other forms of cultural production and dissemination. Hyperlinking is intimately bound to the conception of the Internet as a network, and hyperlinks constitute paths leading users from one location to another. [...] The legal regulation of hyperlinking thus carries with it enormous capacity to interfere with the operation of the Internet, and therefore with access to information, freedom of expression, freedom to conduct business, as well – of course – with business ventures that depend on these types of linkages.[45]

This is equally true in the United States. Linking is fundamental to the essential nature of the Internet. All sorts of websites link to all sorts of content on other websites for all sorts of reasons. That is, in some sense, the point of the Internet. Just to take one example, Youtube licenses millions of audio and video works for performance on its website. Thousands of other websites link to or embed these licensed videos on their own sites. Some of these websites use a hyperlink – the glowing blue text that merely sends users to Youtube to perform the video if they click the link. Other websites use inline linking, embedding, or framing, which are instructions that cause Youtube's servers to perform the video through the other website directly. Given that copyright protects essentially everything on the Internet, adding a making available right would threaten every website that links to material on any other website with the possibility of strict liability for copyright infringement. It would radically disrupt settled legal expectations, and imperil both existing licensing arrangements and prospective investment decisions.

To take another example, in *Cartoon Network, LP v. CSC Holdings, Inc.* ("*Cablevision")*,[46] the Second Circuit addressed whether the provision of a remote digital video-recorder ("dvr") constituted infringement of the public performance right. Copyright owners argued that Cablevision was essentially offering a video-on-demand service that fell within the scope of copyright's public performance right. Cablevision countered that it was merely enabling consumers to record and playback television programs remotely, rather than through a set-top box. Given that a consumer's decision to record and playback through a set-top box constitutes a private, rather than public, performance, so too should a consumer's decision to record and playback through a remote dvr, or so Cablevision argued. Presumably, the question whether a performance is public or private should not depend on the length of the cable running from the dvr to the television. In resolving the case, the Second Circuit sided with Cablevision and held that providing a remote dvr, which individual consumers used to record and playback their own individual copies of television programs, did not violate the public performance right.[47]

Once again, it is unclear whether a court would reach the same conclusion were Congress to give copyright owners the exclusive right to make their works available to the public. It may be that a court would. The making available right still requires that a defendant make the work available to the public, and so the reasoning of the *Cablevision* court, that it is the individual consumer, not Cablevision who is performing the work,[48] may still control.[49] Yet, the change in language would make that unclear. Only through another round of litigation could we know for certain whether such conduct would or would not violate the making available right.[50]

Once again, re-opening this question would create substantial uncertainty and threaten investments in new business models and technological innovation made in reliance on the *Cablevision* decision. Here, the central concern is cloud computing. In *Cablevision*, the Second Circuit held that when a user directs a remote dvr to record a television program, and then later plays it back, that constitutes a private, rather than public performance. Moreover, it remains a private performance even if numerous individuals use the remote dvr to record and playback the same television program, so long as each of them records their own separate copy.[51] Cloud computing works similarly. The cloud provider offers each of its users specific assigned space on its servers. The user can then upload files and subsequently download them to another computer or device. It gives people the ability to access their own documents, e-mails, music collections, and other data seamlessly across multiple devices. I can begin working on a document at my office, continue working on it on my cellphone during my commute, and resume working on it when I get home. Of course, others may be uploading and downloading their own files through their own assigned storage space in the cloud. In some cases, different users may each upload and download their own copies of the same work. I can store on my cloud space an extra, back-up copy of Taylor Swift's *Red*, that I purchased from iTunes, and so can thousands of other users. *Cablevision*'s holding ensures that, so long as each of us is uploading and downloading our own copies from our own assigned space in the cloud, these uploadings and downloadings, taken together, do not become a public performance. It thereby allows a cloud provider to operate without the need for a public performance license and without fear of copyright liability. *Cablevision* thus helps provide the legal certainty companies need to invest in cloud computing.[52]

Even if we thought that reaching the opposite result in either *Cablevision* or *Perfect 10* would have better served copyright's purposes, we have to recognize that we are no longer writing on a clean slate. To reach the degree of legal certainty on these issues that we have has taken years of costly litigation. Along the way, some businesses that simply could not afford the costs of high-stakes copyright litigation were forced to fold. In some instances, businesses folded in the face of the high litigation costs even though their legal positions were eventually vindicated. Veoh, for example, was a video sharing website similar to Youtube. Copyright owners sued the website, as well as its investors, for copyright infringement. After nearly six years of litigation, Veoh prevailed.[53] Even so, it spent its money on litigation, rather than innovation, and remains closed to this day.

Given the costs of uncertainty, it is, in some sense, more important to have an answer on these issues, than it is to have the right answer. Whether right or wrong, these decisions established a legal framework that has facilitated the development of new business models and supported the development of social networking and cloud computing. Yet, these decisions were inextricably and precisely tied to the existing statutory language. If we add a making available right to the statute, whether to replace the existing distribution, public performance, and public display rights, or simply to supplement them, this relatively predictable legal framework, and the resulting certainty, would be gone. Moreover, it would be gone not because Congress had specifically decided that one or another of these decisions was wrong as a policy matter. It would be gone because the "making available" right is so inherently vague and ambiguous that the parties who lost in the first round would have a perfectly plausible basis to re-litigate under the new statutory language. New cases would be brought; we would have to re-litigate previously-settled areas of law;

legitimate businesses would, once again, be forced to close in the face of ruinous litigation expense; and investment in new business models would be stifled.[54]

Giving copyright owners the exclusive right to make their works available to the public would thus come at a very high cost.

CONCLUSION

In conclusion, I oppose giving copyright owners the exclusive right to make their works available to the public for three reasons. First, the right is unnecessary. The existing reproduction, distribution, public performance, and public display rights, together with secondary liability doctrines, already provide equivalent protection and fully satisfy our treaty obligations. Second, the right would not materially advance copyright's constitutionally-delimited purposes. While it might make it easier for copyright owners to sue individual file sharers, it would not stop file sharing, and in terms of encouraging the creation of new works and the dissemination of existing works, file sharing is not the problem that copyright owners would have us believe. Rather than address file sharing that threatens legitimate businesses, a making available right would instead only exacerbate the growing problem of copyright trolls. Third, the right would come at a very substantial cost to the economy. Simply by switching from an existing and legally tested legal doctrine to a new and untested doctrine, adding the making available right would reopen settled issues on the Internet. The resulting uncertainty would force legitimate businesses to close and would stifle investment in new business models and innovative technologies.

End Notes

[1] WIPO Copyright Treaty, art. 6(1), Dec. 20, 1996 (available at http://www.wipo.int/treaties/en/ip/wct/).

[2] WIPO Performances and Phonograms Treaty, art. 12(1), Dec. 20, 1996 (available at http://www.wipo.int/treaties/en/ip/wppt/).

[3] WIPO Copyright Treaty, art. 8.

[4] WIPO Performances and Phonograms Treaty, art. 10.

[5] Diplomatic Conference on Certain Copyright and Neighboring Rights Questions, CRNR/DC/102, 301, Geneva, December 2 to 20, 1996 (noting that Mr. Kushan, of the United States,

"stressed the understanding—which had never been questioned during the preparatory work and would certainly not be questioned by any Delegation participating in the Diplomatic Conference—that those rights might be implemented in national legislation through application of any particular exclusive right, also other than the right of communication to the public or the right of making available to the public, or combination of exclusive rights, as long as the acts described in those Articles were covered by such rights.").

[6] *See* Mihaly Fiscor, *The Spring 1997 Horace S. Manges Lecture – Copyright for the Digital Era: The WIPO Treaties*, 21 COLUM.-VLA J.L. and ARTS 197, 211-12 (1997).

[7] See Letter from Marybeth Peters, The Register of Copyrights of the United States of America, to The Honorable Howard L. Berman, Subcommittee on Courts, the Internet and Intellectual Property (Sept. 25, 2002) ("As you are aware, in implementing the new WIPO Copyright Treaty (WCT) and WIPO Performances and Phonograms Treaty (WPPT) in the Digital Millennium Copyright Act, Congress determined that it was not necessary to add any additional rights to Section 106 of the Copyright Act in order to implement the 'making available' right under Article 8 of the WCT."). See also WIPO Copyright Treaties Implementation Act and Online Copyright Liability Limitation Act, Hearing on H.R. 2281 and H.R. 2180 Before the House Subcommittee on Courts and Intellectual Property of the Committee on the Judiciary, 105th Cong. 43 (1997) (Statement of Marybeth Peters, Register of Copyrights).

[8] 17 U.S.C. § 114 (2013).

[9] WIPO Performances and Phonograms Treaty, arts. 15, 16(1).

[10] In section 106(3), the Act gives the copyright owner the exclusive right "to distribute copies or phonorecords of the copyrighted work to the public." 15 U.S.C. §106(3). In section 101, the Act defines both copies and phonorecords as "material objects" in which a work or sounds are fixed. Courts have accepted without much discussion the proposition that a digital download constitutes a "material object." *See, e.g.*, New York Times Co., Inc. v. Tasini, 533 U.S. 483, 498 (2001) (holding that LEXIS/NEXIS, by selling copies of copyrighted articles through its NEXIS database, had exercised the exclusive right of distribution recognized by Section 106(3)); *In re* Aimster Copyright Litig., 334 F.3d 643, 644 (7th Cir.2003) (accepting without discussion that Internet users who swap computer files containing popular copyrighted music by making and transmitting digital copies commit acts of infringement); A and M Records, Inc. v. Napster, Inc., 239 F.3d 1004, 1014 (9th Cir.2001) (agreeing with district court that downloading and uploading of copyrighted music infringes exclusive rights of reproduction and distribution respectively).

[11] WIPO Copyright Treaty, art. 6(1); WIPO Performances and Phonograms Treaty, art. 12(1).

[12] *See* Twentieth Century Fox Film Corp. v. iCraveTV, 2000 WL 255989, 2000 Copr. L. Dec. 28,030, 53 U.S.P.Q.2d (BNA) 1831 (W.D. Pa. 2000).

[13] *Id.*

[14] *See* Capital Records, Inc. v. Thomas-Rasset, 692 F.3d 899 (8th Cir. 2012) (reinstating jury's award of $222,000 in statutory damages for distributing and reproducing twenty-two songs through file-sharing network); Sony BMG Music Enter. v. Tenenbaum, 660 F.3d 487 (1st Cir. 2011) (affirming finding of copyright infringement against an individual for file sharing and reinstating jury's award of $675,000 in statutory damages), *cert. denied*, 132 S. Ct. 2431 (2012).

[15] *Compare* Atlantic Recording Corp. v. Howell, 554 F. Supp. 2d 976, 983 (D. Az. 2008) (requiring proof of a download to establish violation of the distribution right); Elektra Entm't Group, Inc. v. Barker, 551 F.Supp.2d 234, 242-43 (S.D.N.Y.2008) (same); London-Sire Records, Inc. v. Doe 1, 542 F.Supp.2d 153, 168-69 (D. Mass. 2008) (same), *with* Universal

City Studios Prods. LLP v. Bigwood, 441 F.Supp.2d 185, 190-91 (D. Me. 2006) (holding that making work available on a file sharing network constitutes distribution even without proof of a download); Motown Record Co. v. DePietro, No. 04-CV-2246, 2007 U.S. Dist. LEXIS 11626, at *12, 2007 WL 576284, at *3 (E.D. Pa. Feb. 16, 2007) (same).

[16] *See, e.g.*, John Wiley and Sons, Inc. v. Doe Nos. 1-30, 284 F.R.D. 185 (S.D.N.Y. 2012) ("On May 24, 2012, Wiley filed an *ex parte* application for an order authorizing the issuance of subpoenas on ISPs to obtain subscriber information for the IP addresses identified in Schedule A. (Dkt. No. 2). In support of its application, Wiley filed a declaration of its attorney, William Dunnegan, Esq., explaining that a paralegal at Dunnegan's firm had 'downloaded the copyrighted works listed on Schedule A ... from John Doe Nos. 1–30 using BitTorrent software [and, after doing so,] used a tool available on the Internet to look up the [ISP] for each IP address.' (Declaration of William Dunnegan in Support of Plaintiff's Ex Parte Application for an Order Authorizing the Issuance of Subpoenas on Certain Internet Service Providers to Determine the Identity of Defendants, dated May 24, 2012 ('Dunnegan Decl.') 6 (Dkt. No. 3)).").

[17] This argument represents an example of Frederic Bastiat's Broken Window fallacy. Copyright owners argue that if copyright were broader and file sharing were stopped, they would receive additional revenue. If they received additional revenue, it would in turn support additional employment. Thus, they argue, broader copyright creates jobs. But, as Bastiat showed in his 1850 essay, "*Ce qu'on voit et ce qu'on ne voit pas,*" this is a fallacy. For broader copyright to create jobs in the copyright industries, it must increase revenue to copyright owners. Yet, for the copyright industries to receive more revenue, consumers must pay more for works of authorship. Broader copyright, after all, does not generate revenue from thin air. It has to come from somewhere. If consumers have to pay more for works of authorship, they will have less to spend on everything else. Thus, more revenue for the copyright industries necessarily means less revenue for other sectors of the economy. If more revenue for copyrighted works means more jobs for the copyright industries, presumably less revenue everywhere else means fewer jobs elsewhere in the economy. Thus, even if broader copyright generates more revenue for copyright owners, it does not increase net employment in the economy; it merely shifts employment from one sector to another.

[18] U.S. CONST. ART. I, § 8, cl. 8.

[19] Golan v. Holder, 132 S. Ct. 873, 888-89 (2012); *see also* Harper and Row Pubs., Inc. v. Nation Enters., 471 U.S. 539, 558 (1985) ("[C]opyright supplies the economic incentive to create and disseminate ideas.").

[20] *See* Glynn S. Lunney, Jr., *Fair Use and Market Failure:* Sony *Revisited*, 82 B.U.L. REV. 975, 1028-29 (2002) (estimating that, file sharing on Napster in September 2000, essentially doubled the dissemination of existing music compared to the preexisting market mechanisms).

[21] CISCO, CISCO VISUAL NETWORKING INDEX: FORECAST AND METHODOLOGY, 2011-2016, at 9 (2012); CISCO, CISCO VISUAL NETWORKING INDEX: FORECAST AND METHODOLOGY, 2007-2012, at 4 (2008).

[22] Interestingly, in its most recent index, released in May 2013, Cisco projects that file sharing traffic in North America will grow much more slowly from 2012 to 2017 than it had previously projected. CISCO, CISCO VISUAL NETWORKING INDEX: FORECAST AND METHODOLOGY, 2012-2017, at 11 (2013). Instead of continuing to growth by 15 to 20 percent annually, as Cisco had consistently projected in its 2008, 2009, 2010, 2011, and 2012 indices, in its 2013 index, Cisco projects that file sharing traffic will grow by only

9 percent annually in North America from 2012-2017. *Id.* Rather than double every three years for the foreseeable future, as Figure 1 suggests, Cisco now projects that file sharing traffic is beginning to level out. It is not clear what is behind this slowdown. In its 2013 index, Cisco projects a slowdown in the growth rate for file sharing traffic over the next four years, not just for North America, but worldwide. Indeed, for two of its regions, Africa and the Middle East, and Western Europe, Cisco projects that file sharing traffic will actually start declining, at respective rates of ten and two percent annually, over the next four years. In any event, given that the slowdown is worldwide, the slowing growth rate does not appear to be the result of a legal intervention by any particular country. It may simply be that file sharing is running its intrinsically self-limiting course. Yet, whatever is causing the slowdown in the growth of file sharing traffic, the slowdown itself tends to diminish the need for further legal intervention to address the file sharing issue.

[23] *See* Glynn S. Lunney, Jr., *Fair Use and Market Failure:* Sony *Revisited*, 82 B.U.L. REV. 975, 1028-29 (2002).

[24] *Cf.* Metro-Goldwyn-Mayer Studios, Inc. v. Grokster, Ltd., 545 U.S. 913, 922 (2005) (noting that a study by an expert for the plaintiff showed that "nearly 90% of the files available for download on the FastTrack system were copyrighted works").

[25] This data is from the RIAA Shipment Data (available at www.riaa.com). The year 1973 is as far back as the RIAA data goes.

[26] *See* Birgitte Andersen and Marion Frenz, *The Impact of Music Downloads and P2P File-Sharing on the Purchase of Music: A Study for Industry Canada*, University of London Working Paper (2008) (finding that file sharing increasing sales; twelve additional downloads associated with additional 0.44 CD purchases); Sudip Bhattacharjee, Ram D. Gopal, Kaveepan Lertwachara, James R. Marsden and Rahul Telang, *The Effect of Digital Sharing Technologies on Music Markets: A Survival Analysis of Albums on Ranking Charts*, 53 MANAGEMENT SCIENCE 1359 (2007) (finding that file sharing has no overall effect on length of time song spends on charts); Ram D. Gopal and Sudip Bhattacharjee, *Do Artists Benefit from Online Music Sharing?*, 79 J. BUS. 1503 (2006) (finding that students with faster Internet connections sample more, and that sampling increases the propensity to purchase authorized copies); Martin Peitz and Patrick Waelbroeck, *Why the Music Industry May Gain From Free Downloading: The Role of Sampling*, 24 INT'L J. INDUSTRIAL ORG. 907 (2006) (using macro data from sixteen countries to estimate that file sharing reduced sales by 20 percent); Rafael Rob and Joel Waldfogel, *Piracy on the High C's: Music Downloading, Sales Displacement, and Social Welfare in a Sample of College Students*. 49 J. L. and ECON. 29 (2006) (finding that five unauthorized downloads substitute for a single authorized purchase in their sample); Felix Oberholzer-Gee and Koleman Strumpf, *The Effect of File Sharing on Record Sales: An Empirical Analysis,* 115 J. POL. ECON. 1 (2007) (finding that unauthorized downloads do not reduce authorized purchases); Tatsou Tanaka, *Does File-sharing Reduce CD sales?: A Case of Japan*, Conference Paper Prepared for Conference on IT Innovation, Hitotsubashi University, Tokyo (2004) (finding that file sharing has no effect on sales).

[27] A synchronization license or "sync" license is required when a movie, television program, or advertisement wants to include a musical work and synchronize the music to the visual images.

[28] *Compare* Felix Oberholzer-Gee and Koleman Strumpf, *File Sharing and Copyright*, at 20-21 (2010) (available at http://www.hbs.edu/research/pdf/09-132.pdf) (suggesting that sale of complementary goods has largely offset loss of record sale revenue, but including iPod sales and failing to account for inflation by using a nominal, rather than constant, dollar analysis).

[29] Glynn S. Lunney, Jr., *Empirical Copyright: A Case Study of File Sharing and Music Output* (available on www.ssrn.com).

[30] For other quality-consistent measures of music output, *see* Joel Waldfogel, *Copyright Protection, Technological Change, and the Quality of New Products: Evidence from Recorded Music Since Napster* (NBER Working Paper No. 17503) (2011); Joel Waldfogel, *Bye Bye Miss American Pie? The Supply of New Recorded Music Since Napster*, NBER Working Paper No. 16882) (2011).

[31] While listeners may have a preference for "new," as well as "good," music, there is no evidence that this preference has changed from the pre- to the post-file sharing era.

[32] For similar results using other measures of music quality, see Joel Waldfogel, *And the Band Played On: Digital Disintermediation and the Quality of New Recorded Music* (2012) (available on www.ssrn.com); *see also* Oberholzer-Gee and Strumpf, *supra* note 28, at 2, 24 (noting that book publishing, movie production, and music output have all risen substantially since file sharing began).

[33] *See, e.g.*, NPD Group, *Music File Sharing Declined Significantly in 2012* (Feb. 26, 2012) (available at https://www.npd.com/wps/portal/npd/us/news/press-releases/the-npd-group-music-file-sharing-declinedsignificantly-in-2012/).

[34] *Cf.* Glynn S. Lunney Jr., *The Death of Copyright: Digital Technology, Private Copying, and the Digital Millennium Copyright Act*, 87 VA. L. REV. 813 909 (2001) ("Yet, requiring copyright owners to act directly against ordinary citizens helps ensure that the resulting political battle is more balanced. Rather than a disorganized and unaware populace, copyright owners will confront a fully aroused and fully aware citizenry. Even with their transaction costs and collective action advantages, copyright owners should fear such a confrontation.").

[35] *See Prenda seeded its own porn files via BitTorrent, new affidavit argues*, ARS TECHNICA (June 3, 2013) (available at http://arstechnica.com/tech-policy/2013/06/prenda-seeded-its-own-porn-files-via-bittorrent-new-affidavit-shows.)

[36] As one district judge has explained:

> While it is without question that a valid copyright holder is entitled to seek protection of its intellectual property in federal court, it appears that in at least some of these cases, adult film companies may be misusing the subpoena powers of the court, seeking the identities of the Doe defendants solely to facilitate demand letters and coerce settlement, rather than ultimately serve process and litigate the claims. And while it is true that every defendant to a lawsuit must assess reputational costs in his or her determination of whether to settle or defend an action, the potential for embarrassment in being publicly named as allegedly infringing such salacious works as "Big Butt Oil Orgy 2" or "Illegal Ass 2," may be playing a markedly influential role in encouraging a myriad of Doe defendants to settle once subpoenas are issued – a bargaining chip the adult film companies appear to well understand.

Third Degree Films v. Does 1–47, 286 F.R.D. 188, 190 (D. Mass. 2012) (footnotes omitted).

[37] 508 F.3d 1146 (9th Cir. 2007).

[38] An inline link is coding on a webpage that instructs an Internet browser to display a specific image. The image at issue may be stored on another website's server or on the website's own servers. To the person viewing the page, there is no difference in the appearance of the page whether the image is stored on the website's own servers or on another website's server.

[39] Google was also a named defendant in the case. Although Amazon.com was the first named defendant, when an individual searched for images on Amazon.com, Amazon.com simply inline linked to Google's search results.

[40] *Perfect 10, Inc.*, 508 F.3d at 1159-61.

[41] *Id.* at 1164-68.

[42] *Perfect 10, Inc.*, 508 F.3d at 1161.

[43] *Id.* at 1170-73.

[44] *See, e.g.*, Reference for a preliminary ruling from the Svea hovrätt (Sweden) lodged on 18 October 2012 - Nils Svensson, Sten Sjögren, Madelaine Sahlman, Pia Gadd v Retreiver Sverige AB, (Case C-466/12). Four questions are presented in the case, dealing with different types of linking. The first question concerns whether a hyperlink alone constitutes a "communication to the public." The second question concerns whether a hyperlink constitutes a communication to the public if the host website is open to the public without any access restrictions. The third question concerns whether an inline link, framing, or embedding constitutes a communication to the public. With these links, the image appears to the Internet user as if it comes directly from a given website, even though the image is in fact coming, through the link, from another site. The fourth question concerns the leeway that the member states may have to provide greater protection for communications to the public than is available under the relevant European Directive.

[45] European Copyright Society, Opinion on the Reference to the CJEU in Case C-466/12 *Svensson*, at 1, Feb. 15, 2013 (available at http://www.ivir.nl/news/European_Copyright_Society_Opinion_on_Svensson.pdf).

[46] 536 F.3d 121 (2d Cir. 2008). In keeping with common practice, I will hereafter refer to this case as the *Cablevision* decision.

[47] *Cablevision*, 536 F.3d at 134-40.

[48] *Cablevision*, 536 F.3d at 137 ("And because the RS–DVR system, as designed, only makes transmissions to one subscriber using a copy made by that subscriber, we believe that the universe of people capable of receiving an RS–DVR transmission is the single subscriber whose self-made copy is used to create that transmission.").

[49] In addition, the Diplomatic Conference concerning the WIPO treaties adopted an agreed statement that "that the mere provision of physical facilities for enabling or making a communication does not in itself amount to communication within the meaning of this Treaty (the WCT) or the Berne Convention." *See* Fiscor, *supra* note 6, at 214. Given this statement, a cable company that offered a remote dvr to its customers could argue that it was merely providing the physical facilities that would allow its customers to record and replay television programs.

[50] Courts in Germany and Australia have reached the same conclusion under the making available right as the Second Circuit did in *Cablevision. See* De Wolf and Partners, European Union Study on the Application of Directive 2001/29/EC on Copyright and Related Rights in the Information Society (the "Infosoc Directive") 41-42 (2013).

[51] *See Cablevision*, 536 F.3d at 134-37.

[52] *See* Josh Lerner, *The Impact of Copyright Policy Changes on Venture Capital Investment in Cloud Computing Companies*, Nov. 1, 2011, at 9 (*available at* http://www.analysisgroup.com/uploadedFiles/Publishing/Articles/Lerner_Fall2011_Copyright_Policy_VC_Investments.pdf).

[53] *See* UMG Recordings, Inc. v. Shelter Capital Partners, LLC, 718 F.3d 1006 (9th Cir. 2013).

[54] On the issue of cloud computing, for example, the Oberlandsgericht Hamburg decided in 2008 that the mere upload of protected subject matter to a "cloud service", such as Rapidshare,

amounted to an act of making available. Four years later, it changed its position and held that the mere upload of protected subject matter to a cloud service did not amount to an act of making available. De Wolf and Partners, *supra* note 50, at 35.

Index

D

E

J

K

L

M

S

T